INTENSITIES

INTENSITIES: CONTEMPORARY CONTINENTAL PHILOSOPHY OF RELIGION

Series Editors:
Patrice Haynes and Steven Shakespeare,
both at Liverpool Hope University, UK

This series sits at the forefront of contemporary developments in Continental philosophy of religion, engaging particularly with radical reinterpretations and applications of the Continental canon from Kant to Derrida and beyond but also with significant departures from that tradition. A key area of focus is the emergence of new realist and materialist schools of thought whose potential contribution to philosophy of religion is at an early stage. Rooted in a vibrant tradition of thinking about religion, whilst positioning itself at the cutting edge of emerging agendas, this series has a clear focus on Continental and post-Continental philosophy of religion and complements Ashgate's British Society for Philosophy of Religion series with its more analytic approach.

Other titles in the series:

Re-visioning Gender in Philosophy of Religion
Reason, Love and Epistemic Locatedness
Pamela Sue Anderson

Intensities
Philosophy, Religion and the Affirmation of Life

Edited by

KATHARINE SARAH MOODY
STEVEN SHAKESPEARE

ASHGATE

Published by
Ashgate Publishing Limited
Wey Court East
Union Road
Farnham
Surrey, GU9 7PT
England

Ashgate Publishing Company
Suite 420
101 Cherry Street
Burlington
VT 05401-4405
USA

www.ashgate.com

British Library Cataloguing in Publication Data
Intensities : philosophy, religion and the affirmation of life.
 1. Life. 2. Life – Religious aspects.
 I. Shakespeare, Steven, 1968– II. Moody, Katharine Sarah.
 128–dc23

Library of Congress Cataloging-in-Publication Data
Intensities : philosophy, religion, and the affirmation of life / edited by Steven Shakespeare and Katharine Sarah Moody.
    p. cm.
 Includes index.
 ISBN 978-1-4094-4328-5 (hardcover)—ISBN 978-1-4094-4329-2 (pbk.)—
ISBN 978-1-4094-4330-8 (ebook) 1. Life. 2. Meaning (Philosophy) 3. Spirituality.
 I. Shakespeare, Steven, 1968– II. Moody, Katharine Sarah.

 BD431.I58 2012
 128—dc23

2012018434

ISBN 9781409443285 (hbk)
ISBN 9781409443292 (pbk)
ISBN 9781409443308 (ebk – PDF)
ISBN 9781409472292 (ebk – ePUB)

MIX
Paper from
responsible sources
FSC
www.fsc.org
FSC® C018575

Printed and bound in Great Britain by the
MPG Books Group, UK.

Contents

SECTION THREE: LIFE AND SPIRITUALITY

Notes on Contributors

Pamela Sue Anderson is Reader in Philosophy of Religion, University of Oxford, and Fellow in Philosophy, Regent's Park College, Oxford. Anderson has published in Continental philosophy, and especially on Kant, Ricoeur and Michèle Le Doeuff. Her books include *Ricoeur and Kant* (Scholars Press, 1993), *A Feminist Philosophy of Religion: The Rationality and Myths of Religious Belief* (Blackwell, 1998), *Feminist Philosophy of Religion*, co-edited with Beverley Clack (Routledge, 2004), *New Topics in Feminist Philosophy of Religion* (Springer Press, 2010), *Re-visioning Gender in Philosophy of Religion: Reason, Love and Epistemic Locatedness* (forthcoming 2012) and *Kant and Theology*, co-authored with Jordan Bell (Continuum, 2010).

John D. Caputo is the Thomas J. Watson Professor Emeritus of Religion at Syracuse University and the David R. Cook Professor Emeritus of Philosophy at Villanova. His latest book, *The Insistence of God: A Theology of 'Perhaps'*, which will appear in 2013, is a sequel to *The Weakness of God: A Theology of the Event* (Indiana University Press, 2006). He is also the author of *What Would Jesus Deconstruct? The Good News of Postmodernism for the Church* (Baker Academic, 2007), *On Religion* (Routledge, 2001) and *The Prayers and Tears of Jacques Derrida: Religion without Religion* (Indiana University Press, 1997).

Don Cupitt is Life Fellow at Emmanuel College, Cambridge and the author of many books, including *Taking Leave of God* (SCM Press, 1980), *The Sea of Faith* (3rd edn, SCM Press, 2003 [1984]), *The Long Legged Fly* (SCM Press, 1987), *The Last Philosophy* (SCM Press, 1995), *Philosophy's Own Religion* (SCM Press, 2000), *Life, Life* (Polebridge, 2003) and *The Fountain: A Secular Theology* (SCM Press, 2010).

Lorenz Moises J. Festin is a priest of the Archdiocese of Manila. He earned his doctorate degree in philosophy in 1998 from the Pontifica Università Gregoriana in Rome, Italy. He is currently the dean of the San Carlos Seminary, College of Philosophy in Makati, Philippines. He is also an associate professor at De La Salle University in Manila, where he teaches philosophy and theology.

Philip Goodchild is Professor of Religion and Philosophy in the Department of Theology and Religious Studies, University of Nottingham, UK. He is the author of *Gilles Deleuze and the Question of Philosophy* (Fairleigh Dickinson University Press, 1996), *Deleuze and Guattari: An Introduction to the Politics of Desire*

(Sage, 1996), *Capitalism and Religion: The Price of Piety* (Routledge, 2002) and *The Theology of Money* (Duke University Press, 2007). He is also currently a Senior Fellow of the Rethinking Capitalism Initiative, University of California Santa Cruz.

Alison Martin is Senior Lecturer in French Language at Nottingham Trent University. Her previous publications include *Luce Irigaray and the Question of the Divine* (Maney, 2000) and 'Beauvoir and the Transcendence of Natality', in Pamela Sue Anderson (ed.), *New Topics in Feminist Philosophy of Religion: Contestations and Transcendence Incarnate* (Springer, 2010), pp. 249–60.

Katharine Sarah Moody (PhD Lancaster University 2010) is the author of *Truth as Event: Radical Theology and Emerging Christianity* (forthcoming Ashgate, 2013). Other publications on deconstruction, materialism and contemporary Christianity include 'Retrospective Speculative Philosophy: Looking for Traces of Žižek's Communist Collective in Emerging Christian Praxis', *Political Theology* 13/2 (2012): 182–98 and 'Between Deconstruction and Speculation: John D. Caputo and A/Theological Materialism', in Clayton Crockett, B. Keith Putt and Jeffrey W. Robbins (eds), *The Future of Continental Philosophy of Religion* (forthcoming).

John Reader (PhD University of Wales, Bangor) is Rector of the Ironstone Benefice in the Diocese of Oxford and a Senior Honorary Research Fellow with the William Temple Foundation (University of Chester, UK). His books include *Reconstructing Practical Theology* (Ashgate, 2008), *Encountering the New Theological Space* co-edited with Chris Baker (Ashgate, 2009), *Christianity and the New Social Order* with John Atherton and Chris Baker (SPCK, 2011), *Theological Reflection for Human Flourishing* with Helen Cameron, Victoria Slater and Chris Rowland (SCM Press, 2012) and *Heteropia: Alternative Pathways to Social Justice* with Caroline Baillie and Jens Kabo (Zero Books, 2012).

Steven Shakespeare is Senior Lecturer in Philosophy at Liverpool Hope University and co-facilitator of the Association for Continental Philosophy of Religion. His published work includes *Kierkegaard, Language and the Reality of God* (Ashgate, 2001), *Radical Orthodoxy: A Critical Introduction* (SPCK, 2007), *Derrida and Theology* (Continuum, 2009) and *Beyond Human: From Animality to Transhumanism*, co-edited with Claire Molloy and Charlie Blake (Continuum, 2011).

Brian Sudlow is Lecturer in French with Translation Studies at Aston University, Birmingham. He is the author of *Catholic Literature and Secularisation in France and England 1880–1914* (Manchester University Press, 2011) and is keenly interested in the comparative and interpretative uses of René Girard's mimetic theory.

Neil Turnbull is currently Principal Lecturer in Philosophy at Nottingham Trent University. He was awarded his PhD in 2001 and has since published on a number of philosophical issues in books and academic journals such as *Theory, Culture and Society*, *Telos*, *Space and Culture*, and *New Formations*.

Kenneth Jason Wardley is a librarian at the University of Edinburgh, where he is also a doctoral researcher in the School of Divinity, New College. His research interests are in Continental philosophy of religion, phenomenology and theological anthropology. He has published articles on metaphysics, thanatology, liturgy and transcendence.

Acknowledgements

The origin of many of the contributions to this volume lies in the inaugural conference of the Association for Continental Philosophy of Religion, held at Liverpool Hope University in 2009. The editors would like to acknowledge all who took part in that conference, especially Dr Patrice Haynes, the principal organizer, and Liverpool Hope University, who provided financial support for the event. They would also like to thank the staff at Ashgate, especially Sarah Lloyd for her support, patience and good sense.

Introduction
Irritating Life

Katharine Sarah Moody and Steven Shakespeare

> I have always been interested in this theme of survival, the meaning of which is *not to be added on* to living and dying. It is originary: life *is* living on, life *is* survival [la vie *est* survie].[1]

Life is a duplicitous affair. Insistent but nebulous, the idea of life haunts philosophy. It does so, perhaps, because of its inherent dynamism. Never simply one 'thing', life is a process of exchange, metabolism, ingestion, reproduction, excretion. It always lives off its own unliving origins and its return to the inorganic. Life is never simply separate from death. It is born from the decay of such fixed dualities. In his final published interview, Jacques Derrida notes the fascination of life's duplicity. To live is to live on: survival is not merely an extension of a univocal conception of life. The slippage of time and difference disturbs any moment of self-presence from the outset. Life is always in motion. In relating to itself, it never simply coincides with itself. The trace always lives on in the absence of its origin, the sign is always read in the wake of the death of its author (even when, in an empirical sense, its author is very much alive). Life drifts, mortally wounded.

This is more than an interesting intellectual conundrum or piece of speculative ingenuity, however. It is also the realization that life is a negotiation, an interpretation of traces, and that here lies the possibility of affirmation. The complicity between death and life is not necessarily a morbid alliance. As Derrida remarks, 'I would not want to encourage an interpretation that situates surviving on the side of death and the past rather than life and the future. No, deconstruction is always on the side of the *yes*, on the side of the affirmation of life.'[2] Derrida even speaks of 'an unconditional affirmation of life' in which survival is 'the most intense life possible'.[3]

How then do we move from the idea of life as internally divided, caught in the shifting web of contingent differences, to an affirmation without conditions, to an intensity that reaches the limits of the possible? This is a question which the contributors to this volume address in different registers, sometimes in tension with one another. For all, however, the pressing issue is how to say 'yes' to life, to intensify life in an age when life has become spectacle, commodity and brand. Can we move from commonplaces ('live for the day!') to articulate the affirmation of

---

[1]   Jacques Derrida, *Learning to Live Finally: The Last Interview* (Basingstoke and New York: Palgrave Macmillan, 2007), p. 26.

[2]   Ibid., p. 51.

[3]   Ibid., p. 52.

life as a radical, even revolutionary, act? Is the affirmation itself – the declaration, attestation or testimony to belief, faith, trust or love, which constitutes the (political) subject in many contemporary philosophical engagements with religion and, especially, St Paul – the act through which life is truly lived? If, as Derrida suggests, life is survival, then perhaps life is the decision to survive? And yet how might such a 'firm decision'[4] of affirmation be made, given the very conditions of life? 'How would it be possible for me to experience my life-impulse not as a foreign automatism, as a blind "compulsion to repeat", making me transgress the law, with the unacknowledged complicity of the law itself, but as a fully subjectivized, positive "Yes" to my life?'[5]

Such a prospect appears beguiling, but it raises a critical question. From what standpoint can we affirm life? From where can we achieve this 'yes'? Is it a matter of life somehow relating to and intensifying itself through immanent means? Or can life only really be valued from the outside, through an appeal to some kind of transcendent perspective? Of course, we do not have to simply accept the terms of this split. Derrida's notion of survival seems to elude both horns of this dilemma. To live on is both to continue and to go beyond, complicating the boundary line between immanence and transcendence. Nevertheless, Derrida's talk of a future, or the radical openness of what is to come, will surely not satisfy those who demand a more 'robust' ontology, in which the matter of this world only has value because it is created and given by a supernatural source.[6] Such persistent debates call us to reconsider some of the seminal moments of thinking about life from the philosophical tradition. Many of the essays in this collection offer such points of orientation. Our task in this introduction is simply to offer a narrative which goes some way towards contextualizing the volume. In the Afterword, we will briefly consider what lines of thought could be pursued in future research.

The fastidious nature of Kant's critical philosophy hardly makes it seem a likely bedfellow for Romanticism. And yet it is Kant's *Critique of Judgement* which does so much to underline the importance of organic and aesthetic forms for thought. Faced with the division between his theoretical and practical uses of reason, Kant's engagement with ideas of purpose and beauty is not simply an afterthought or discrete concern. The third critique opens the question of the

---

[4]   In 'Living On', Derrida remarks that the punctuation in 'living, living on [*vivre, survivre*]' marks a relation not of equation nor of opposition between 'living' and 'living on' but, rather, the 'pause' before a 'firm decision' to live on after living, to survive, is made. Jacques Derrida, 'Living On', trans. James Hulbert, in Harold Bloom, Paul de Man, Jacques Derrida, Geoffrey H. Hartman and J. Hillis Miller, *Deconstruction and Criticism* (London: Routledge, 1979), p. 135.

[5]   Slavoj Žižek, 'Paul and the Truth Event', in John Milbank, Slavoj Žižek and Creston Davis, *Paul's New Moment: Continental Philosophy and the Future of Christian Theology* (Grand Rapids, MI: Brazos Press, 2010), p. 97.

[6]   See, for example, John Milbank's theological materialism in Creston Davis (ed.), *The Monstrosity of Christ: Paradox or Dialectic?* (Cambridge, MA: MIT Press, 2009).

supersensible basis which links theoretical knowledge with moral action. For our purposes, what is most significant is the privileged place given to the organism. It is the organism which presents us with a potential bridge between an explanation of nature on purely mechanical grounds and one which appeals to a transcendent principle of soul or spirit. The organism does not derive its purposiveness from external relationships, or from a divine spirit injected into nature from without. Neither can it be accounted for mechanically, since

> a machine has only *motive* force. But an organized being has within it *formative* force, and a formative force that this being imparts to the kinds of matter that lack it (thereby organizing them). This force is a formative force that propagates itself – a force that a mere ability [of one thing] to have [another] (i.e. mechanism) cannot explain.[7]

Organic life is more than, other than, machine; but it would be a mistake to think it is wholly other than inorganic nature. It is not that in the organism the motive force relating cause and effect is lacking, but that this force turns upon itself, loops back in reciprocal interchange and formation, producing a whole greater than the sum of its parts: '*An organized product of nature is one in which everything is a purpose and reciprocally also a means.*'[8]

The crux for Kant is that the idea of the organism must remain 'regulative' – a guiding idea or a limit concept,[9] rather than one that gives us theoretical knowledge of reality in itself. We have to continue using mechanical and purposive ways of judging natural entities, and, ultimately, we 'are quite unable to prove that organized natural products cannot be produced through the mere mechanism of nature'.[10] Unification can only be found in the supersensible basis of all things, a basis which must remain forever inaccessible to us. We must, and do, subordinate mechanical modes of explaining life to teleological ones, but the 'supplement' of mechanism must always haunt our attempts to do so.[11]

The organism as the privileged instance of life becomes a vanishing concept, even as it articulates a fundamental aporia common to ideas such as consciousness, freedom and creativity (Derrida's analysis of invention is illustrative[12]): the conditions which make these phenomena possible also make them impossible. Consciousness, for example, presumes a subjective point of view which cannot

---

[7]   Immanuel Kant, *Critique of Judgment* (Indianapolis: Hackett Publishing Company, 1987), p. 253.

[8]   Ibid., p. 255.

[9]   See Eugene Thacker, *After Life* (Chicago: University of Chicago Press, 2010), pp. 242–9.

[10]   Kant, *Critique of Judgment*, p. 269.

[11]   Ibid., p. 299.

[12]   Jacques Derrida, 'Psyche: Invention of the Other', in *Psyche: Inventions of the Other*, vol. 1 (Stanford: Stanford University Press, 2007), pp. 1–47.

be accounted for by any objective description of brain states or the like; and yet the subjective view is nothing, could not even arise as possible, without those objective conditions. If consciousness does not arrive as a divine spark from the blue, how can it mysteriously emerge from presuppositions wholly alien to its qualitative nature? Of course, philosophers of mind will take a variety of stands on this issue, ranging from eliminativist materialism to theistic idealism; but it is hard to shake off the sense that all of them fail as explanations, since all must beg the question. The conclusion ('consciousness is accounted for by x') determines the kind of evidence that will even be considered as decisive.

In that sense, we have hardly moved beyond Kant in accounting for the nature of life and Kant himself indicates the scope of the problem. When considering aesthetic judgements about art, we seem well removed from the kind of considerations that must apply to our understanding of natural organisms. However, here too we find the tension between mechanical and purposive or free modes of explanation: 'there is no fine art that does not have as its essential condition something mechanical'.[13] Earlier, Kant describes this tension more fully:

> It is advisable, however, to remind ourselves that in all the free arts there is yet a need for something in the order of a constraint, or, as it is called, a *mechanism*. (In poetry, for example, it is correctness and richness of language, as well as prosody and meter). Without this the *spirit*, which in art must be *free* and alone animates the work, would have no body at all and would evaporate completely.[14]

Here, in these pages which defined the creative nature of genius for the Romantic movement, we find that even a Goethe can create nothing without the machine body; that spirit's animation of art is constituted by constraint. If animation and life go together, then we can infer that life, be it aesthetic or organic, is nothing without this friction. Life is incarnation, understood not as the enfleshing of God in human form, but as the inseparable, inexplicable complication of machine and free purpose.

Kant's statement of the problem thus remains seminal. It set the agenda for speculative idealism, not least for Hegel's treatment of the concept of life in *The Science of Logic*. Whilst an adequate account of that treatment is beyond the scope of this introduction, several features of it are worth noting.

First, life appears in a privileged position, near the end of the *Logic*, in the section entitled 'The Idea'. Here, concept and reality are united, for the concept has itself as its own reality. The previous section, 'Objectivity', comprises concepts of mechanism, chemism and teleology, a progression from externally related objects to freely posited purpose. The Kantian inheritance is striking; that truth begins to emerge most fully with the idea of life, even more so. For Hegel, the idea of life (and he is clear he is dealing with a logical concept, not natural life conditioned

---

13   Ibid., p. 178.
14   Ibid., p. 171.

by the reality of inorganic objects, or life in the service of a transcendent spirit) is 'in and for itself absolute *universality*'.[15] In its diversity, life is permeated by the rational concept, like an omnipresent soul. The concept remains at one with itself in all the manifold determinations of life. Life manifests itself first through the living individual, purely simple, determining itself, 'the initiating self-moving *principle*'.[16] As we would expect of Hegel, the idea of life must traverse a complex history, in which it fully arrives at its own meaning, pointing forward to the overcoming of all splits between objectivity and subjectivity. Here, life, the organism, becomes a moving image or focal point for the whole content of the absolute. For Hegel, life is not added on to logic, because logic itself lives: only the idea that determines itself, and initiates its own movement, can be a truly comprehensive thought.

At the same time, Hegel's realism militates against any serene progression to perfect knowledge. The living individual has universality only in immediate form, not realized and known as such. It possesses sensibility as a 'purely internal pulsation',[17] a kind of autoaffection locked up within itself. This is unlocked through 'irritability', when what is immediately felt is referred to something external. This abstract outside is then further determined in the stage of 'singularity': here irritability is conceived as the living being's own passage into externality – and so into reproduction. The living being must be ruptured; life must become irritability and then excess or even ecstasy. Hegel's description of how this relates to the foregoing stages of mechanism and chemical relationships is worth quoting at length:

> The mechanical and chemical factor in the process is a beginning of the dissolution of the living thing. Since life is the truth of these processes, and as living being it is therefore the concrete existence of this truth and the power over the processes, it infringes upon the latter, permeates them as their universality, and their product is entirely determined by it. This transformation of them into the living individual constitutes the turning back of this individual into itself, with the result that the production that as such would be the transition into an other becomes reproduction, a reproduction in which the living being posits itself as self-identical *for-itself*.[18]

There is a clear direction here: from merely external relations, mechanical productions, to self-conscious reproductions. And yet the qualitative change remains conditioned by its base components. Life is nothing without the machinic, it is the machine turned back upon itself, realizing its end in reproduction. Can the irritability ever be finally expunged from reflection? Can the reproduction of

---

[15]   Georg Wilhelm Friedrich Hegel, *The Science of Logic* (Cambridge: Cambridge University Press, 2010), p. 678.

[16]   Ibid., p. 680.

[17]   Ibid., p. 682.

[18]   Ibid., p. 686.

life ever lose its reference to the production of singular others, inaccessible to one another in their subjective point of view, and their singular accountability? Perhaps our expectations of Hegel are wrong: it is not that the limitations of life must be overcome in order to 'arrive' at some fully transparent 'truth', but rather that the truth lies precisely in the living process itself, with all its material, shifting, elusive, unliving elements included.

The concept of irritability, though not necessarily central for Hegel, is suggestive of this whole dynamic. In the wake of such discoveries as galvanism, both scientists and philosophers of nature were led to speculate on the principle of life and its relationship to electrical and chemical flows. Irritability straddles the divide between passive reception of stimuli and active response. For Schelling, irritability's '*ultimate* condition is organic *duplicity*'.[19] The organism relates to an external world because it is divided in itself (and thereby, the world is also divided in itself). The importance of the concept of irritability thus lies in its pivotal and ambiguous place in understanding life, the organism and the task of thinking. It signifies not so much a resolution of the dilemma of how to characterize life, but a concentrated statement of the underlying antagonism that constitutes life as such. It calls for an irritated thinking, rather than a process of rationalization which aims at a totalizing conceptual grasp.

To affirm life, then, is not to transport oneself to an imaginary outside; but nor is it to rest in the pure spontaneity and self-reference of an immanent process. Nietzsche's famous thought experiment of the eternal return can be read along these lines. Nietzsche asks: Can we say 'yes' to our life being endlessly repeated in every detail? Is there a moment of rapture so intense that it makes up for all the attendant miseries and misfortunes we have known? His own response to nihilism veers between a kind of biologically based naturalism and a 'purer' sovereign decision to revalue all inherited values, which cannot be constrained by any pre-critical idea of nature.[20] The dangers of either approach – an uncritical social Darwinism and a celebration of elitist hierarchy – are well known. Perhaps the appeal to a sovereign moment of ecstasy simply underlines this romanticization of vital force and domination.

But what if we take a more Hegelian approach to Nietzsche's scenario? In this case, the 'yes' to life is also a frank refusal to wish away or sentimentalize the negativity which we experience in living. Life is not an object or process independent of our subjective stance towards it. What life is, what it means, depends upon the way we live in thought and in action. *This* is the true moment of sovereignty, not some Darwinian-aristocratic experience of raw power. It is a moment always internally divided, never resting in a fixed position. And it always assumes a responsibility towards life, rather than prostrating itself before some supposedly objective force. In other words, perhaps this 'yes' to life also offers something of a 'no'.

---

[19] F.W.J. Schelling, *First Outline of a System of the Philosophy of* Nature (New York: State University of New York Press, 2004), p. 121.

[20] Friedrich Nietzsche, *The Gay Science* (New York: Vintage Books, 1974), p. 273.

On the story we are telling, then, life is affirmed as conflicted, and as a conflict whose meaning and shape only emerges through our engagement with it, ethically and politically. The mechanical and inorganic elements of life are not simply suppressed; it is actually their part in the process which prevents life being confused with some abstract, asocial, disembodied spirit. This narrative of life thus departs from vitalism, the scientific and philosophical movement which, through the nineteenth and early twentieth centuries, posited the existence of an immaterial life-force. And yet this is not simply an embrace of 'materialism' either, as if we *knew* what matter was. In contemporary debates about its origin, nature and artificial reproduction, life is much more likely to be conceived of as information. Life is transmitted and expanded through codes, which blur the line between the physical and the non-physical, and, ultimately, between the natural and the cultural. Life and meaning are not two things: the living process invites a hermeneutics of life which is never neutral and disengaged.[21]

In this light, Žižek is right to note that the 'reversal' of idealism associated with Feuerbach and Marx needs to be seen in a more complex light.[22] Typically, these radical thinkers are seen as opposing the way Hegel subordinates the real processes of material history to a suprahistorical consciousness or Spirit. The solution is to return our attention from theory to practice, to dispel the mystifying ideologies which distract us from and devalue concrete human life. However, Žižek argues that Marx himself recognizes that this is too simplistic. Capitalism creates a new kind of relationship to nature and labour. Through the idea of the commodity, we discover that value is socially engineered from the very outset. If life is commodified, it is not that we can escape from this into a purely 'natural' and objective meaning of life. To fight the commodity form, to resist it, to realize that labour creates value, is not to deny the social construction of value, but to take it in a revolutionary direction. The key insight is, again, that the emancipation of life cannot occur except through the risk of revolutionary agency. The subjective stance on life, its affirmation or negation, cannot be evaded. For Marx of course, it must take concrete form in class struggle. But that struggle is itself not just a pre-existing fact: it comes into being because we take sides in it. In this sense, there is no absolute distinction between affirming life (as given) and creating life (as new). And any act of affirmation takes place in a context of class struggle, where the very meaning of life is at stake. What we fight over changes in the fight.

We are thus brought back to the question of affirmation: *what* is being affirmed and *how*? The thesis we are advancing is that the *what* (the content of life as lived or thought) cannot be understood in abstraction from the *how*. This helps us to trouble the distinction we made earlier, between those philosophies of life

---

[21]   See Leonard Lawlor, *The Implications of Immanence: Toward a New Concept of Life* (New York: Fordham University Press, 2006); Margaret A. Boden (ed.), *The Philosophy of Artificial Life* (Oxford: Oxford University Press, 1996); and John Johnston, *The Allure of Machinic Life: Cybernetics, Artificial Life and the New AI* (Cambridge, MA: MIT Press, 2008).

[22]   Slavoj Žižek, *Living in the End Times* (London: Verso, 2011), p. 201.

which assume a transcendent point of reference and those which understand the life process in purely immanent terms. Take a paradigmatic instance of an immanent philosophy, that of Deleuze and Guattari. In *A Thousand Plateaus* and elsewhere, they advance a nonhierarchical and acentred thinking, which traces the ways in which the fundamental processes of life are always breaking out of fixed and organic forms. Machinic and abstract processes are indispensable to the way in which life breaks with pre-existing territories and differentiates itself anew. In this way of thinking, what matters is new possibilities, creative intensities, not reaching some kind of 'beyond'. The absolute is not a form, but a deformation, life's exuberance constantly breaking the bounds of 'organization'.[23]

In his history of the modern subject, Foucault writes: 'For millennia, man remained what he was for Aristotle: a living animal with the additional capacity for a political existence; modern man is an animal whose politics places his existence as a living being in question.'[24] As Deleuze and Guattari have suggested, the contemporary political machine of global capitalism manifests itself in specific strata – inorganic (or geological), organic (biological) and alloplastic (social) – which stratify life and determine the forms of subjective possibility open to it. Modes of organization, such as corporatization, structure what we say, who we are, the constitution of our bodies and our bodily practices, and our unconscious desires, in order to configure and codify life into forms that are especially recognizable to the consumer market and expedient for its efficient operation.[25] Foucault's analysis of the ways in which the art of government regulates a population through the exercise of power over life illustrates how a political state of affairs seeks to 'optimize a state of life'.[26] Sovereign power had the right to life and death, manifest in the power to *make die and let live* (in other words, the question was to kill or not to kill), but the technologies of power that emerged in recent centuries established a hold over all aspects of human life in order to *make live and let die*. These techniques were both disciplinary, ruling by dissolving a multiplicity into individual bodies that can be manipulated and rendered both submissive and useful to governmentality, and biopolitical, ruling through bioregulation, replacing a multiplicity of bodies with the general biological processes of a population, which could then be controlled politically through the regulation of health and hygiene, birth rate and life expectancy, and so on. Biopower succeeds, then, Foucault notes, 'in covering the whole surface that lies between the organic and the biological,

---

[23]   Gilles Deleuze and Felix Guattari, *A Thousand Plateaus* (London: Continuum, 2004), pp. 60–3. Cf. Keith Ansell-Pearson, *Germinal Life: The Difference and Repetition of Deleuze* (Abingdon and New York: Routledge, 1999).

[24]   Michel Foucault, 'Right of Death and Power over Life, in Paul Rainbow (ed.), *The Foucault Reader* (New York: Pantheon Books, 1984), p. 265.

[25]   See, for example, Deleuze and Guattari, *A Thousand Plateaus*, pp. 504–7.

[26]   Michael Foucault, *'Society Must Be Defended': Lectures at the Collège de France, 1975–76*, Mauro Bertani and Alessandro Fontana (eds), trans. David Macey (London: Penguin, 2003), p. 246.

between body and population',[27] between the inorganic machine and the organism. Biopower thus determines how life should live, what the possibilities for life are and what an affirmation of life can look like.

How *should* life live?

This is a question that philosophy, ancient and modern, has often sought to answer. 'The question of *how one should live* involves a particular way of approaching life. It views life as having a shape: a life – a human life – is a whole that might be approached by way of asking how it should unfold.'[28] The question of *how one should act*, however, becomes 'less concerned with the overall shape of one's life', instead seeking to determine whether one is acting correctly, thus distinguishing one's actions from one's life as a whole whilst still rooting one's obligations in the life and will of God.[29] In light of the death of God, however, the question must shift from how one *should* live (or act), with the associated notion of 'transcendent values' by which 'modes of existence' can be 'compared, selected and judged',[30] to how one *might* live – a question that Todd May rightly observes is never far from Deleuze's mind.[31] It is a more thoroughly immanentist question.

How *might* life live?

This is a question that affirms that 'there is always the possibility of changing'.[32] In its power over life, the biopolitical affirmation, optimization or furtherance of life and of life chances in the service of productivity, becomes life denying, justifying racism, war and genocide. But dissatisfaction with the hegemonic organization of life within global capitalism and the desire for alternative modes of living and being, for new possibilities for social, political and economic life, are never far from media headlines. The question, 'How might life live?' – and attendant questions such as, 'How might I live?' 'Who might I be?'[33] 'What might I do?'

---

[27] Foucault, *'Society Must Be Defended'*, p. 253.

[28] Todd May, *Gilles Deleuze: An Introduction* (Cambridge: Cambridge University Press, [2005] 2008), p. 4; our emphases.

[29] May, *Gilles Deleuze*, pp. 5–6.

[30] Gilles Deleuze and Félix Guatarri, *What is Philosophy?* trans. Graham Burchell and Hugh Tomlinson (London: Verso, 1994), p. 74.

[31] May, *Gilles Deleuze*, p. 3.

[32] Michel Foucault, 'Sex, Power and the Politics of Identity', in Paul Rainbow (ed.), *Essential Works of Foucault: Ethics, Subjectivity, Truth* (New York: The New Press, 1997), p. 167.

[33] The various technologies that Foucault documents (of madness, for example) are mechanisms for determining the answer to the question, 'Who am I?' According to John Caputo, 'Foucault's idea is not only *not* to answer this question in a determinate way but to see to it that no one else is allowed to answer it, or rather to answer it on behalf of anyone else and above all to enforce their answer.' John D. Caputo, 'On Not Knowing Who We Are: Madness, Hermeneutics, and the Night of Truth in Foucault', in *More Radical Hermeneutics: On Not Knowing Who We Are* (Bloomington and Indianapolis: Indiana University Press, 2000), p. 30.

'What might bodies be capable of?' 'What's in my power?'[34] – might offer hope for the invention of something new. It might open lines of thought and action that are also 'lines of flight' from the strata that order life within a 'striated grid' and open up onto a 'smooth space' that creates, rather than captures, contains and constrains, possibilities for living (Deleuze and Guattari). Or it might form 'strategic games' within existing power relations that provide sites of resistance (Foucault).

The anarchic political potential of such a line of thought is clear, and Deleuze characterizes these processes of escape from striation in terms directly relevant to this volume: 'We will say of pure immanence that it is A LIFE, and nothing else … A life is the immanence of immanence, absolute immanence: it is complete power, complete bliss.'[35] This immanence of life rules out any pre-existing organization or end goal, but also gives life something of an absolute character: 'A life is everywhere … : an immanent life carrying with it the events and singularities that are merely actualized in subjects and objects'.[36] However, if we read this as making subjects and objects into mere surface manifestations of a universal flow, problems arise. Not least of these is practical: where does the political agency for creativity and resistance come from if all is immersed into the impersonal flow of life? But there is also a theoretical issue: the distinction between a flow and what that flow carries with it, or between surface and depth, appears inconsistent with a thoroughgoing immanentism. How then do we develop a critical and practically engaged thinking, that does not reduce life to an object, or ignore its political definition and potential? This is a question that several of the essays in this volume take up.

But for now we can at least claim that the affirmation of life might require or demand a form of resistance. If we might say 'yes' to life, to what might we say 'no'? If we answer, 'to that which is not life' or 'to that which is less than life', we can ask, 'What is that?' – Is it death? Is it what Jantzen calls 'the death-dealing structures of modernity'?[37] – and 'How might it be resisted?' Like the *what* and the *how* of the affirmation of life, we also claim that these two questions (of the *what* and the *how* of resistance) cannot be treated in isolation, either. What and how, both at the same time.[38]

---

[34]   On these last two questions see especially Deleuze's work on Spinoza. He writes, '*We do not even know of what a body is capable*, says Spinoza.' Gilles Deleuze, *Expressionism in Philosophy: Spinoza*, trans. Martin Joughin (New York: Zone Press, 1990 [1968]), p. 226.

[35]   Gilles Deleuze, *Pure Immanence: Essays on a Life* (Cambridge, MA: MIT Press, 2002), p. 27.

[36]   Ibid., p. 29.

[37]   Grace Jantzen, 'Flourishing: Towards an Ethic of Natality', *Feminist Theory*, 2/2 (2001): 229.

[38]   The question of the *who* of life, of affirmation and resistance, is also raised by this volume.

We began with words from an interview with Derrida, published two months before his death. We can end with words from Foucault, interviewed in 1984, the year before his death, on resistance and creativity:

> [R]esistance is not solely a negation but a creative process. To create and recreate, to transform the situation, to participate actively in the process, that is to resist. ... Yes, that is the way I would put it. To say no is the minimum form of resistance. But naturally, at times that is very important. You have to say no as a decisive form of resistance.[39]

Life *is* survival, living on. And survival is not defined by death, but by life, by a decision *for* life. Yet perhaps such an affirmation is a form of negation – a resisting, creative and affirmative negation. Yes and no, both at the same time. Life is conflicted. Never simply one, life is duplicitous.

***

The Essays

This volume seeks to take up this strange and urgent affirmation in three parts. In the first, 'The Politics of Life', questions of biopower and subjectivity are considered through feminist and political readings. In 'Life and the Limits of Thinking', contributors explore the ways in which life resists assimilation into thought and what thinking and action might be provoked by this. Finally, 'Life and Spirituality' considers what it might mean to think anew of philosophy as a way of life or a spiritual exercise, and whether it would be shaped and directed by a transcendent focus or given intensity through its immersion in the immanent world.

The Politics of Life

Following Deleuze, an immanent philosophy is concerned with what life can do, rather than with the transcendent values to which life should be compared, and the evaluation of life proceeds through an examination of the intensities it creates or the movements it lays out. These possibilities of and for life make questions of life a question of politics, and Pamela Sue Anderson highlights two divergent interpretations of the central 'myth' of woman as the Other in Beauvoir's *The Second Sex*, in order to argue for a feminist immanent philosophy of life that eschews what Le Doeuff identifies as the dogma of transcendent or absolute alterity formed by a tradition of French Hegelianism. Beauvoir writes that, just as a 'subject posits itself only in opposition; it asserts itself as the essential and sets up the other as inessential, as the object', the other has 'an opposing reciprocal

---

[39] Foucault, 'Sex, Power and the Politics of Identity', p. 168.

claim' to identity, to essentiality and Oneness, such that there is a relationship of reciprocity between the same and the other, the One and the Other. Yet this reciprocity is not recognized between the sexes; woman does not turn 'into the One' by positing an Other.[40] The question of interpreting this Hegelian-Kojèvian-Beauvoirian relation between the same and the other – and the failure of woman to create her Other – might be said to signify the difference between transcendent and immanent feminist philosophies and politics of life. For example, in Irigaray's philosophy of sexual difference, women have failed to achieve female subjectivity because they need their own sexually specific transcendent Other to do so and, through such a process of deification, they will become divine women. This symmetry between the becoming-divine of both men and women requires sexual difference, then, the maintenance of predetermined heterosexual forms of subjectivity, interrelation and becoming, as well as a transcendent philosophy of male and female apotheosis. As such, it is conservative or conformist, 'fixated' politically, Anderson concludes, on 'a fixed feminine subject rather than a mobile feminist subject'. In contrast, Le Deouff claims that Beauvoir asserts a crucial exception to the Hegelian-Kojèvian dogma that the categories of same and other are fundamental to human thought: 'women', Anderson summarizes, 'do not (need to) posit an Other'. For her, the measures, or the 'minimal conditions' of, feminist philosophy are neither the reduction of the Other to the Same nor the elevation of the Other to the Absolute, rather they become the rejection of subjection to otherness and the recognition of the unique, as well as the intensification of life's immanent (rather than transcendent) values and the mobilization (rather than fixation) of the subject.

The question of life becomes a question of subjectivity for Brian Sudlow also. Who lives? Who is the subject of life? Is it that life lives? Or that there is a (divine) subject who lives? Perhaps, however, 'life does not live' (Adorno's epigram to *Minima Moralia*)?[41] Perhaps there are forms of life that are but a simulacrum of authentic life, such that 'Life' is 'lost' in the living (T.S. Eliot),[42] with what survives this loss of Life being subject to biopower (Foucault)? And, if so, then, as Agamben suggests, perhaps life in general (*zoe*) is shaped by the particular form(s) of life (*bios*), of living, that are enabled or limited by the biopolitical disciplines through which modern sovereignties are constituted? For Agamben, life is only *included* in the political through its *exclusion* (and perfection), through a transformation of *zoe* into *bios*. The figure of *homo sacer*, that individual life placed beyond human and divine law by sovereign power's self-constituting act of exclusion, models what Sudlow characterizes as that 'excluded life' arising from Agamben's *zoe-bios* distinction and produced by the biopolitical conditions of sovereignty: bare

40   Simone de Beauvoir, *The Second Sex*, trans. Constance Borde and Sheila Malovany-Chevallier (London: Jonathan Cape, 2009), pp. 6–7.
41   Theodor Adorno, *Minima Moralia: Reflections from Damaged Life* (London: Verso, 2005 [1951]), p. 19.
42   T.S. Eliot, *Collected Poems 1909–1962* (London: Faber and Faber, 2002), p. 140.

life. Moving from several criticisms of this distinction and interpretation of *homo sacer*, Sudlow notes their consciously 'intra-anthropic' character to ask how life might live beyond the limits of such a 'hegemonic episteme'. While characterizing Girardian mimesis as an equally intra-anthropic relation between human agents – in which the resultant mimetic rivalry and violence are either unlimited (the limitlessness of general or profane life, *zoe*) or limited (brought under a cohesive or sacred framework for life, *bios*) – Sudlow suggests that Girard introduces a third possibility for life beyond that of the profane and the sacred. In the *divine* life, the mimetic violence and scapegoating of life under the (sacred) conditions of biopoliticization are subject to an intervention of love, through which, Sudlow suggests, a new form of life as 'theandric' is modelled, one that offers the possibility of (a lost) life lived in relation with the divine.

John Reader, too, locates in the current political and economic context a specific concept of life as subject to, and the object of, biopolitical forces to which (we are told) there are no alternatives, no possibilities for freedom, creativity, self-determination or hope. He suggests, therefore, that now is the time for a politics of life that can restore a sense of 'new direction', of opposition to the 'life denying' forces of global neo-liberal capitalism. And this requires, he argues, 'an expanded portrait of human life'. Beginning from recent developments that seek to account for innovation and change beyond biological determinism, Reader introduces Whitehead's philosophy of organism to suggest that life is restless, desiring the creation of alterity; 'life is a matter of transformation rather than preservation, a striving for something other than what already exists'. Life is not, then, predetermined by its present structures but has the potential to produce alternative possibilities. For Reader, this means that human being's creativity is pre-rational or pre-autonomous, terms which indicate the limits of rationality, of human being's ability to function rationally and the commitments within human life that pre-exist reason, autonomy and subjectivity. For Badiou, this pre-autonomous dimension of human being is a form of pre-cognitive fidelity to a cause, through which subjectivity emerges. But Reader wonders to what extent such notions of pre-autonomy limit understandings of human subjectivity *precisely to the pre-autonomous* and whether such a limitation of human being precludes the kind of political involvement at a rational level that could effect change. He asks, 'What remains of any notion of human autonomy and the human being as agent?' and, 'How does one develop a discourse capable of acknowledging the presence of values and ethical stances before it is so late in the process that they are bound to be ineffective?' To answer this latter question, he turns to Latour, whose understanding of matters of concern as complex assemblages highlights for Reader both that fidelities and commitments are embedded in 'earlier' stages than is commonly recognized and allowed by public discourse, and that such attachments are necessarily multiple and messy, interconnected and interconnecting, entangled and entangling. As such, political decisions, actions and policies always involve the entanglement of the pre-autonomous and innovative with the autonomous dimensions of human being. What this means for Reader is that, rather than detaching the pre-autonomous commitments from subjectivity or denying life's creative potential for the new and the alternate, political discourse must admit to the public sphere of reason those matters of concern to which actants are faithful.

For Alison Martin, Jantzen identifies a similar philosophical and cultural narrative, one of violence and death, that dominates discourse and practice and that delimits possibilities for change. Martin documents Jantzen's analysis of death as the pathological and neurotic obsession of recent European history and thought, highlighting (Kojève's) French Hegelianism, in which the emergence of human subjectivity is 'a life and death struggle' that determines subjectivity and otherness, and Freudian psychoanalysis, where even birth is 'always already shot through with death' in the form of both symbolic castration by the father and immersion in the mother. To overcome this cultural 'preoccupation' with death and violence, Jantzen suggests a therapeutic model of bringing to consciousness the structures shaping cultural possibilities. Such an analysis exposes the Western constructions of masculinity that have, in Martin's words, 'structured the symbolic as an obsessive concern with death' and the Western suppression of possibilities connected to the maternal and natal. For Jantzen, following Arendt, natality is, Martin summarizes, an 'existential predisposition towards life', an alternative symbolic to that of the necrophilic contemporary *habitus*; it is ripe with possibilities for new and liberatory beginnings, for human flourishing and freedom, and for the affirmation of life rather than death and of justice and hope rather than violence. However, while Martin recognizes that Jantzen's therapeutic strategy is a powerful tool within intellectual analysis, she argues that it 'has limitations in relation to the social'. Jantzen's notion of the natal appears ahistorical in comparison with her historical analysis of the cultural embeddedness and embodiment of death and violence. For Martin, the 'germ' of a transcendent state of peace, reconciliation, harmony or beauty cannot be intrinsically contained within the immanent conditions of being born, of natality; models for transformation 'require social structures to support them, and forms of political organization and action to realize these'. Natality becomes, then, a symbol for 'the absolutely undetermined yet simultaneously absolutely conditioned state of being human', and thus for the conditions of being born, of life, and the social and political conditions of living, 'that may induce peace or that may not'.

Life and the Limits of Thinking

The obsession with death identified by Martin provides a bridge to John D. Caputo's essay, in which he argues that 'theology has been spooked by death'. The transcendence desired by theology is too often a denial of life, and particularly of moral bodies, of flesh. Its dream of eternal life actually represents a profound necrophilia. For Caputo, on the contrary, 'to take a stand for life is to stand for and with flesh'. Caputo's strategy is to take Christianity 'at its word'. Orthodox theology too often suppresses the radical implications of the doctrine of incarnation, preserving God's impassible transcendence and making the humanity of God a mere passing show. For Caputo, this is nothing other than Gnosticism, against which he poses a genuinely incarnational theology. This means taking seriously the becoming flesh of God, where 'flesh' is not a perfectly formed body, but the vulnerable seat of passivity, affectivity and feeling. Caputo draws out the connections between the incorruptible body dreamed of by classical theology and the artificially produced cybernetic body which is the fetish of transhumanism. In each case, the dream of imperishability remains intact, even if the means of attaining these dreams differ. Through readings of Dickens, Deleuze and *Slumdog Millionaire*, Caputo offers an alternative account of the flesh as alive with possibility. Resurrection becomes an earthly reality, since 'in my view it is fragile flesh that constitutes life's treasure, life's fragile absolute, and it is there that our heart should be'. This is a thinking of life that takes sides, that stands with the 'slumdogs' who need life now, not a fantasy of heavenly escape: 'If thinking is not affirmation, and if affirmation is not the affirmation of life, if it is not "for life", then it is worth nothing, or less than nothing because it is for the other side of life.' In this weak theology, this refusal of ultimate guarantees, we are solicited to make justice real, for '[t]he name of God is the name of a deed'.

If Caputo contests orthodox theology's denial of the flesh, Neil Turnbull takes on a growing philosophical orthodoxy that it is time to 'forget Wittgenstein'. Turnbull responds that Wittgenstein's 'social vitalism' offers an important contribution to recent thinking on what it means to live well. Turnbull argues that 'for Wittgenstein it is not *language* that ought to be the main concern of the philosopher but the "language-relatedness" of *life*'. On this view, Wittgenstein does nothing less than contribute to a 'philosophical project that strives to heal the modern fracturing of the lived world'. In an intriguing connection with Caputo's association of God and deed, Wittgenstein is read as saying that 'it is only through the lived deed that we can discern the dynamic unity of life'. Turnbull follows the evolution of Wittgenstein's understanding of life through his work. He insists that the famous phrase 'forms of life' is not a label applied to social and cultural contexts, but is, rather, about the way life 'is *informed*; given shape, direction and ultimately purpose'. The Wittgenstein of *The Tractatus* seeks the overcoming of false separations between self, world and life, a life which 'is not a predicate of subject'. Life cannot be given a meaning pointing beyond the world, since it is coextensive with it. It is only through misconceiving this relation that life becomes a problem for us. In a sense, 'life' comes to stand for this misrecognition, this flawed 'point of view' on the world. Wittgenstein's later work takes another tack: here, life is not the source of its own problem but a given, a self-evident certainty, the 'tacit dimension that we forget but cannot go beyond in all of our cognitions'. Now the problems and illusions are rooted in a model that tries to hook language up with the 'world', rather than seeing language as a formation of life. Life is reconceived in terms of a 'social ontology', 'the primordial connection(s) upon which language acts as a means for reweaving life into meaning'. Turnbull notes intriguing connections with Neoplatonic and earlier Greek philosophy, in the emphasis upon life as 'formative, simple and immediate activity, irreducible to all our analyses', and the understanding of philosophy as a way of life. Life is 'immanent-transcendent', neither reduced to nor going beyond a bounded world. Philosophy turns to practice, a collective practice that seeks to return us to life rather than seeking to get beyond it. Wittgenstein thus offers a profound challenge to modern philosophies still obsessed with the model of subjects relating to the world.

This reworking of subjectivity via life is apparent in a different way in the following chapter, which is more open to life being informed by encounter with the transcendent. Kenneth Jason Wardley opens his essay by acknowledging: 'It may seem odd – perverse even – to include an essay on boredom and fatigue in a book subtitled the "affirmation of life". And yet they are part of our everyday lives'. Wardley suggests that such moods are marginalized by philosophers after the more enticing game of anguish and joy. In theological terms, they are often seen as symptoms of a culpable lack of interest and motivation (as when the young man drops off during Paul's extended talk and falls to his death, 'the first recorded incident in the history of the Christian church in which a member of the congregation is bored to death by the preaching'). For Barth and others, boredom is an affliction of the modern age, an uninterested turning away from the pressing issues of life and its meaning. Wardley asks whether such experiences do in fact close a person off from fundamental questions, or whether they offer moments of emptiness in which we can be addressed anew by Being. He notes how, for Lacoste, the background fatigue of life straddles our consciousness and our inescapable animality. There is a heaviness to our experience in these states, which is also a 'dispossession of the self when subjectivity is bracketed out in and by the world'. Lacoste notes that it is especially important to pray when tired, acknowledging the felt experience of our embodied life. Such practices can dislodge the prejudice that life should be defined in terms of active agency. Giving priority to affective and embodied experience offers 'possibilities of human freedom that precede and exceed the merely conceptual or discursive'. Wardley cites Lubac's claim that there is a truth 'which is lived before it is known'.[43] Boredom and tiredness bear witness to an encounter with the world and with God that cannot be limited to intellect or an act of will. The liturgical act of keeping vigil offers one manifestation of ways in which experiencing the heaviness of time can decentre the human subject and help us resist the commodification of life. Reflecting on boredom and fatigue, Wardley concludes, is both 'a call to impurity' and an 'affirmation of life', resisting boundaries between faith and reason, theology and philosophy.

Life and Spirituality

Human life, Lorenz Moises J. Festin suggests, is essentially spiritual. Illustrating the ways in which Aristotle and Aquinas are asking questions of how human life can be understood – What is human being's constitution? What are its characteristic

---

[43]   Henri de Lubac, *The Discovery of God*, trans. Alexander Dru (London: Darton, Longman & Todd, 1960), p. 59.

function, activity and end? What accounts for its tendency towards transcendence? – Festin begins by presenting Aristotle's thinking of life as the actualization of the particular potentialities possessed by the soul of the life form in question. This means that the characteristic function (*ergon*) of the human soul is reason, a potentiality actualized through the contemplative life. The goal (*telos*) of human life is *eudaimonia* (happiness), understood as an activity (*energeia*) that is 'complete at every moment' of its 'unfolding'. On Festin's reading, this actualization of the potentiality of reason is complete at every stage of reasoning, just as seeing is the actualization of a capacity that happens at every moment of sight. While this suggests that many of the activities that human beings engage in might actualize *eudaimonia*, reason opens human life to the transcendent, such that Aristotle nevertheless commends the contemplative life. Since reason is understood by him to be 'an aperture' on that which transcends materiality, 'the decisive factor in human being's happiness' is, then, for Aquinas, 'no longer its *ergon* or characteristic capacity but that to which this actualizing pursuit is directed'. In other words, in order to attain happiness, reason – the 'divine element' in the human subject – must be supplemented by that transcendent 'object' to which it is directed: God. Thus, both human being's characteristic function and its end are spiritual, both having 'the marks of divinity'. Festin therefore concludes that human reason and intelligence are 'spiritual powers', employed in a great many of our daily activities but directing human being beyond the concerns of its everyday life.

While ancient philosophers such as Aristotle privilege the life of the mind, the contemplative life, over the life of the body, for Don Cupitt modern philosophy offers more thoroughly immanent understandings of human thought and life. Cupitt has offered two such philosophies of life, the first of which is an 'Energetic Spinozism', seeking to overcome such dualisms as mind and body through a philosophical representation of the world as a stream of contingent readings of the world and a simultaneous poetic yet pragmatic evocation of the world as an arena for the pursuit of a certain way of living. In this philosophy, the ambivalence and anxiety that results from the conflicting forces of life can find partial resolution and relief, Cupitt suggests, through expressive life-activities, such that redemption is to be found in works of beauty and other experiences of 'ecstatic immanence'. But while this philosophy comes to the reader with the suggestion that it be read aloud, slowly, to be paused over in the hope that 'a feeling of religious happiness' is formed by its very performance, Cupitt also acknowledges that such an immanent or 'democratic' philosophy may require more explicit reference to the form of *religion* in order to be more attractive as a philosophy of *life* – and this because of what he sees as a demonstrable linguistic shift wherein the term 'life' comes increasingly to occupy the fluid positions in the stream of language formerly occupied by that of 'God'. In the second philosophy of life offered by Cupitt, then, life *is* God. On the one hand, the love of life is the love of God and, on the other, the love of God or neighbour is 'generalized without limit until it becomes the love of all life'. This more 'advanced' philosophy of life would, then, become a *religion* of life, a 'religion of ordinary life' that Cupitt sees as becoming the 'effective religion of ordinary people'. It consists not so much in the interiority of the contemplative life, but in the exteriority of the expressive life, a solar life in which we come out, giving out and giving over our lives to others in a living-by-self-giving and a living-by-dying, just as the sun 'lives by expending itself'.

Finally, Philip Goodchild asks whether the contemplative life, the life of the philosopher, of reason, can truly be *a way of life* and, as such, a spiritual exercise, given the constraints of life itself. He wonders whether a 'thoughtful life begins when life lacks meaning', since suffering is, as Weil notes, that which moves thought or sets the mind in motion. In the face of life, then, philosophy would thus be a movement, 'a task to be undertaken', a form of life rather than a form of knowledge. Following Deleuze, an 'immanentist revolution' in philosophy attends to 'life within thought, within the forces that form thought as such', that set the mind to thinking. Goodchild therefore builds upon the work of McGhee, for whom the 'real task' of philosophy is to examine experiences of life.[44] This is a philosophy of *religion* not only because it concerns interiority and inwardness, but because understanding 'comes, as it were, from outside'[45] and the mind is 'set in motion *by* ... and, more radically, *towards*' such experiences of externality in the philosophical endeavour.[46] For McGhee, reason is not the characteristic function of the soul (as it was for Aristotle) but, rather, is that which 'moves or engages us'.[47] For Goodchild, then, after the death of God – the death of 'God' as a dynamic concept that evokes and provokes, that 'impels the mind towards it' (as for Aristotle, Aquinas, Anselm and Augustine) – philosophy of religion is 'no longer concerned primarily with the question of the existence of God; it has to be concerned with the conditions under which the mind is set in motion'. To the extent that the concept of life has replaced that of God in setting the mind in motion, a thinking of the concept of life within the philosophy of religion would be, Goodchild argues, 'at once intensification, attention and awakening'. But, if the thinking of God has been shaped by religious practices, he asks what practices might shape a thinking of life. In other words, what practices shape a philosopher's way of life? This question leads Goodchild back to the question of whether philosophy as a way of life might be truly possible, given the constraints of life itself. For the life of the philosopher is, he notes, shaped 'by the demands, more internalized than ever, of the management of thought within the multicultural university in contemporary global credit capitalism'.

---

[44]   Michael McGhee, *Transformations of Mind* (Cambridge: Cambridge University Press, 2000), p. 23.

[45]   Ibid., p. 115.

[46]   Ibid., p. 120.

[47]   Ibid., p. 29.

SECTION ONE
The Politics of Life

Chapter 1
Believing in This Life:
French Philosophy after Beauvoir

Pamela Sue Anderson

Introduction

In 1949, Simone de Beauvoir published her twentieth-century classic of feminist philosophy, *Le Deuxième sexe*.[1] The year before this, Gilles Deleuze had earned his *agrégation* in philosophy and was a teacher at the *lycée* Louis-le-Grand in Paris. He was already on his way to becoming one of the most significant twentieth-century philosophers of life. His philosophy is often called 'immanent' because of a concern for what life can do rather than for what is transcendent. In 1991, Gilles Deleuze and Félix Guatarri published *Qu'est-ce que la philosophie*?[2] They argue:

> There is not the slightest reason for thinking that modes of existence need transcendent values by which they could be compared, selected and judged relative to one another … A possibility of life is evaluated through itself in the movements it lays out and the intensities it creates on a plane of immanence: what is not laid out or created is rejected … [T]here are never any criteria other than the tenor of existence, the intensification of life.[3]

So, a possibility of life is explored through 'the intensities it creates' and 'the movements it lays out' on a plane of immanence. This 'intensification of life' replaces transcendent values and inspires a radical movement away from fixed forms.

The contention of the present chapter is that both Beauvoir and Deleuze prepare the way for the feminist philosopher Michèle Le Doeuff to dismiss the twentieth-century French preoccupation with Hegelian readings of a transcendent other, a normative (male) subject and a hierarchal structure of patriarchy.[4] After the Hegelianism which had dominated intellectual thinking in Paris before and during

---

[1]   Simone de Beauvoir, *Le Deuxième sexe* (Paris: Éditions Gallimard, 1949).

[2]   Gilles Deleuze and Félix Guatarri, *Qu'est-ce que la philosophie*? (Paris: Les Éditions de Minuit, 1991).

[3]   Gilles Deleuze and Félix Guatarri, *What is Philosophy?* trans. Graham Burchell and Hugh Tomlinson (London: Verso, 1994), p. 74.

[4]   Michèle Le Doeuff, *Hipparchia's Choice: An Essay Concerning Women, Philosophy, etc.*, trans. Trista Selous, 2nd edn, with an 'Epilogue 2006' (New York: Columbia University

the German occupation,[5] Deleuze offers to French philosophy something new: he contends that 'conceptual personae' constitute points of view according to which planes of immanence become distinguishable and creative.[6] And then, following in the wake of both Beauvoir's feminist philosophy and Deleuze's immanent philosophy, Le Doeuff intensifies life with a conceptual persona – that is, 'the woman-philosopher' – who generates new concepts on a plane of immanence.

This chapter will demonstrate that, unlike her near contemporary Luce Irigaray, Le Doeuff does not follow those other feminists and other philosophers who were caught up in seemingly endless rereadings of Hegel's phenomenology.[7] To the contrary, Le Doeuff accuses a 'French-style' German phenomenology of being responsible for a dogma of otherness that damages women and philosophy.[8] As will be argued here, Irigaray falls under Le Doeuff's accusation: she re-enforces an extreme version of the French Hegelian reading of the same and the other. The danger for the Irigarayan feminist is to rely upon, even while trying to reject, the transcendent values and patriarchal structures by which sexually different modes of existence are 'compared, selected and judged relative to one another'.[9]

For Irigaray, men and women must have their own sexually specific transcendent ideals which maintain predetermined forms of subjectivity.[10] Each subjectivity 'finds' (but as if 'creating' for the first time) a transcendent Other for his or her sexually specific mode of existence. Female subjectivity and male subjectivity become fully as 'divine women' and 'divine men', respectively.[11] In this light, Irigaray claims that sexual difference is required to maintain otherness beyond the sameness of one's own sex.[12] Disagreeing with a(n Irigarayan) feminism of sexual difference, Le Doeuff develops instead a conceptual persona for a philosophy of immanence, leading into ever-greater intensities and movements in our individual

---

Press, 2007), p. 107; cf. Simone de Beauvoir, *The Second Sex*, trans. Constance Borde and Sheila Malovaney-Chevallier (London: Jonathan Cape 2009), pp. 6–7.

[5]   For background, see Bruce Baugh, *French Hegel* (London: Routledge, 2003).

[6]   Deleuze and Guatarri, *What is Philosophy?*, pp. 75–6.

[7]   Twentieth-century Marxism, psychoanalysis, existentialism and phenomenology in France reflect their respective engagements with Hegel; for further background see Alexandre Kojève, *Introduction à la lecture de Hegel* (Paris: Gallimard, 1947); Judith Butler, *Subjects of Desire: Hegelian Reflections in Twentieth-Century France* (New York: Columbia University Press, 1987).

[8]   Le Doeuff, *Hipparchia's Choice*, p. 107.

[9]   Deleuze and Guatarri, *What is Philosophy?* p. 74.

[10]   Luce Irigaray, 'Divine Women', in *Genealogies and Sexes*, trans. Gillian C. Gill (New York: Columbia University Press 1993), pp. 55–72; 'Toward a Divine in the Feminine', in Gillian Howie and J'annine Jobling (eds), *Women and the Divine: Touching Transcendence* (New York: Palgrave Macmillan 2009), pp. 13–26.

[11]   Irigaray, 'Toward a Divine in the Feminine', pp. 14–16.

[12]   Luce Irigaray, 'Questions to Emmanuel Levinas', in Margaret Whitford (ed.), *The Kristeva Reader* (Oxford: Blackwell, 1991), pp. 178–89.

and collective relations with each other. For Le Doeuff, in order to live fully in joy and in hope human subjects do not project a transcendent ideal; above all, they do not strive to be divine men and divine women.

As will be argued in this chapter, Le Doeuff asserts her subtle yet profound rejection of the French Hegelian philosophy which ultimately pursued the death of the Other. Moreover, although some philosophers have read Beauvoir as accepting that Hegelian struggle of the master (self) and the slave (other) which culminates in the death of that Other, Le Doeuff points to the moment (in *The Second Sex*) when Beauvoir explicitly rejects the category of Other. It will be necessary for my argument here to elucidate that moment.

In brief, we will find that the French reader of Hegel's *Phenomenology of Spirit* in *The Second Sex* has either remained – like Irigaray – preoccupied by the relation of the self to the transcendent or absolute Other[13] or rejected – like Le Doeuff – the very question of otherness for something more creative and immanent in this life. Le Doeuff chooses to reject the category of Other (and so, alterity), finding specific support for this from Beauvoir.[14] So, in contrast to Irigaray, Le Doeuff turns away from the Left-Bank Parisian preoccupation with the Other; she explicitly dismisses 'the "French-style" German phenomenology [which] became a dogma' for fifty years or more.[15] To generate a critical focus, this chapter stresses Irigaray's and Le Doeuff's conflicting responses to 'the myth of the Other' in *The Second Sex*.[16]

French Feminist Interpretations of Beauvoir's Text

Le Doeuff reads the myth as 'the dogma' of the Other in *The Second Sex*.[17] Here it is worthwhile considering how Le Doeuff gives political value to the reader – that is, 'the self' – who strives 'to dialogue with' Beauvoir's text. The Le Doeuffian 'reading self' becomes 'mobilized',[18] and a Le Doeuffian 'philosophical dialogue' with Beauvoir's myth (of the Other) offers us one model for a feminist interpretation of philosophical texts and of political contexts. This model is distinguishable as an alternative to another feminist interpretative model which, as Le Doeuff herself claims, seeks to 'rewrite', or 'construct', the original text in 'a more conformist version of it'.[19] With this (latter) model of interpretation of the text, the identity of the self is 'fixated' politically as unchanging and not, as in the Le Doeuffian model, mobilized politically for change.

---

[13]   Beauvoir, *The Second Sex*, pp. 5–17; cf. Emmanuel Levinas, *Time and the* Other, trans. Richard A. Cohen (Pittsburgh, PA: Duquesne University Press, 1987), pp. 81–94.

[14]   Beauvoir, *The Second Sex*, pp. 5–9; Le Doeuff, *Hipparchia's Choice*, pp. 107–8.

[15]   Le Doeuff, *Hipparchia's Choice*, p. 107; and for a more complete quotation, see below.

[16]   Beauvoir, *The Second Sex*, especially pp. 5–17 and 164–7.

[17]   Le Doeuff, *Hipparchia's Choice*, p. 107.

[18]   Le Doeuff, 'Engaging with Simone de Beauvoir', pp. 17–18.

[19]   Ibid.

I will assume some background in French feminist interpretations of the profound and urgent questions which have been raised about Beauvoir's dogma of the Other, but will also fill in some gaps on Hegel before turning to my present proposal concerning the movements and intensities in a philosophy of life.

A crucial, critical question is, how do we respond to the dramatic conservative swing – or, what Le Doeuff herself would call, 'conformist' constructions – in current French-influenced interpretations of feminist issues, especially of self–other relations. To take an example, the popularization of a conservative, or conformist, trend of 'theologizing'[20] has been spear-headed by a recent Irigarayan feminist trend for sexual difference which accepts a dogma of (compulsory) heterosexuality and seeks to create a theology of divine women, alongside an already existing theology of divine men. Although I prefer not to get into the question of what has been called in a negative sense 'theologizing', this label does point to a problematic which prevents the reading self from mobilizing herself. The problem rests in reviving a once-orthodox dogma of concepts to do with deification, recalling the transcendental ideal of a man-god. In this case, deification involves actively projecting sexual types for becoming divine women and divine men.

Le Doeuff herself objects to this contemporary quest for the deification of women as a form of 'female apotheosis'.[21] In turn, her objection raises the question whether becoming divine women in any orthodox sense could be a 'feminist' task. In response, Le Doeuff urges women and critically thinking men to take seriously the political and philosophical need for identifying the minimal condition of 'feminist'. One condition for claiming to be a 'feminist' would be the possibility of disagreement; that is, if a feminist philosopher claims to be politically engaged in acting and thinking for individual women, then it would follow that a feminist philosophy of life would have to allow for disagreements about the conditions of life most suitable for women in their uniqueness and concrete differences.

Disagreements are necessary for change; the best outcome would generate the possibility of new cognitive insights, new concepts and personae. In general, philosophical disagreements about 'life' should be reflectively and critically open to dialogue; these are crucial conditions for changing minds and lives. In particular, there would be the possibility of, in Deleuzian terms, 'new planes of immanence'; and this means that, in Le Doeuff and in others who follow Deleuze, dialogue partners would not assume that agreement depends on transcendent values, or on a quest for transcendence of this life. At this stage we turn to the philosophical question of the (transcendent) Other as it appears in Beauvoir, *The Second Sex*.

At this point, it is necessary to introduce the Irigarayan and the Le Doeuffian interpretations of Beauvoir's central myth of woman as the Other. The Irigarayan

---

[20] Anthony Paul Smith and Daniel Whistler, 'Editors' Introduction', *After the Postsecular and the Postmodern: New Essays in Continental Philosophy of Religion* (Newcastle upon Tyne: Cambridge Scholars Publishing, 2010), pp. 1–25.

[21] Pamela Sue Anderson, 'Transcendence and Feminist Philosophy', in Howie and Jobling, *Women and the Divine: Touching Transcendence*, pp. 33–4.

reading of Beauvoir is difficult to sketch, not least because of the great range of things which could be said about the multiple mimetic readings of Irigaray's other/ woman. Irigaray does not just give one reading of the Other. She explores alterity in the texts of many different Western philosophers. So alongside what she says about Beauvoir on the Other, Irigaray writes varying and often conflicting things about alterity, depending upon what text of philosophy she reads, so to speak, disruptively; that is, she reads with her distinctive style of mimetic disruption by and for the Other. The question is whether the so-called disruption changes anything: men stay the same and so do women except that she becomes visible; her sexual difference remains but is made clear.

The French (Reading of) Hegel and Beauvoir's Category of the Other

In one sense, like Beauvoir, Irigaray addresses the significance of the Other in both French Hegelian appropriations of the master–slave (or, 'the lord and the bondsman'[22]) relationship, and, for example, Emmanuel Levinas's account of the absolute other.[23] However, unlike Beauvoir, Irigaray in *Speculum of the Other Woman* interprets Hegel as part of her own critical disagreements with Lacanian psycholinguistics and the significance of the 'invisibility' of woman in our social-symbolic world.[24] Lacan himself, having attended Alexandre Kojève's seminars on Hegel in 1930s Paris, was directly influenced by French Hegelianism, and so, too, was Irigaray, in her disagreements with him on the other and sexual difference. In another sense, unlike Beauvoir, Irigaray in 'Questions to Emmanuel Levinas' offers a necessary addition to, and not a mere dismissal of, Levinas's ethics of alterity in which the feminine is the absolute other; Irigaray claims that there is no alterity/otherness without sexual difference.[25] Crucially, for Irigaray, the problem is not otherness but the lack of sexual difference.

The Le Doeuffian reading of Beauvoir is not difficult to present. Le Doeuff provides the necessary, critical focus by singling out a central passage on the category of Other in *The Second Sex*. But notice the subtle nature of Le Doeuff's account: she selects a passage in Beauvoir's text which also already reflects Beauvoir's own feminist interpretation of French Hegelianism generally, including her own otherwise Hegelian experience of life; that is, Le Doeuff reads Beauvoir as overturning what Beauvoir herself might actually experience as (the) Other in the oppressive master–slave (self–other) relations between men and women in

---

[22]   G.W.F. Hegel, *The Phenomenology of Spirit.* trans. A.V. Miller (Oxford: Oxford University Press, 1977), pp. 119–39.

[23]   Levinas, *Time and the Other*, pp. 81–94.

[24]   Luce Irigaray, *Speculum of the Other Woman.* trans. Gillian C. Gill (Ithaca, NY: Cornell University Press, 1985).

[25]   Irigaray, 'Questions to Emmanuel Levinas', pp. 178ff.

1940s France. Let me explain more in order to understand Le Doeuff's feminist, political and philosophical point here.

The French philosophical context makes all the difference to an explanation of Le Doeuff and of Irigaray on Beauvoir's Other. Starting in the 1930s in Parisian academic and intellectual circles, a French line of novel appropriations of Hegel's *Phenomenology of Spirit*, especially of the master–slave dialectic, is developed, notably by Professors Jean Wahl and Jean Hyppolite at the Sorbonne, but also, as just stated, by Kojève's now famous seminars on Hegel at the *École Pratique des Hautes Études* which were attended by George Bataille, Jacques Lacan, Jean-Paul Sartre and many other well-known Parisian intellectuals who would, in turn, influence Beauvoir, Irigaray, Le Doeuff and numerous other philosophers, theorists and thinkers in a range of human sciences.[26] In light of this complex history of reception of Hegel in French twentieth-century philosophy alone, the critical question to be posed is: do Beauvoir and the French philosophers who have relied upon the Beauvoirian myth of the Other require that alterity be 'the fundamental category of human thought'? To answer, we turn to the critical passage in *The Second Sex*.

Beauvoir begins the passage of concern with a bold assertion: 'The category of *Other* is as original as consciousness itself'.[27] She continues to explain that the duality between self and other can be found in the most 'primitive' societies and in the most 'ancient' mythologies; yet she adds: 'this division did not always fall into the category of the division of the sexes, it was not based on any empirical given'.[28] Whether sun and moon, or day and night, in a primitive society, Beauvoir concludes there was 'no feminine element'. So, whether left and right, or God and Lucifer, Beauvoir asserts that 'alterity' was 'the fundamental category of human thought'.[29]

Beauvoir goes on to stress that 'no group ever defines itself as *One* without immediately setting up the *Other* opposite itself'.[30] Her examples include the native of a country who views the inhabitants of other countries as 'foreigners'; the Jews as the 'others' of anti-Semites; the blacks as the 'others' of racist Americans and so on. It seems that, according to Beauvoir, there exists, in Kojèvean terms, 'a fundamental hostility to any other consciousness'; this hostility is found in consciousness itself. The logic is that a subject posits itself only in opposition: 'it asserts itself as the essential and sets up the other as inessential, as the object'.[31] In addition, the other consciousness also has an opposing claim. As Beauvoir tells the story,

---

[26]   Pamela Sue Anderson, 'The Other', in Nicholas Adams, George Pattison and Graham Ward (eds), *The Oxford Handbook of Theology and Modern European Thought* (Oxford: Oxford University Press, forthcoming 2012); Baugh, *French Hegel*; Butler, *Subjects of Desire*.

[27]   Beauvoir, *The Second Sex*, p. 6.

[28]   Ibid.

[29]   Ibid.

[30]   Ibid., emphasis added.

[31]   Ibid., p. 7.

travelling, a local is shocked to realise that in neighbouring countries locals view him
as a foreigner: between villages, clans, nations and classes there are wars, potlatches,
agreements, treaties and struggles that remove the absolute meaning from the idea
of the other and bring out its relativity; whether one likes it or not, individuals and
groups have no choice but to recognise the reciprocity of their relation.[32]

She, then, makes a crucial claim 'that between the sexes this reciprocity has not
been put forward'; instead, one of the terms has been asserted as 'the only essential
one'; and the latter is 'pure alterity'.[33] She asks, 'Why do women not contest male
sovereignty?' A further question follows:

No subject posits itself spontaneously and at once as the inessential from the
outset; *it is not the Other who, defining itself as Other, defines the One; the Other
is posited as Other by the One positing itself as One.* But in order for the Other
not to turn into the One, the Other has to submit to this foreign point of view.
Where does this submission in woman come from?

... It is often numerical inequality that confers this privilege: the majority
imposes its law on or persecutes the minority. *But women are not a minority.*[34]

Thus, we recognize the influence on twentieth-century French philosophers –
amongst whom Beauvoir is increasingly recognized as a notable figure – of, in
particular, Kojève's seminars on Hegel.

The crucial feature of feminist interpretations of Beauvoir's distinctively French
reading of the Hegelian other is their reaction to Kojèvean interpretations of otherness.
Kojève's own reading of Hegel's dialectic in terms of the desire for recognition and
historical change is only loosely drawn from Hegel's *Phenomenology of Spirit* and
what Kojève describes as 'the bloody battle'. Kojève was probably the first to give a
central role to human desire in an inevitable struggle between the self and the other,
in which negation plays a decisive role, ending in death.

Political Responses to Woman as 'the Other', not 'the One'

As found in the previous section, Beauvoir uncovers two problematic assumptions
concerning (1) woman as the Other who is 'posited as Other by the One positing
itself as One'; and yet (2) woman as *not* turning 'into the One' by positing 'an Other'.
Insofar as women accept the One's perspective, they take on the male perspective of
themselves as other; but the question is, can women resist becoming this exception?
In other words, we need to ask how Beauvoir should be interpreted here.

---

[32]   Ibid.
[33]   Ibid.
[34]   Ibid., emphases added.

Irigaray's and Le Doeuff's differing interpretations of the French Hegelian dialectic of the same and the other are manifest in their conflicting conceptions of the role of 'the Other' in philosophy and, notably, the role of 'the feminine' posited as the 'absolute Other'.[35] It is worth asking whether Irigarayan and Le Doeuffian feminist politics and their implicit disagreements are exaggerated. When it comes to the Other is the issue merely a matter of interpretation? If so, then could there be agreement on the necessary condition(s) for contemporary feminism? Nevertheless, the answer 'no' to the first of the two questions is worth a defence; if no, then the second question could not arise.

As already mentioned, Le Doeuff urges her readers to engage in philosophical 'dialogue' by interpreting for themselves the history of texts, especially those by the few women in the history of Western philosophy. Beauvoir's text serves as her paradigm for how women can have philosophical dialogues both in solitude with texts (including those by other women philosophers) and in political contexts within collective life.[36] Le Doeuff illustrates the political value of feminism in philosophical dialogues with Beauvoir's theoretical argument *against* defining woman as the Other. If we turn to *The Second Sex*, we find that Beauvoir's theoretical objection to positing woman as the absolutely other clearly motivates her practical action for justice in self–other relations. In addressing the role of the Other, Beauvoir singles out *Time and the Other*, where Levinas asserts that 'I think the absolutely contrary contrary [*le contraire absolument contraire*], whose contrariety is in no way affected by the relationship that can be established between it and its correlative, the contrariety that permits its terms to remain absolutely other, is the *feminine*'.[37] In *The Second Sex* Beauvoir admits both the theoretical problem with this 'definition' of the absolutely other and the practical sense in which European women accepted the role which had been assigned to them as the Other. The critical question is whether the French (Kojèvean) reading of the struggle between the same and the other – as a paradigm of post-Hegelianism for twentieth-century French intellectuals – is successfully broken and undermined by Beauvoir in pointing to a simple fact: the 'failure' of woman to create her own Other.

In fact, we find that a political debate about otherness in French feminist philosophy becomes apparent in Kojève, Beauvoir, Irigaray and Le Doeuff, but each responds in their own distinctive ways to the dialectic of same and other. They disagree about the outcome of the Hegelian dialectical process, especially on the question of subjection. Which of them successfully, in Le Doeuff's terms, 'unhooks'[38] women from their subjection as the Other of the men who have been the masters in the history of Western philosophy? In their respective interpretations of this subjection of the female Other to the self-same subject of intellectual thought,

---

[35]   Levinas, *Time and the Other*, p. 85.

[36]   Michèle Le Doeuff, 'Women in Dialogue and in Solitude', *Journal of Romance Studies* 5.2 (Summer 2005): 1–15.

[37]   Levinas, *Time and the Other*, p. 85.

[38]   Le Doeuff, *Hipparchia's Choice*, p. 107.

the French feminist voices of Irigaray and of Le Doeuff have rung loud and clear. Yet their words propose political responses to otherness which do not agree with each other. In particular, while Le Doeuff replaces the dialectic of the same and the other with personal and political dialogue in individual and collective life, Irigaray promotes her feminist dialectic of sexual difference as a necessary dimension (however invisible under patriarchy) for any politics of otherness. Le Doeuff may agree with the object of feminist critique as 'the same' which dominates 'the other'. However, unlike Irigaray, her philosophical and political response to woman being treating as other is not compatible with seeking the invisible other in the social unconscious of a masculine philosophical order.

In sharp contrast to Irigaray, Le Doeuff interprets the passage from *The Second Sex* as denying that otherness (alterity) is a fundamental category of all human thought. Le Doeuff's criticism of otherness as a fundamental category attributes this mistake specifically to, again, 'a "French-style" … dogma' from 'Kojève's catechism … on the Left Bank of the Seine'.[39] Le Doeuff also explains the practical significance in Beauvoir's crucial acknowledgement of a decisive exception to Kojève's dogma. Beauvoir, in Le Doeuff's words, 'unhooks herself or turns away from what she nevertheless regards as an indisputable theoretical position', and she 'reintroduces an element which reopens the space of a problem: the notion of reciprocity'. [40] If each consciousness regards the other as another, then 'the other consciousness sets up a reciprocal claim'.[41] It appears that there is no Other in absolute terms; and yet, there is one exception to this rule: 'between the sexes this reciprocity has not been established because women have not (yet) done the same back to those who set them up as Others'.[42] Le Doeuff concludes that, in terms of method, 'Simone de Beauvoir's technique, her *metis*, her craftiness with and towards the doctrinal philosophy she has accepted … is a technique of reintroduction which undermines the structure'.[43]

Critical interpretations of woman as the Other by French feminist philosophers from Beauvoir to Irigaray and to Le Doeuff move European philosophy to the heart of twentieth-century gender debates and sexual politics well beyond Paris. We find this heart represented by Judith Butler when she returns to the question of the 'Other'. As Butler says, retrospectively in 2004, 'the Other seemed to me, as it did for Simone de Beauvoir, to be the point of departure for thinking politically about subordination and exclusion: … in asking about the Other … I turned to the modern source of the understanding of Otherness: Hegel himself'.[44]

---

[39] Ibid.

[40] Ibid.

[41] Beauvoir, *Le Deuxième sexe*, p. 19; also see pp. 16–20.

[42] Le Doeuff, *Hipparchia's Choice*, p. 107–8; cf. Beauvoir, *The Second Sex*, pp. 5–11.

[43] Le Doeuff, *Hipparchia's Choice*, p. 108.

[44] Judith Butler, 'Can the Other of Philosophy Speak?', in *Undoing Gender* (London and New York: Routledge, 2004), p. 240.

Generally, the history of modern European philosophy is not complete, or near its *telos*, until it either raises the Other to a highly privileged position as the absolute or reduces the Other to the same. But for woman as the Other, this is a no-win choice. Following after Kojève, neither the Irigarayan deification of the feminine other nor the Lacanian invisibility of woman in post-Hegelian discourse offers a lasting solution to the problem of the oppression of female subjects. A distinctive measure – to which this chapter will return – remains necessary for feminist philosophy; this measure is not the same or the absolute. Instead, the measure is more appropriately the unique, ensuring the many concrete differences between individual subjects.

Admittedly, Irigaray challenges the negative Lacanian interpretation of woman's invisibility. In *Speculum of the Other Woman*, she unearths an invisible unconscious space of female *jouissance* in the struggle of the male subject and his other. Irigaray's practice of disruptive mimesis appears, for example, in her mime of Hegel's Antigone as the 'eternal irony of the community'.[45] With this mime, Irigaray claims to uncover a female language of desire, constituting the invisible substructure on which the social-symbolic structure, that is, 'the male economy of the same', of exclusive relations between men, still rests. In fact, in her most recent writings, Irigaray strongly advocates that women 'create' (apparently, in this sense, 'find') their own (projected) God, in order to become sovereign subjects; that is, she advocates a divine in the feminine as the ideal for the female subject.[46] So, to become divine women is decisive for Irigaray's ethics of sexual difference.[47]

The Irigarayan imperative to become divine as male or as female assumes that the Kojèvean logic of the subject, who requires the Other as the ideal of its own gender, should be extended to women. There is, then, not only one sexually specific subject who is male, but there are two subjects; and each of the two types of subjects needs a God of his or her own gender, in order to become fully as (in Irigaray's more recent terms, 'sexuate') subjects. The becoming of the sex/gender ideals, which distinguish sexual difference, would acknowledge the love between mother and daughter as well as that between father and son; it is on sexually specific ideals that the contemporary Irigarayan calls for an ethics and, in fact, a theology of sexual difference.

The present contention is that a problematic result of Irigaray's interpretation of otherness as requiring sexual difference is to resume wittingly or unwittingly the Hegelian dialectic of self and other. This is most apparent when Irigaray urges woman to create a god(dess) as the absolute other for her own gender. Irigaray's divine in the feminine moves close to Hegel's idealization of femininity as a

---

[45]   Irigaray, *Speculum of the Other Woman*, pp. 214–26; cf. Pamela Sue Anderson, *A Feminist Philosophy of Religion: the Rationality and Myths of Religious Belief* (Oxford: Blackwell, 1998), pp. 194–200.

[46]   Irigaray, 'Toward a Divine in the Feminine', pp. 13–26.

[47]   Luce Irigaray, *An Ethics of Sexual Difference*, trans. Carolyn Burke and Gillian C. Gill (London: Athlone Press, 1993), pp. 117–29.

transcendent value[48] and Levinas's feminine as the absolute other.[49] Like the Father-Son God who is the absolute for the (love) relations of male subjects in Christianity, Irigaray's deification of the mother-daughter becomes the absolute for the (love) relations of female subjects in her theologizing. Together the male and female theologizing of sexual stereotype privileges two sexes and so heterosexuality. The dialectical 'logic' of Irigarayan sexual difference, with male and female divinities, does not eradicate the Other from its separate sphere of life. Instead, Irigaray's most recent theology conforms to traditional heterosexual relations.

After all, we might say that this conformity to an orthodox theology of sexual difference is what Le Doeuff has in mind when she speaks of a 'conformist construction' of a fixed feminine subject rather than a mobile feminist subject. It would then follow that Irigaray's ethics of sexual difference would leave men undisturbed by women who develop in their separate sexually specific lives. Yet surely this Irigarayan interpretation of a philosophy of life is precisely what 'modern' (non-Hegelian) European feminist philosophers aimed to abolish: a separate sphere of life where women could get on with their chores (for men and children) without disturbing the male thinker and male politics.[50]

In sharp contrast to Irigaray's feminist imperatives, neither Beauvoir nor Le Doeuff seeks anything like Irigaray's 'solution' to the problem of the Other for women. As already stated, Le Doeuff argues explicitly against female apotheosis.[51] She interprets Beauvoir as supporting her claim that women do not (need to) posit an Other. Le Doeuff argues, with this support from Beauvoir, that the deification of female subjects will only return us to the Hegelian objectification of femininity; and this is a negative implication of the projection of a god(dess) for women. Le Doeuff's distinctive feminist politics urges women to celebrate the diversity of women and of men; but for her this means that the dignity of each woman and of each man requires that each of them be given unique, cognitive and political value. These values are not fixed biologically by sex differences, but of course they will be gendered to some degree, just not fixed by transcendent bi-gendered types; that is, something like those stereotypes fixed by normative Roman Catholic assumptions of heterosexuality and of sex functioning to fulfil norms of compulsory reproduction.

---

48   On femininity, see Hegel, *Phenomenology of Spirit*, p. 288.

49   Levinas, *Time and the Other*, pp. 84–90.

50   Le Doeuff, *Hipparchia's Choice*, pp. 227–8; Daniel Whistler, 'The Abandoned Fiancée, Against Subjection', in Pamela S. Anderson (ed.) *New Topics in Feminist Philosophy of Religion: Contestations and Transcendence Incarnate* (Dordrecht: Springer, 2010), pp. 128–30.

51   Anderson, 'Transcendence and Feminist Philosophy', pp. 33–7.

On Friendship, Reciprocity and Immanent Life

For Le Doeuff, the result of fixing the subject's relation to an (absolute) Other fits a pernicious French Hegelian story. Le Doeuff insists that it is simply wrong to suppose that otherness is a fundamental category of *all* human thought. It is also wrong to portray the Other as a necessary part in a dialectic of negation and subjection. To what place does a rejection of this story and the dialectic lead? If Beauvoir is saying that women can have freedom without subjection, then she can lead us to freedom; and this is the freedom which, as Le Doeuff claims, makes female subjects of all kinds free to create friendships without dependence on any male master: no longer is the woman subjected. Liberated from the slavery of same–other relations she has freedom and the possibility of life.

If Le Doeuffian and Beauvoirian philosophies of life are to bring about equal relations between subjects as friends who dialogue and attend to each other, then appeals to an absolute Other must necessarily be given up. Ultimately, we find a minimal condition for contemporary 'feminists': the freedom to think for oneself, to disagree and to live life's intensities and movements for the possibilities they generate. Daniel Whistler finds Le Doeuff's rejection of the master–slave dialectic moves us closer to a Deleuzian possibility.[52] As Whistler explains:

> Key to Le Doeuff's rejection of the master/slave dialectic and its more subtle manifestations is her rejection of the notion of otherness (on which Hegelian dialectic is based). Against the crude duality of same and other, Le Doeuff (following Beauvoir) posits 'the ideal of reciprocity'.[53] 'No morality is possible without at least the principle of reciprocity, without mutual recognition'.[54] While for Hegel such 'mutual recognition' is merely an ideal, Le Doeuff – [who says] 'incorrigible meliorist that I am'[55] – believes it reachable. *Subjection is not necessary; equality is a possibility.*[56]

In other words, encouraging friendship, hence, autonomy and dialogue, and not subjection and heteronomy, would be the way forward for a (feminist) philosophy

---

[52]   Whistler, 'The Abandoned Fiancée', pp. 127–45.

[53]   Le Doeuff, *Hipparchia's Choice*, pp. 107–8. Note that 'reciprocity' is used in more than one sense by Beauvoir. According to Penelope Deutscher, Le Doeuff reads reciprocity in a (Beauvoirian) positive sense of recognition; that is, she sees reciprocity in 'recognition that the other is difficult to understand and necessarily exceeds my capacities of comprehension', see Penelope Deutscher, *The Philosophy of Simone de Beauvoir: Ambiguity, Conversion, Resistance* (Cambridge: Cambridge University Press, 2008), p. 164 fn. 20.

[54]   Le Doeuff, *Hipparchia's Choice*, p. 187.

[55]   Michèle Le Doeuff, *The Sex of Knowing*, trans. Kathryn Hamer and Lorraine Code (New York: Continuum, 2003), p. 68.

[56]   Whistler 'The Abandoned Fiancée, p. 129, emphasis added; cf. Le Doeuff, *Hipparchia's Choice*, p. 320.

of life; this is a life which is free from subjection to otherness. The aim of life would be to generate Le Doeuffian friendships of autonomous subjects who would gain cognitive insights through dialogue, while listening yet never allowing anyone else to think in one's place. These friendships would flourish as each subject listens and learns about the diverse and concrete differences which mark each of us, individually and collectively.

Whistler's interpretation of Le Doeuff as an 'incorrigible meliorist', that is, an always hopeful feminist, is well worth further exploration. Feminists and philosophers (of life) today can discover that Le Doeuff's philosophy self-consciously resonates not only with Beauvoir, but with Deleuze who clearly rejected the Parisian fashion of Hegelian struggles between the subject and the other.

In *Hipparchia's Choice*, Le Doeuff creates the imaginary for 'a woman-philosopher' which, as mentioned earlier, Deleuze himself would identify as a conceptual persona.[57] In response to a correspondence with Deleuze, Le Doeuff acknowledges that 'The philosophical world is a *milieu* and each of us is like a living creature dialectically engaged with its environment.'[58] She seems to agree that, in Deleuzian terms, we philosophize on a plane of immanence which can be creative as new possibilities of life are invented and the power of a new conceptual persona stretches out before and around us.[59] Basically, Deleuze, first, describes 'a plane of immanence' and, next, explains how the conceptual persona and plane of immanence 'presuppose each other'. In the highly significant words of Deleuze and Guattari:

> Sometimes the person seems to precede the plane, sometimes to come after it – that is, it appears twice; it intervenes twice ... [T]he conceptual persona with its personalized features intervenes between chaos and the diagrammatic features of the plane of immanence and also between the plane and the intensive features of the concepts that happen to populate it ... Conceptual personae constitute points of view according to which planes of immanence are distinguished from one another or brought together, but they also constitute the conditions under which each plane finds itself filled with concepts of the same group ... But this is a very complex game [as if a handful of dice are thrown on a table by the persona] ... The conceptual persona is needed to create concepts on the plane, just as the plane itself needs to be laid out.[60]

Le Doeuff's increasing visibility in Anglo-American feminism seems equally to be due to changes in the contemporary politics of interpretation, especially when

---

[57]   Le Doeuff, *Hipparchia's Choice*, p. 319. Subsequently, Deleuze identifies the conceptual persona of the woman-philosopher in Le Doeuff, *L'Etude et le rouet*, see Deleuze and Guatarri, *What is Philosophy?* pp. 69–81 and 222 fn. 7.

[58]   Le Doeuff, *Hipparchia's Choice*, p. 320.

[59]   Deleuze and Guattari, *What is Philosophy?* pp. 71ff.

[60]   Ibid., pp. 75–6.

it comes to the French feminist interpretations of the same and the Other. The long-popularized French feminist response to Hegel, associated with a feminism of sexual difference, most notably with Irigaray's ethics of sexual difference, may have gone too far in its conformism, to its theologizing, in deifying women according to their own gender (like men who have been deified according to their own gender ideal). For some of us, it is difficult to call this Irigarayan trend 'feminism'.[61] At least for me, 'the politics' of sexual difference has seemed to turn into its opposite: the theologizing of fixed heterosexual norms of male and female relations. What sort of politics of interpretation advocates divine men and divine women? Certainly it is not what everyone would expect of 'feminisms'!

Rejection of the Duality of the Same and the Other: New Movements in this Life

It becomes noteworthy – in light of the previous section – that ever since 1980 when Le Doeuff published a collection of essays in *The Philosophical Imaginary*, she has been critical of philosophical appeals to the Other. Moreover, today in 'a spirit of secularism', Le Doeuff is urging a resistance to female apotheosis. As Le Doeuff's well-known interpretation of *The Second Sex* makes clear: she has no time for Kojèvean phenomenology when it comes to the Hegelian dialectic of same and other. Her reaction can be heard resounding as here:

> Eeek! Kojève's catechism certainly has set the tone for the century on the Left Bank of the Seine … Lacan, Levinas, Levi-Strauss, Simone de Beauvoir and a few others all took their bearings from it, directly or indirectly, and thus 'French-style' German phenomenology became a dogma, in other words an obvious truth to be taught. According to this dogma, human thought has a universal structure which can be observed equally well among the Bororo peoples as among the tribe of St Germain-des-Près … an ultra-simple structure and so minimal that in practice it is most difficult to establish its absolute absence anywhere … I shall not try to prove that there are some thoughts which escape this duality of the Same and the Other. Suffice it to say that it is trivial, or rather so crude that we cannot legitimately regard it as a 'fundamental category'; for what can be founded on such a summary logic? What is really thought in the various forms of thinking requires many other things. It is not this poor duality which makes Newton's theory into one which thinks something through or makes Marx or Tocqueville into political thinkers.[62]

---

[61]　For more on Le Doeuff's relation to Deleuze (and her alternative model to the Hegelian master–slave dialectic), see Whistler, 'The Abandoned Fiancée', pp. 128–30.

[62]　Le Doeuff, *Hipparchia's Choice*, p. 107.

With the triviality of this 'logic', in telling us nothing about actual thinking in its glorious details and uniqueness, whether in physics or biological theory or politics, Le Doeuff persuasively insists that otherness is not a fundamental category of all human thought. As a result, Le Doeuff reads any feminist, or other French, philosophical appeals to 'the Other' as a mere foil for the superiority of what is considered 'the Same' – whether it be philosophy, rationality or masculinity.

In *Hipparchia's Choice*, Le Doeuff applies her criticism specifically to the feminisms of difference. She argues that to define women as the Other is to advocate an abstract difference between man and woman at the expense of the differences that exist between particular women and the differences that sometimes do not exist between particular men and particular women. In her words: 'To look for a language in which "women can speak their sex" is, in fact, to reduce this diversity [between women] to a sameness, to speak in terms of a single femininity.'[63] This is not only a problem for a feminist politics of sexual difference. According to Le Doeuff, it is a problem for any philosophy of the Other:

> The ideology of difference ... arises from a contradiction. It starts by assuming that the existence of difference is valued, but then, by concentrating on one particular difference, it turns against its original programme, suppressing all differences which might exist on either side of the great dividing line [between same and other] which it has drawn. The only consistent way to give value to the fact of difference is to uncover differences by their thousands.[64]

So Beauvoir uncovers the myth of the Other; Le Doeuff turns to Beauvoir, not only to overcome the hegemony of the Other but to criticize an 'ideology of difference' premised on an asymmetrical reciprocity. Le Doeuff interprets Beauvoir's commitment both to the ideal of 'reciprocity'[65] (where mutual recognition is a fact to be presupposed and not, as in Hegel, an ideal to strive violently for) and also to the ideal of thinking which is 'tied to the factual'; this thinking enables us to 'pluralise' and ultimately, to 'undermine' the category of Other/alterity.[66]

Again, turning to Le Doeuff's own words, see how she dramatically distinguishes Beauvoir's feminism from that of Irigaray:

> Those [women] who feel strong and hope to find employment, a place in the professional world, and a satisfactory level of material independence prefer Simone de Beauvoir; those who are less sure probably need someone to talk to them in positive terms about a domestic destiny [are] ... reading Luce Irigaray.[67]

---

63   Ibid., p. 227.
64   Ibid., p. 228.
65   Ibid., p. 108.
66   Ibid., pp. 108 and 133.
67   Le Doeuff, *The Sex of Knowing*, pp. 65–6.

This is clearly a political statement for a politics of choice! Yet Le Doeuff moves on to present her own alternative for a politics of interpretations in terms of a dialogue which is available to every woman and every man. This is a distinctive sort of 'philosophical dialogue' which pays careful, yet critical attention to the interpretation of particular texts. Her politics of interpretation aims to represent the Other differently, in a range of (historical-social) locations and styles of thinking. Instead of a search for an ever new dialectics of same/other, the Le Doeuffian dialogue aims to read texts outside of either the Hegelian or the Levinasian tradition of the Other. For example, Le Doeuff herself returns to earlier historical periods such as the seventeenth century with her focus on Gabrielle Suchon, searching for political alternatives for feminists which will transform 'the abstract Other' into a plurality of diverse and concrete subjects.[68]

Le Doeuff's claim that otherness is not the fundamental category contains the core idea of her feminist politics in the context of modern European philosophy. As seen, Le Doeuff does not follow the assumptions concerning otherness, or the same and the other, which preoccupied other twentieth-century French philosophers, namely Hegelianism. Instead, she shows an affinity with Deleuze's rejection of Hegel's theory of negation and practice of subjection (of the Other). She chooses to learn from Deleuze rather than either the feminisms of sexual difference or the politics of French (Kojevean) phenomenology. I suggest that Le Doeuff learns to, in Deleuze's term, 'believe'[69] in life's possibilities of movements and intensities; she learns, again in Deleuze's terms, 'to give birth to new modes of existence, closer to animals, rocks', and so, to nature, the world and all living things.[70] We should not be surprised to find freedom (for all women and men) in a rejection of the conservative theologizing which continues to contaminate French philosophy and the sexual lives of (conservative) women and men today.

Le Doeuff rightly and increasingly admits her affinity with and gratitude to Deleuze. Whistler is right to discover the heart of Le Doeuff's departure from the French Hegelians, including the feminism of sexual difference, as follows:

> The first chapter of the second part of Hegel's *Phenomenology of Spirit* – 'Independence and Dependence of Self-consciousness' – has left a remarkable legacy on modern [European] thought … it is only through being subjected that one can initially become a subject: coming to self-consciousness is the privilege of the slave – the dominated are to be envied for they are the real human. It, of course, needs no great insight to see how such an ethical model can be used as a justification for the worst forms of oppression of both women and men.

---

[68]   Le Doeuff, 'Women in Dialogue and in Solitude', pp. 1–15.
[69]   Deleuze and Guatarri, *What is Philosophy?*, p. 74.
[70]   Ibid., pp. 74–5.

... Against the Hegelian master/slave dialectic I oppose Michèle Le Doeuff's 'model of radical friendship' for the development of subjectivity.[71]

This confirms that Le Doeuffian politics could be said to have, to repeat, as one of its feminist mottos: 'subjection is *not* necessary, while equality is a possibility'! Or, as he also asserts, 'friendship and so, dialogue (not bondage and so, heteronomy) ... is the way of self-consciousness for Le Doeuff'.[72]

 To end with the point which Le Doeuff – but apparently, not Irigaray – draws from *The Second Sex*. Beauvoir presents the exception of woman as the Other who is 'posited as Other by the One positing itself as One'; but who does *not* 'turn into the One' by positing an Other.[73] In other words, the Hegelian patriarchal 'logic' is broken, just as women resist accepting and promoting subjection in life as the Other. It remains a truism that a Le Doeuffian politics of interpretation offers the possibility of equality, while the politics of Irigarayan interpretation presupposes the forms of sexual difference. The latter may be the 'popular' choice of the twenty-first century feminine 'feminist' of sexual difference; but the price paid for this popularity may block a philosophy of life. In her decisive terms, Le Doeuff concludes that in Irigaray's texts we find female and male identities of predetermined (biological) sex-roles organized into patriarchal structures: 'Everywhere you find respect for the mother and for nature. In fact, in [Irigaray's] writing we find the three "c"s (*K*s) ... cooking (*Kuche*) with Hestia, children (*Kinder*) with the right to motherhood and the church (*Kirche*) with leaden references to edifying (female) deities'.[74]

Conclusion

To conclude, I leave the reading self with a choice between two feminist (political) approaches to a philosophy of life: the first approach offers a chance to recognize a divine in the feminine, to become female and male subjects in preformed sexually specific spheres of life; and the second approach offers the chance to be mobilized by life's intensities and movements rather than determined by transcendent sexual stereotypes. If the alternatives for this choice are fair, then we have two distinct philosophies of life. Only one of them seems to promise the intensification of a life's possibilities, along with movements of creativity, which give new colour to the tenor of our present existence.

 Mobilization, or fixation! Consider carefully how a possibility of life is evaluated. According to Deleuze, we find a possibility of life 'in the movements

---

[71]   Whistler, 'The Abandoned Fiancée', p. 128.

[72]   Ibid., p. 129.

[73]   Anderson, 'The Other'.

[74]   Le Doeuff, *The Sex of Knowing*, pp. 65–6.

it lays out and the intensities it creates on a plane of immanence'.[75] So, why not follow a Le Doeuffian reading of Beauvoir? And also, like Le Doeuff, take up a Deleuzian imperative to recharge immanence and not reassert transcendence? This could mean energizing life in this world, not projecting life into another world of transcendent values. Let us be philosophers, including women and men, who believe in this life!

---

[75]   Deleuze and Guatarri, *What is Philosophy?* p. 74.

Chapter 2

Agamben, Girard and the Life that Does Not Live

Brian Sudlow

'Life does not live', the epigram deployed by Theodor Adorno at the start of *Minima Moralia*, embodied Adorno's conviction that life could not flourish at a time when production superseded it in importance.[1] In the dedication to this very work, Adorno observes caustically: 'Our perspective of life has passed into an ideology which conceals the fact that there is life no longer'.[2] The *Minima Moralia* reflect on the fallout of this ideology in the bourgeois-created, consumer-led Western societies of the mid-twentieth century. Undoubtedly, his other source of pessimism in this work can be located in the long shadow of the concentration camp, the gloom of which had reached Adorno in his US exile during World War II: 'The subject still feels sure of its autonomy, but the nullity demonstrated to subjects by the concentration camp is already overtaking the form of subjectivity itself'.[3] Paradoxically, as if the subject's autonomy were always dependent on social recognition, this collapse of subjectivity resulted from the impact which total exclusion from the community had had on the individual within the paradigm of the camp. Indeed, what could be more isolating, and thereby more destructive for the individual, than to be thrust beyond the realms of recognized humanity, subject to unbridled violence, and exiled to the darkness outside human and divine law where Giorgio Agamben will locate his *homo sacer*?

It is right to elect major cultural commentators like Adorno as our interlocutors, as we seek to try to understand ourselves, our history and our very own life. However bad the concentration camps were, nevertheless, the pre-Holocaust world itself was far from Edenic. Without wishing to mobilize the Holocaust for any cause whatsoever, one cannot help drawing correlations between the isolation and death which it so emblematically represents to Adorno's mind and to ours, and the forms of isolation, dislocation and death – beyond the alienating effects of overproduction lamented by Adorno – experienced by many Western people

---

[1]   Theodor Adorno, *Minima Moralia: Reflections from Damaged Life* (London: Verso, 2005 [1951]), p. 19. The epigram is in fact a quotation from Ferdinand Kürnberger, an obscure Viennese writer whose only previous claim to fame was to have been cited by Wittgenstein at the opening of his *Tractatus Logico-Philosophicus*.

[2]   Ibid., p. 15.

[3]   Ibid., p. 16.

within the fifty years that preceded and coincided with it. Applying Adorno's concern with life to their case, we could ask how life might live for those who, like the Surrealists and the Dadaists, embraced Nietzsche's announcement of the death of God and turned increasingly towards the realms of absurdity, expressing the isolation of the thinking mind from Christian, deist or even rationalist teleologies. How might life live for those who endured the daily horror of trench warfare and witnessed first-hand the transformation of northern France and the Low Countries into the greatest open charnel house until that time? How might life live also, for those who, confronted with such isolation, dislocation and death, were turning away from the Enlightenment's unfulfilled promises of progress and asking, with T.S. Eliot in *Choruses from The Rock*, 'Where is the Life we have lost in living?'[4] Eliot's rhetorical question suggests that the life 'that does not live' has in fact been disguised by a simulacrum of life which has obscured true life in a flurry of inauthentic activity. More significantly, however, it also implies that the recovery of that lost life is not as remote a possibility as Adorno's judgement seems to assume.

Unquestionably, therefore, Adorno's anxieties about a life ruined by production and devastated by the disintegration of subjectivity find many correlations within modernity. The problem this chapter faces, however, is that to search for an answer to Adorno's question about life while ignoring the problem of life as posed by Eliot in 1934 – that some kinds of living are the enemies of an authentic life – promises a counsel merely for survival. Moreover, the problem of life necessarily raises the problem of the subject: who lives? Is it in fact life that lives, or do life and the problems associated with it not inevitably raise again the possibility of the divine subject who in the Christian tradition claims to be *Life* itself?

In order to elaborate answers to such questions, this chapter will first consider the subject and the matter of life as embodied by Giorgio Agamben's *homo sacer*, a figure embedded in the experience of the Holocaust and emblematic also of the emergence of biopolitics as announced by Michel Foucault. Agamben's view of the subject of life is written into his analysis of how the very existence of sovereignty is founded on the power to exclude that subject, the *homo sacer*. His proposition for the matter of life, on the other hand, is contained in his critique of how the Western tradition of political thought has divided what he will call *bios* from *zoe*, a distinction which stands in need of rigorous questioning.

A ready foil for this analysis of Agamben is found in the work of René Girard. Girard's work has been contrasted several times with Agamben's in recent scholarship but not yet in ways that address this key question of life. While Colby Dickinson has analysed the correlations between Agamben and Girard on the topic of mimesis, and Christopher A. Fox has considered the ways in which these two major critics have distinguished and differentiated politics and religion, Frederiek Depoortere has cast doubts over the solidity of Agamben's analysis of *homo sacer* and turns to Girard's reading of the figure of the scapegoat as a means of clarifying

---

4   T.S. Eliot, *Collected Poems 1909–1962* (London: Faber and Faber, 2002), p. 140.

the difficulties posed by Agamben.[5] By analysing still further the terrain which separates Agamben from Girard, this chapter will seek to reassess what exactly Agamben and Girard propose as the life that can live, and what the divergences between their findings signify.

Agamben's Bare Life

For Agamben, there is no sense in which the subject of political life, the 'who' of living, is anything else than the anthropic agent or agents; this is true, even though part of Agamben's philosophical work has been to dismantle what he calls the anthropological machinery which has historically sought to conceptualize humanity ontologically, rather than as a cultural construct.[6] Whatever Ἄνθρωπος ultimately means, the anthropic agent, whom Agamben will come to reinterpret from the perspective of the *homo sacer*, remains for Agamben the central figure of political life in the contemporary period with all its biopolitical possibilities. There are no other knowing agents who can contribute to this project for life.

Agamben's concern in his *Homo Sacer: Sovereign Power and Bare Life* is to unpack and develop the notion of biopolitics first broached by Michel Foucault in his history of sexuality and developed further in later writings and lectures. For Foucault, the threshold of biological modernity, signalled by the themacity of sexuality which arose during the Enlightenment, was also marked by a sea change which saw the simple living body becoming central to the state's political strategies. As Foucault argued in his 1978–79 lectures at the *Collège de France*, biopolitics emerged in the eighteenth century as governments began 'to rationalise the problems posed ... by phenomena characteristic of a set of living beings forming a population: health, hygiene, birth rate, life expectancy, race'.[7] Capitalism itself, claims Foucault, was in part rendered possible by the kinds of discipline which biopolitical control made possible.

For Agamben, the impact of this biopolitical shift on the cultural episteme – the cluster of relations between discourses which express a culture's self-understanding – 'constitutes the decisive event of modernity' and colours all strands of modern

---

[5]   Frederiek Depoortere, 'Reading Giorgio Agamben's *Homo Sacer* with René Girard', *Philosophy Today* (2011): 108–17; Colby Dickinson, 'Beyond Violence, Beyond the Text: The Role of Gesture in Walter Benjamin and Giorgio Agamben, and its Affinity with the Work of René Girard', *Heythrop Journal*, 52 (2011): 952–61; Christopher A. Fox, 'Sacrificial Pasts and Messianic Futures: Religion as a Political Prospect in René Girard and Giorgio Agamben', *Philosophy and Social Criticism*, 33/5 (2007): 563–95.

[6]   See, for example, Giorgio Agamben, *The Open: Man and Animal*, trans. Kevin Attell (Stanford: Stanford University Press, 2004 [2002]).

[7]   Michel Foucault, *The Birth of Biopolitics: Lectures at the Collège de France, 1978–1979*, Michel Sennellart (ed.), trans. Graham Burchell (Basingstoke: Palgrave Macmillan, 2008 [2004]), p. 315.

politics, even the most extreme, with all the enigmas that they pose for life itself.[8]
Yet, far from being content with this conceptualization of biopolitics as a uniquely
modern phenomenon, Agamben discovers a foreshadowing of biopoliticization
in two instances of classical thought and culture, both of which cast light on the
perennial political problem of the state of exception, especially because of the
processes to which they subject life itself. Life and its differentiation from death
have always been a central consideration of how sovereignty is constituted, but
the foregrounding of biological life under the conditions of biopolitics allows
Agamben to pose the question of sovereignty again in a different light.

Accordingly, Agamben notes that the Greeks originally used two words for
life: *zoe* and *bios*. *Zoe* denotes just life in general or bare life, as Agamben comes
to call it; *bios*, on the other hand, is a particular kind of life, perfected individually
by virtue and socially by politics. The entire Western tradition of politics which
has incorporated bare life into the city through individual or political virtue has,
Agamben argues, achieved this inclusion paradoxically through an act of exclusion.
Bare life, or *zoe*, is included or co-opted into the political domain because of its
potential to supply the raw lifeline of a particular *bios*, but excluded by the same
token because it does not remain itself.[9]

The importance of this initially linguistic distinction of *zoe* and *bios* does
not appear clear until we consider the second adumbration of biopolitics which
Agamben detects in classical culture: the figure of the *homo sacer*. In the writings
of Pompeius Festus, a grammarian and etymologist of the second century AD, the
homo sacer is defined as

> the one whom the people have judged on account of a crime. It is not permitted
> to sacrifice this man, yet he who kills him will not be condemned for homicide;
> in the first tribunitian law, in fact, it is noted that 'if someone kills the one who
> is sacred according to the plebiscite, it will not be considered homicide'. This is
> why it is customary for a bad or impure man to be called sacred.[10]

The use of the word 'sacred' in the context of purity and impurity requires
contextualization. In its original meaning, 'sacred' denotes in fact that which
is set aside or reserved for use in relation to worship. Such an action, however,
exposes the sacred object to interpretation through the categories of cleanness
and uncleanness. The ambivalence of the sacred, thus conceived, appears in the
work of numerous early anthropologists, notably William Robertson Smith and
Emile Durkheim. Now, while the concept of taboo is often used to manage this
ambivalence, Agamben rejects this as a way of explaining the phenomenon of the
homo sacer. Instead, he argues that *homo sacer* was a category which emerged when

---

Giorgio Agamben, *Homo Sacer: Sovereign Power and Bare Life*, trans. Daniel
Heller-Roazen (Stanford: Stanford University Press, 1998 [1995]), p. 4.

Ibid., pp. 9 and 11.

[10]   Cited in ibid., p. 71.

sovereign power posed an act that was self-constituting by placing an individual beyond human and divine law. The *homo sacer* is beyond human law because his homicide is unpunishable; it would not be unfaithful to Agamben's thought to say that the homicide of the *homo sacer* is in fact literally an act of pesticide. Yet *homo sacer* is also beyond divine law, argues Agamben, because he cannot become the victim of a sacrifice; the paradox being that the *homo sacer* represents a sacredness which is antithetical to the domain of the gods. Agamben concludes that the *homo sacer* thus lies beyond the sacred and the profane, the province of divine law and the province of human law, and that this exclusion, ordained by sovereign power in a self-constituting act, produces or reveals the bare life or *zoe* that it co-opts. The *homo sacer* thus models the excluded life which Agamben claims emerges from the *zoe–bios* distinction. Together, they render more explicit the production of bare life which, Agamben argues, is at the heart of biopolitics.[11]

Critical welcome for this theory in relation to life, death and sovereignty has been significant and has crossed disciplinary boundaries.[12] On the other hand, the sternest critique of Agamben's analysis questions his understanding of the primary sources. In Frederiek Depoortere's 2011 article on *homo sacer*, he argues that Agamben's argument fails to account fully for the fact that in the original Latin sources the *homo sacer* is one who has committed a heinous crime. Agamben's claim is that such crimes constitute 'the originary exception in which human life is included in the political order in being exposed to an unlimited capacity to be killed'.[13] Depoortere's response is that Agamben provides no substantial proof of this; in his view, 'it seems more accurate to accept what the sources explicitly say and to consider *sacratio* [that is the condition of the *homo sacer*] to be the punishment for a number of severe crimes, crimes that … affect the foundational relationships of Roman society'.[14] However life is included in the political order, therefore, it is not through the mechanism that Agamben has wrongly attributed to the figure of the *homo sacer*, at least in Depoortere's analysis of the primaries.

Depoortere's objection is not the only one which can be made against Agamben's analysis and his characterization of the Western political tradition as perennially biopolitical. Even if we accepted Agamben's analysis of *homo sacer* as a figure of Roman culture, why should we also accept that the theological or jurisprudential postulates of Roman society have the same effects as those of Christianity which was a dominant influence on the tradition of Western politics and whose grand projects have included the recovery of the excluded and the exaltation of the humbled? In fact, the entire tradition of sanctuary laws, not only in their Christian forms but even in their Roman forerunners, seems to offer a refutation of Agamben's reading of *homo sacer*. While sanctuary law is thought by

---

[11]   Ibid., pp. 71–4.

[12]   See, for example, Andrew Norris (ed.), *Politics, Metaphysics and Death: Essays on Giorgio Agamben's* Homo Sacer (Durham, NC: Duke University Press, 2005).

[13]   Agamben, *Homo Sacer*, p. 85.

[14]   Depoortere, 'Reading Giorgio Agamben's *Homo Sacer*', p. 111.

some to have achieved its apogee precisely in the absence of properly constituted sovereign power, other readings of the sources find sanctuary, and the attendant practices of *intercessio*, clemency and pardon, to be deeply inscribed in Greek, Roman and Christian legal traditions which are at the same time predicated on clear conceptualizations of sovereign power.[15] Given the thousand years of jurisprudential history in which sanctuary legislation was implemented widely across Europe, the idea that sovereign power generally constitutes itself through some self-constituting act of excluding the *homo sacer* is entirely moot.[16]

Another objection to Agamben's arguments can be formulated as follows. Agamben's treatment of the distinction of *zoe* and *bios* posits that *zoe* is excluded by *bios*, yet this proposition seems to obfuscate rather than clarify the relationship. *Bios* proposes not only to include but to perfect *zoe*, the biological resources of which far from exhaust human potential; indeed the idea that *bios* excludes *zoe* fails to account for all the benefits which *bios*, as a chosen form of life, can bring to *zoe* or bare life. In the case of ancient Greece, for example, from the language of which Agamben draws the distinction, the *bios* represented by medical science and culture is the very antithesis of a supposed exclusion of natural or pure bodily *zoe*. Rather than excluding *zoe*, Greek medical culture (or we might say a life perfected by medical *bios*) '[lifted] men up from the bestial level', according to Helen King.[17] Moreover, while the sharp distinction of *zoe* and *bios* clearly serves Agamben's argument about sovereign power, at the same time it leads Agamben into creating a simplistic dichotomy which sits uneasily with the intertwining narratives of *zoe* and *bios* that shape Greek conceptualizations of the body and of the relationship of physicality to the human.[18] Thus, a conceptualization of life as divided between *zoe* and *bios*, the latter being differentiated by the exclusion of the former, is by no means assured.

Yet if Agamben's analysis of biopolitics does not provide an answer to Adorno's question about life in terms of political science, it at least provides an observational and situational one: life is 'this' in the period of biopolitics. More crucially, the airbrushing of Christian legal tradition from his analysis of the constitutive elements of sovereignty suggests that the *kind of life* which Agamben observes in the *zoe–bios* distinction, and in his reading of *homo sacer*, is essentially, exclusively and deliberately intra-anthropic – intra-anthropic because estranged from the vistas

---

[15]   Karl Shoemaker, *Crime and Sanctuary in the Middle Ages 500–1400* (New York: Fordham University Press, 2011).

[16]   Even after consultation with Colby Dickinson, Andrew Norris and Leland de la Durantaye, all leading Agamben scholars, this author could find no trace of Agamben ever having engaged with the tradition of sanctuary law.

[17]   Helen King, 'The Origins of Medicine in the Second Century AD', in Simon Goldhill and Robin Osborne (eds), *Rethinking Revolutions Through Ancient Greece* (Cambridge: Cambridge University Press, 2006), p. 262.

[18]   Brooke Holmes, *The Symptom and the Subject: The Emergence of the Physical Body in Ancient Greece* (Princeton: Princeton University Press, 2010).

which theological conceptualizations of the human subject appeal to. In placing the state of exception in the context of biopolitics, Agamben has thus succeeded in giving an account of sovereign power divorced from the kind of theological moderation which sanctuary practices exemplify. Now, while it is unsustainable in a European context to airbrush Christian legal tradition from a plenary history of how sovereignty is constituted, it is also undeniable that there has been an erosion of the influence of Christian legal dispositions over the public square since the early modern period. In other words, the secularization of legislative provision in European culture has in many ways run parallel to the turn towards biopolitics.

At this point in the argument, the question, thereby, naturally arises: if in the contemporary period of biopolitics the reduction of the human to the bodily is what fascist and liberal democratic societies share in common (as Agamben argues), might their own intra-anthropic limits be the reason why the former could wreak such outward destruction on life, after the other has felt such inward destruction (as Adorno and Eliot observed)? How indeed might life live if it is locked within the limits which biopoliticization places *de facto* on human life, whether by liberal democratic society or by fascist dictatorship? In this light, the conclusion of Agamben's study of *homo sacer* in which he evokes a variety of nameless terrains and biopolitical cases to generate the ways and forms of a new biopolitics appears fruitless.[19] Biopolitical life, even when purged of what Agamben considers to be the toxic exclusion of *zoe*, remains exclusively intra-anthropic because the biopolitical space is circumscribed by the action of human agents alone. Moreover, looking for a form of life whose *bios* is only its own *zoe*, as Agamben endeavours to do, suggests the possibility of dispensing with inclusion and exclusion without at the same time accounting for the purpose that is fulfilled by these actions. For if we regard *zoe* or bare life only as the result of an act of exclusion, we have surely forgotten that all choices, regardless of their objects, involve the exclusion of alternatives and of stasis. If, after all, every choice could be invalidated simply because it necessarily involved the exclusion of something else, we would arrive at a *reductio ad absurdum* in which no political choice (let alone any other choice) is possible at all.

Forms of Bare Life in the Anthropology of René Girard?

In Girardian mimetic theory, what accounts for the existence of sovereign power and all social institutions is not any act of inclusion or exclusion but the need to control the effects of imitative behaviour between individuals. All life within the category of human culture is, according to Girard, made up of the patterns which emerge from the dangerous playing out of mimetically learnt desire in the social arena.

Unlike Agamben, whose analysis of bare life is an attempt to reveal a third domain which is neither sacred nor profane, Girard first frames the profane and

---

[19]   Agamben, *Homo Sacer*, p. 187.

the sacred as the spaces in which mimetic pressures respectively unfold and are relieved, before discovering in Christianity a *tertium quid* which offers a real encounter with a life which is divine but not sacred in the sense that Girard lends to the word. By way of furthering our study of the 'life [that] does not live', we will consider here the Girardian profane and sacred and their points of tension with Agamben's analysis, and in the next section we will turn our attention to the third possibility for life, as set out by Girard in what is arguably his most important work, *Des Choses cachées depuis la fondation du monde*.

Girard's fullest account of mimetic desire actually appears in his first work, *Le Mensonge romantique et la Vérité Romanesque*.[20] In the first section of *Des Choses cachées*, however, he retraces some of the key steps which characterize his reflections on this area. Girard's profane occupies the arena of mimetic desire as yet uninhibited by taboo, myth, ritual or scapegoating. Therein, Girard argues, all subjective desire emerges from the imitation of the desires of others. Subjects initiate the generation of desire by observing the possession of some good by a third person (the model) and by calibrating their own desires against the measure provided by this model.[21] The collision of wills which this imitation gives rise to is what Girard classes as mimetic rivalry, a pathology which usually escalates into a condition of violence, leading eventually to the mimetic crisis wherein the subject and model become monstrous doubles of each other, contending first over the good desired, before finally their rivalry itself becomes the theme of their relations. For Girard, the characterization of desire as imitative served initially as a literary theory; it explained for him how certain writers, notably Stendhal, Flaubert and Dostoyevsky in the nineteenth century, had challenged the Romantic view of desire as auto-generative. The development of his theory of desire and its links to violence came about through further explorations which Girard conducted in classical mythology, as his work took a cultural and anthropological turn in his later study *La Violence et le Sacré*.[22]

Clearly, there are objections that could be made to this account of desire – not least because of the perpetual chain of desire and imitation that it requires – and to Girard's claim that these processes point the way towards the origins of all cultural institutions. We shall return to the Girardian account of the origins of institutions below. Nevertheless, if we consider mimesis in relation to the question of life, as it arises in Agamben's analysis of biopolitics, we might say that mimesis is Girard's fundamentally intra-anthropic principle since it posits the notion that desire arises from contact with the desires of other human agents. As Colby Dickinson has observed, there are some correlations here between Agamben and Girard, especially given Agamben's reading of Walter Benjamin's analysis of mimesis,

---

[20]   René Girard, *Le Mensonge romantique et la Vérité Romanesque* (Paris: Grasset, 1961).

[21]   René Girard, *Des Choses cachées depuis la fondation du monde* (Paris: Grasset, 2004 [1978]), p. 18.

[22]   René Girard, *La Violence et le Sacré* (Paris: Grasset, 1972).

language and violence. In developing his reflections on the consequences of the act of exclusion, notably in relation to how humanity is differentiated from animality, Agamben has even tried to associate the state in which the *homo sacer* lives with a state where mimesis has not yet entered in. As *zoe* or bare life precedes *bios* and its attendant vices, so for Agamben gesture could precede mimesis and the *bios* to which it leads. The importance of pre-mimetic gesture, as Agamben sees it, is that it 'breaks with the false alternative between ends and means that paralyzes morality and presents instead means that, as such, evade the orbit of mediality without becoming, for that reason, ends'.[23] In this condition, as Dickinson sums it up, 'not only are we capable of living without a sovereign politics, enslaved to our mimetic heritage, we are, if we embrace it, capable of living in a realm of pure gesture beyond language as we have known it'.[24]

In attributing such power to gesture, however, Agamben is only trying to escape the problems which he believes mimesis triggers: the forms of exclusion which produce sovereign power and the differentiation of humanity from animality. And yet, in what would such gesture consist if mimesis were not involved? Since the communication which gesture evokes would necessitate the sharing (and therefore the mimetic passage) of signs without which there could be no mutuality, Agamben's vision of the role that gesture might play in a purified condition of biopolitics risks again suffering a *reductio ad absurdum*. More to the point, from a Girardian perspective, the evasion of mimesis would require the resurrection of the *mensonge romantique* or the Romantic lie whose claims to originality are based on a veiling of the role of imitation in the generation of culture. Nevertheless, in linking mimesis and political or social structures as sources of coercion, Agamben perhaps unwittingly echoes the passage which Girard sees between profane mimesis and its sacred solutions. If bare life or *zoe*, the life prior to *bios*, might in Girardian terms be labelled as the life of unorganized mimesis, in which the processes of desire and imitation are unchecked and free to run wild, then *bios* can be associated with the way in which, according to Girard, mimetic desires have historically been brought to order within some sacred framework.

At the climax of the Girardian profane, the point at which the mimetic rivalry and the violence it engenders risk destroying all who stand in their path, Girard detects mechanisms – including sacred royalty, animal domestication and ritual hunting, sexual taboos and funerals[25] – which, he is convinced, are scattered across all cultures in various ways and guises. These sacred rites or institutions restore order by confronting and evacuating the dangers posed by the profane realm of imitative desire and its attendant violence. Moreover, in Girard's schema these manifestations of the sacred are all in one way or another ruled by the process of scapegoating in which an individual becomes the object of the common aggression

---

[23] Giorgio Agamben, *Means without Ends: Notes on Politics*, trans. Vicenzo Binetti and Cesare Casarino (Minneapolis: University of Minnesota Press, 2000 [1996]), p. 57.

[24] Dickinson, 'Beyond Violence, Beyond the Text', p. 957.

[25] Girard, *Des Choses cachées*, pp. 68–113.

of a community, hitherto divided by unpurged mimetic conflict and subsequently restored to peace and cohesion through the effects of the persecution of the scapegoat. To crown it all, this entire domain of the Girardian sacred is sustained by the emergence of myths that conceal from the community the acts of violence which ensure the community's cohesion. The dilemma that the Girardian sacred thus poses for life is that, like the Girardian profane, it evokes violence; one of the reasons why *La Violence et le Sacré* upon its publication was hailed by some as an atheistic text was that it seemed to give expression to the oft-repeated complaint against religion that it is the cause of war or conflict. Unlike the Girardian profane, however, the Girardian sacred seeks to displace violence though ritual canalization and to conceal it and its purgation through the generation of myth.

Now, Girard's scapegoat undoubtedly bears some resemblance to Agamben's *homo sacer* with regard to his exclusion from the community. Moreover, while Girard describes the erection of sacred institutions as the result of trying to control mimetic violence, he is by no means saying that they offer an authentic form of life, any more than Agamben is content with the act which he believes founds sovereignty by excluding *homo sacer*. In this respect alone Agamben and Girard might agree.

Nevertheless, there is another subtle difference between them even here. By the very process of bearing the burdens of the community's violence, the Girardian scapegoat, unlike Agamben's *homo sacer*, becomes something unholy *and* holy; unholy or *sacer* because it is the target of the pent-up aggression of the community in mimetic crisis, and holy or *sanctus* because its death or exclusion is associated by the community with a return of harmony and the re-establishment of unity. In this light, Christopher Fox's attempt to establish correlations between Agamben and Girard rather oversteps the mark for the sake of synthesis, and in other ways misses Agamben's intentions.[26] True, as we have noted, Girard's scapegoat seems to represent an excluded life like the *homo sacer*. Claiming, however, as Fox does, that both Girard and Agamben turn to religion in the search for tools to deconstruct the indissoluble dichotomy of friend–enemy (as defined by Carl Schmitt) fails to highlight sufficiently Agamben's secularist agenda. This agenda is most clearly inscribed in the annexation of Pauline messianism which Agamben undertakes in *The Time that Remains: A Commentary on the Letter to the Romans* and in which he seeks to create a kind of temporal axis along which bare life and biopolitics can find their chronological coordinates.[27] The time that remains for Paul before the *eschaton* and the second coming of Christ is mobilized by Agamben as a way of describing an excluded moment. This is expressed by Paul in the Greek *hos me*, but Agamben understands it not as a gaze towards some future destiny (with its supposed indifference to the present) but as a time of indistinction, the chronological analogue of the indistinct space in which *homo sacer* dwells.

---

[26]   Fox, 'Sacrificial Pasts and Messianic Futures', p. 586.

[27]   Giorgio Agamben, *The Time That Remains: A Commentary on the Letter to the Romans*, trans. Patricia Dailey (Stanford: Stanford University Press, 2005 [2000]).

Fox's conclusion that this argument represents a use of religion – rather than a *détournement* which is aimed specifically at bringing under secular control the 'hunchback dwarf' of theology whose doctrines (says Agamben, echoing Walter Benjamin) act like puppet strings on materialist thought[28] – is itself intra-anthropic in its assumptions since it appears not to interrogate fully the uses to which religion is being put. Fox acknowledges that Agamben and Girard both challenge Schmitt's reading of the friend–enemy division as the basis for political life, but claims that while Agamben, 'disrupts the binary categories that underlie politics and ideology',[29] Girard only restores that binary division as an unconscious coda to his theories. Yet the truth of the matter is almost the exact contrary: Girard does indeed break the binary division of friend–enemy not through the creation of some indeterminate state of pre-mimetic gesture wherein such rivalry is supposedly overcome, but rather by introducing a third agent, the divine life, as a factor within the constitution of human community.

Life as Human Life plus Divine Life

Girard's singularity as an anthropologist in the contemporary period is that not only is he averse to the deconstruction of the human – the dismantling of the 'anthropological machine', as Agamben calls it[30] – he is also quite prepared to undermine the idea that the social and physical sciences can offer no insight into matters spiritual. It is not that Girard thinks Christianity is a religion whose faith is rationally demonstrable; rather, he sees himself as an enemy of that kind of social science according to which 'if an argument is favourable to Christianity, no matter its lack of importance or its justifications, it cannot be scientific'.[31] Girard, in other words, is open to the possibility that anthropological science can point to a kind of life for humanity which is not purely and exclusively intra-anthropic.

Girard has written several works in recent years about God, Christianity and culture, notably *Dieu existe-t-il?* and *Christianisme et modernité* (2009) with Gianno Vattimo. It was *Des Choses cachées depuis la fondation du monde*, however, which established the *grandes lignes* of his thinking about Christianity. In the biblical accounts of Cain and Abel, in the persecution of Joseph by his brothers and, ultimately, in the crucifixion and resurrection of Christ, acts of mimetic violence or apparent scapegoating unfold. The violence they contain, however, is not disguised but condemned, and in the case of Joseph and Jesus, the conflict is solved through an act of self-renunciation and forgiveness obviating the processes of revenge and retaliation inscribed in the mimetic conflict. Instead

---

28   Ibid., pp. 138–9.

29   Fox, 'Sacrificial Pasts and Messianic Futures', p. 589.

30   Agamben, *The Open*, p. 33.

31   René Girard, *Les Origines de la Culture: Entretiens avec Pierpaolo Antonello et João Cezar de Castro Rocha* (Paris: Hachette, 2004), p. 265, my translation.

of rivalry and violence being avoided through taboo and ritual, cleansed through scapegoating and concealed through myth, their cause is removed by an action which resembles the generous nature of a selfless love, rather than the self-regarding nature of exacting psychological catharsis.

In fact, Girard contends that in the evangelical accounts of the death of Christ, the numinous atmosphere associated with sacred rites of purely human origin is deliberately eschewed. This eschewal, and its apparently profane implications, point not to a demystified zone, as if Girard's reading of the gospel was really a return to a theology of Ernest Renan – even if there are clear tensions between Girard's historico-critical readings of the Christian scriptures and Christian doctrine; he has in fact modified certain of his theses, notably concerning sacrifice, after dialogue with theologians such as Raymond Schwager[32] – but rather indicate a turning from violence in what is called *la surtranscendance de l'amour* (the supra-transcendence of love) and in which Girard finds the presence of the divine.[33] The utter uniqueness of this solution to mimesis and violence is, for Girard, proof enough that it is the work of an agent who is more than human, since only an extra-human (or supra-human) perspective is capable of bringing humans to an awareness of the dangers of mimesis. Faced with the question of life, this *surtranscendance* offers to the 'life [that] does not live' a way out of its dilemma by modelling a new form of living in which the intra-anthropic domain is forced to open up to possibilities that are divine in origin.

It is right to point out here that Girard firstly sees such a possibility as an anthropological observation, though undoubtedly for Girard it is also a postulate of faith. Still, while the mechanisms that deflect violence through ritual and myth show the deployment of strategies against mimetic hostility in human communities, it is only the freedom of the Judeo-Christian scriptures from these dynamics which, in Girard's argument, allows them to act as a lens through which to judge all cultures mired in the logic of the scapegoat. We might even say that their avoidance of myth amounts in fact to the raw material of revelation since they seek to unveil an action and initiative – a life! – which begins as a divine intervention. This is how we can explain Girard's term *la surtranscendance de l'amour*: in *la surtranscendance* there is expressed a reality above the human construction of sacred gods, and in *l'amour* there is a relationship to the divine which begins in a divine initiative.

Hence, Girard's thought expands or reconceptualizes intra-anthropic living – those relations which exhaust the juridico-political thinking of Schmitt as well as Agamben and many others – by pointing to an encounter with what we can dare to call the theandric possibilities made available in the Christian paradigm. By theandric we mean not those possibilities which are associated with the

---

[32]   Raymund Schwager, *Must there be Scapegoats? Violence and Redemption in the Bible*, trans. Maria L. Assad (San Francisco: Harper and Row, 1987).

[33]   Girard, *Des Choses cachées*, p. 317.

perichoresis of Christ, but theandric by analogy – a relatedness, a shared *life* – which is proposed between God and humanity.

Conclusion

How might life live for Agamben and Girard? There is a curious paradox in answering this question insofar as Girard's and Agamben's arguments take them beyond the domains of the sacred and the profane. Yet there is this difference also: beyond Agamben's profane and sacred lies the realm of biopolitics, and a project in which bare life, *zoe*, must find a *bios* that does not exclude *zoe* as its founding principle. Life can only live for Agamben on those terms. Beyond Girard's realm of the sacred and profane, on the other hand, lies a solution to the threat which mimetic conflict poses to life, a solution that offers the possibility of relatedness to the divine. Life lives, for Girard, when the *surtranscendance de l'amour* breaks through the sentence of perpetual conflict which purely intra-anthropic relations impose on human life and human living. In Girardian terms, this *surtranscendance* surely is the *Life* which Eliot felt that we had lost in living.

Likewise, the life that Girard identifies beyond the profane and the sacred raises many issues, not the least of which lies in the perennial problem of the credibility of Christian postulates to a humanist academy. Even if the Christian solution to mimesis is unique, is that necessarily a proof of its divine origins? Another problem which critics have not been slow to point out is the often violent character of Christian history. Since there is not space here to deal with all such objections, let us simply try to position Girard's thought in relation to the domain of the intra-anthropic which is, after all, the hegemonic episteme of the twenty-first century in the West.

In *Also sprach Zarathustra*, Nietzsche, with whose philosophy Girard is in constant dialogue, proclaimed the death of God.[34] Thereby he did not, of course, mean the death of a divinity as such but the end of God as what later philosophers would call a cultural construct. Nietzsche's successors have, as Gabriel Marcel observes in *Les Hommes contre l'Humain*, also sought to announce the death of humanity; thereby, again, Marcel did not so much mean the death of humanity as a race – though *Les Hommes contre l'Humain* was written in the shadow of the mushroom clouds of Nagasaki and Hiroshima – but rather the death of humanity in its Western conceptualization.[35] Now, Agamben's *homo sacer* corresponds to these two conceptual deaths insofar as it attempts to give expression to a human life placed beyond human and divine conceptualizations. We are all, Agamben says, *homines sacri*. Still, in the light of such an observation, and in the light of the frequent hostility of the academy to matters religious, perhaps Girard's

---

[34] Friedrich Nietzsche, *Also sprach Zarathustra* (Berlin: Akademie Verlag, 2000 [1883–85]).

[35] Gabriel Marcel, *Les Hommes contre l'Humain* (Paris: La Colombe, 1952).

importance lies first in whether his thought genuinely encounters this problem of the deconstruction of the Western notion of humanity; second, whether it offers some genuine alternative to Adorno's 'life [that] does not live'; and third, whether it can posit instead the credibility, the recovery or we might say the resurrection of possibilities that offer to draw Agamben's *homo sacer* out of its exclusion and back into a theandric life.

Chapter 3

Entangled Fidelities: Reassembling the Human

John Reader

Introduction

The argument of this chapter is that we currently lack a credible public discourse for ethical engagement in political life because our culture insists on maintaining an impoverished understanding of human subjectivity. The predominant view of what it is to be human is reductionist and inadequate, relying too exclusively upon a rationalist interpretation supportive of and emboldened by a specific political philosophy and economic configuration. What is required, therefore, is an expanded portrait of human life that is able to acknowledge how and when ethical and value-based concerns do, in reality, impinge upon political and economic debates. In order to achieve this, the chapter will draw upon a number of recent philosophical sources, illustrating my own particular version of human subjectivity.

The initial stage of this will be to utilize ideas from Derrida and Levinas to suggest that there is what I call a pre-autonomous dimension to human being, and this will then be linked to the political philosophy of Badiou. My final philosophical source will be Latour and his developing discourse of reassembling, which I hope will lead to a more adequate understanding both of human nature itself and then the reality of political processes. I will take creative ideas from each of these thinkers in order to construct my own portrait of human subjectivity, but at each stage assessing their work in terms of practical political implications and the way in which a politics of life might be assembled. The result will be suggestions for a more adequate public discourse that is able to take into account how ethical concerns are always already contained within political debates and policy formation. Before the start of the journey proper, though, it is important to register some ideas which ground the discussion in a wider social and historical context.

The Life-Denying Impact of Contemporary Politics

At the time of writing, as the developing crisis in the Eurozone continues to unfold, with the risks of recession still looming large and the probability that the centre of economic power is shifting inexorably towards China, one might be forgiven for thinking that one is listening to a recorded message from many of our politicians.

Virtually every challenge to their policy prescriptions is met with 'our priority has to be to reduce the budget deficit' combined with the mantra that 'there is no alternative'. The psychological impact of this upon the lives of ordinary people, who find themselves at the sharp end of redundancies in the public sector and the withdrawal of public services and the shrinking of many a welfare state, is that we have become the passive victims of some infernal economic machine over which nobody has any control. Whenever anyone dares to challenge this, we are told that countries have no choice but to be seen to be tackling their budget deficits, as the alternative is a downgrading of their status by the rating agencies and therefore their cost of future borrowing will be increased, further exacerbating the existing downturn in economic activity. Meanwhile those closer to the top of the economic heap continue to reap the benefits of what remains of the turbo stage of global capitalism, whilst protestors continue to gather in the streets of major US and UK cities and riots break out in Greece and beyond.

What we experience therefore is a public presentation which suggests that we are subjects – or more accurately, the objects – of an inexorable and uncontrollable economic machine, to which our only possible responses are either mute compliance or unfocussed resistance. This can only be received as a life-denying experience which robs most people of any sense of control or autonomy. It is certainly the case that some groups of protestors are keen to formulate alternative policies or to suggest that the whole economic system is in need of dramatic reform, but how exactly this can be effective when no real global alternative to neo-liberalism has much public currency is not obvious. As long as 'there is no alternative' is the reality of what most people feel, there is little prospect of avoiding long-term global economic downturn if not outright recession, or the social unrest that will inevitably follow. If ever there was a moment when we need a politics of life to restore some sense of hope and new direction, this is surely it.

If one had to describe this political context and the views of human subjectivity that underpin it, one would use such terms as 'deterministic', 'reductionist', 'linear-thinking' and 'uncreative', and designate their impacts upon human life as paralysing and oppressive. Yet such self-understandings of human life are in stark contrast to much that is now to be found within some scientific disciplines. Before turning to the explicitly philosophical it is to one of these that I will refer. There are currently some very interesting debates taking place within biology which offer clues to an alternative approach.[1] Although theories of natural selection hold sway within the discipline, there are examples of supplementary ideas which suggest that a mechanistic causality needs to be understood alongside notions of processes which involve reciprocity and feedback, and some sort of innovation or 'decision'.[2] In other words, in contrast to the mainstream Darwinist view, genetic inheritance

---

[1]   Steven Shaviro, 'Interstitial Life: Remarks on Causality and Purpose in Biology', in Peter Gaffney (ed.), *The Force of the Virtual: Deleuze, Science and Philosophy* (Minneapolis: University of Minnesota Press, 2010), pp. 133–46.

[2]   Ibid., p. 141.

combined with occasional random mutation is not sufficient to account for biological variation. If they were sufficient then our understanding of life would be that it is essentially conservative and organized for the purposes of self-preservation and self-reproduction. It is very difficult then to view innovation and change as anything other than forced adaptive reactions to environmental pressures. As with the interpretation of economic activity discussed earlier, life becomes a matter of inescapable compulsion rather than an outpouring of creative energy.

Shaviro suggests that a possible philosophical source of an alternative approach is to be found in the work of Whitehead and his philosophy of organism.[3] Like both Kant and Deleuze, he posits a double causality: efficient and final. Final causality works alongside the efficient and is the decision by means of which an actual entity becomes what it is (concresces). There is therefore scope for freedom, creativity and contingency which allows for the emergence of the unexpected. Every entity has some possibility of self-determination and self-actualization. Whitehead describes life itself as 'the origination of conceptual novelty' stemming from a principle of unrest and the desire for the creation of something different. Particularly with living beings, this thirst to press beyond the already existing is a defining characteristic without which it is impossible to understand or explain the human capacity for change and innovation. So life is a matter of transformation rather than preservation, a striving for something other than what already exists. It is a bid for freedom, the intense experience of desiring that which is not yet, and then the capacity to make unforeseen decisions.

Even in the animal kingdom there is evidence that all living organisms make decisions that are not causally programmed or predetermined, as each single cell has the 'intelligence' required to make decisions on its own. What Whitehead's theory does suggest, though, is that it is not cognition which makes the decisions possible but the other way around: the decisions come first. 'We don't make decisions because we are free and responsible; rather we are free and responsible because – and precisely to the extent that – we make decisions.'[4]

What does this tell us about 'life' if it is an accurate account? It tells us that our creativity is initially something pre-rational or pre-autonomous, that there are non-linear and spontaneous processes at work which challenge any view that life is somehow predetermined and predictable, and that an element of randomness is in fact of evolutionary value – it enables beings to adapt and respond in order to survive. Inflexible organisms tend to perish, whilst it is the flexible ones who stand a better chance of surviving. Life has evolved so as to crave, and to generate, novelty. It is in the interstices, or the spaces, that what is merely potential or virtual resides, and it is because of this we can say that life remains open to other possibilities, not fully determined by what has gone before.

It seems to me that these insights from the field of biology are of deep significance and offer a critical perspective on the forms of economic and political

---

3   Ibid., p. 142.

4   Ibid., p. 144.

determinism that currently dominate our responses to the global financial crisis. It is and has to be possible that there are always alternatives, that things can be different. So one needs to ask in whose interests it might be that we are lead to believe otherwise. It also suggests that we must retain an understanding of human subjectivity that takes the potential for creativity and innovation seriously and include in the dimensions of what it is to be human an element of transformation and novelty. I will offer as ways of describing this at this stage, terms such as 'transpersonal', 'transhuman' and 'post-autonomous', but will explain these in greater detail as the philosophical exposition progresses. But even now one can see that a politics of life, a practice and interpretation that builds upon an empirically-based view of what it is to be human, creates a challenge to the oppressive and deterministic views which shape much of our current politics.

Pre-Autonomy and Politics

Is there empirical evidence for the ways in which human beings actually make decisions, particularly when it comes to political issues? The work of Damasio from within the discipline of neuroscience and as used by the sociologist Castells has much to offer here.[5] Damasio's research has shown that the divisions that we assume operate between reason and emotion are to be brought into question and that the reality when it comes to decision making is that if one is impaired then the other also suffers. Hence human action takes place through a process that involves emotions, feelings and reasoning components. Emotions thus play a double role in decision making. On the one hand, they covertly activate the emotional experiences related to the issue that is the object of the decision making. On the other, they can directly act on the process of decision making, by prompting the subject to feel in the way that she does. The result of this is that people tend to select information in ways that favour the decision that they are inclined to make. We are likely to look for information that confirms our existing beliefs and habits and less likely to search out and give credibility to evidence that might challenge the positions we have already adopted. When there is a conflict between emotion and cognition, the evidence suggests that people tend to believe what they want to believe. This is certainly a powerful explanation for the way in which the media function and for how politicians are able to manipulate public opinion.

None of this is exactly surprising, but it does point to the importance of what I now want to describe as the pre-autonomous dimension of human subjectivity and therefore the limits of the rationality which we so readily attribute to ourselves when it comes to matters of economics and politics, where the assumption is that we are indeed rational utility maximizers who always know and then operate on the basis of what is in our best interests. None of this is to argue that our behaviour

---

[5]   Manuel Castells, *Communication Power* (Oxford: Oxford University Press, 2011), pp. 140 ff.

is determined in advance or open to reliable prediction, but it does show that if our behaviour is to change then appeals to the purely rational dimension of ourselves are going to be more limited than we care to recognize.[6] I will now support this with reference to more overtly philosophical sources.

In analysing how decisions come to be made and positions adopted, one factor that needs to be taken into account is how much most of us take on trust. In part this is a matter of necessity in that the details of many matters of concern or issues are so complex and potentially overwhelming that we are more inclined to address them by asking first whose interpretations are to be trusted than by examining the details ourselves. This makes good sense as there is often neither the time nor the capacity to enter into such issues at the required depth. Environmental concerns are an obvious example of this, where the complexities of the scientific arguments and the research that lies behind them are beyond the skills of most of us, however much we attempt to come to grips with them. All this does, however, is to push the crucial question further back in the decision making process. How do we know who to trust and how does one make that particular decision? It seems likely that the answer is similar to that offered by Castells. We tend to trust those whose views already coincide with and confirm the positions we have already adopted. If one is temperamentally inclined to believe that climate change and environmental dangers are of major concern, then one is likely to give more credibility to those who advocate appropriate responses to this than to those who argue that the whole debate is overblown and represents the interests of a particular academic elite. This is not to say that positions cannot and will not change, or that arguments have no place in the judgements we make, but that our initial inclination is more likely to be in tune with our pre-existing beliefs.

The philosophical support for this interpretation of what it is to be human is to be found, in part at least, in the work of Derrida and Levinas. My own interest in this came from a study of faith and reason, contrasting the work of these two French philosophers with the more rationalistic and cognitive approach of Habermas. The conclusion I reached was that elements of both positions were required to reach a fuller understanding of human subjectivity, so this is not a matter of adopting one of these positions at the expense of the other, but of arguing that both pre-autonomy and an understanding of autonomy are necessary.[7]

The initial criticism of Habermas is that he is essentially too optimistic over what it is possible for humans to achieve through the exercise of their critical faculties and reflexivity. There are dimensions of ourselves that remain opaque and beyond the clear articulation of language and thought, and yet which continue to shape our beliefs and responses. Whether or not we employ a Freudian or other psychotherapeutic terminology to describe this, our experience seems to be that we cannot always offer

---

[6]   For a recent contribution to this debate from within psychology see Daniel Kahnemann, *Thinking Fast and Slow* (London: Allen Lane, 2011).

[7]   John Reader, *Blurred Encounters: A Reasoned Practice of Faith* (Cardiff: Aureus Publishing, 2005), pp. 100–6.

convincing rational explanations of why we do the things we do. Thus there is a limit to our capacity to function in a solely rational manner, and the term that describes this is 'pre-autonomy': that which precedes and also undergirds our sense of who we are and which also, up to a point, shapes our views and decisions.

In a study of religion, Derrida argues that this is reflected in a deeper level of connection between reason and religion. Before there can be either reason or religion both will have to respond to what Derrida refers to as an encounter with the other. Both of them already presuppose a trust and confidence in a particular way of looking at the world. Whether this is a trust in a scientific or rationalistic world view, or indeed in a faith-based interpretation of the world and human life, one or other of these prior commitments has to be in place before a further encounter can begin. Only once this exists can an element of rational argument impinge upon the ensuing debates. Derrida describes this as 'acquiescing to the testimony of the other'.[8] This does not necessarily refer to the other as another human being, but it is likely that the influence or example of another person will have been significant in this process at some stage.

One can supplement this understanding with reference to Levinas, who was searching for a terminology that more adequately describes our relationships with one another and the depth of the moral demands that we place on another, and might prevent the sort of atrocities that he experienced during the Holocaust.[9] He offers rather extreme interpretations of such familiar terms as 'hospitality', 'hostage', 'substitution' and 'proximity'. In doing this he is suggesting that our responses to others are always already deeply embedded in this pre-autonomous dimension of what it is to be human, and that these are in place well before we then start to articulate or rationalize our behaviour in relationships. We are 'exposed' to the other and in proximity to the other even before what we describe as human subjectivity begins to function. One does not become aware of oneself and then subsequently discover that one is in proximity to another, but rather being in proximity is itself a precondition for becoming aware of oneself. Although it needs to be acknowledged that Levinas is stretching the use of these terms beyond their normal application, I would still argue that he is pointing to a dimension of human subjectivity that is not properly taken into account as yet.

A politically charged example of the need to recognize the pre-autonomous dimension occurred during the 2001 Foot-and-mouth disease outbreak in the UK. As this disease spread through the stock of UK farms it became clear that, for some farmers at least, this was the source of what could only be termed a bereavement. Even though most animals eventually go for slaughter and consumption, what came to the surface was that there was a relationship between farmer and livestock for which there was no public discourse and which could not be acknowledged or registered by the political authorities dealing with the outbreak. A complaint

---

[8]   Jacques Derrida and Gianni Vattimo, *Religion* (Cambridge: Polity Press, 1998), p. 55.

[9]   Emmanuel Levinas, *Otherwise than Being or Beyond Essence* (Pittsburgh: Duquesne University Press, 2002).

to No. 10 Downing Street pointing this out was met with a standard 'rational' and economically based answer that current UK agricultural policy was determined by relationships and agreement with the European Union. Any human (pre-autonomous) dimension to what was happening received no attention or acknowledgement. Very much like the animals themselves, the farmers were seen as numbers on a spreadsheet, rather than as fellow beings with feelings and in relationship. As I argue from the outset, the culture at this political level lacks a convincing and adequate public discourse which can take into account the various dimensions of human subjectivity, hence it is dehumanizing and oppressive. As will be seen in due course this question can also be extended to the relationship between humans and non-humans as we examine the work of Latour.

Badiou, Human Subjectivity and Politics

Given the constraints of this short chapter it is not possible to do justice to the breadth of Badiou's thought, but only to focus on three aspects which contribute to the overall topic of a more suitable public discourse. First, his view of human subjectivity, then the political implications of this, and then his notion of fidelity and what that might offer to the wider debate. Clearly these are all connected, but for the purposes of this exercise they will be treated separately.

In a recent contribution to a text of collected essays on the future of communism, Badiou offers a clear summary of his understanding of how the human subject is configured within political processes. 'A political truth is a concrete, time-specific sequence in which a new thought and practice of collective emancipation arise, exist and eventually disappear'.[10] (He gives the examples of the French Revolution, the People's War of Liberation in China, and the Bolshevik Revolution.) Every truth procedure prescribes a Subject of this truth, a Subject who cannot be reduced to an individual. In other words, it is through this incorporation into the wider cause and the placing of oneself in the service of what is to be fought for and achieved that a degree of subjectivity is to be established. Any notion that subjectivity is attained through some process of self-realization is discounted from the beginning. This is nothing to do with cognition, as the subject does not know the truth of what they are involved in, but rather that some aspect of what they are doing produces a truth within that situation. Badiou is keen to counter the traditional humanistic theories of human subjectivity as, in his view, these lead only to a stance that fails to distinguish humans from animals who might only pursue what is in their own best interests and pleasures. Like the philosophies of life referred to earlier, Badiou wants to show how humans are creative, innovative and can become agents of change. The subject is the presence of novelty in a situation, something like a location or point of intersection where different components come together and something new can therefore emerge.

---

[10] Alain Badiou, 'The Idea of Communism', in Costa Douzanis and Slavoj Žižek (eds), *The Idea of Communism* (London: Verso, 2010), p. 2.

So it is clear that in Badiou's thought, the subject is not the same as a free conscious agent, one who is knowingly in control of the political processes in which he or she is engaged. Subjectivity is what emerges as a result of participating in an action or process of creation that is greater than the subject itself. Whilst one can see the power and attraction of such an idea it surely raises some important questions. Is it the case then that individuals are not to be valued as such, but only to the extent that they are engaged in some appropriate political activity? What remains of any notion of human autonomy and the human being as agent? Is this in fact another form of pre-autonomy where already existing and possibly predetermined patterns of behaviour are all that matters and any idea of the exercise of one's critical faculties is discounted as somehow illegitimate? One can set that alongside alternative views which argue that one most truly becomes oneself when one is fully absorbed by and engaged in an activity that takes one beyond oneself, but this does not seem to be quite what Badiou is saying. It is as if, by wanting to show how what is new and radically different can emerge as a result of human action and thus combat the reactionary forces in contemporary culture, Badiou has to stretch the understanding of human subjectivity to a point where one wonders exactly what remains.

I would argue that there is something contradictory about his position. In addition to suggesting that we are somehow less than fully human when we are not engaged in his version of political activity, his own position is surely based on a rational and autonomous judgement which cannot be taken into account by his own stance on what makes us human subjects. How can Badiou himself consistently argue for his version of human subjectivity unless he himself is always already engaged in exactly the type of political action that he is advocating? He may believe that this is what he is doing, but then how can he justify the role of rational argumentation from within that position, or prevent this from being such an elitist stance that most others are immediately excluded from it? I suggest that what Badiou offers is a form of pre-autonomy that reveals the limitation of pursuing this at the expense of other understandings of what it is to be human. Nevertheless, there is still something in this that one can recognize as being part of what it can be to be human – the role of faithfulness and commitment to a cause which transcends the individual.

So where does this approach take Badiou in practical political terms? According to one commentator, it leads him away from struggles for democracy and direct engagement with mainstream political processes and into what are apparently more marginal activities.[11] His becomes a strategy of subtraction and of separating from the obvious, even from those movements that claim to be carrying forward the Marxist ideals through left-wing political action. So it is no longer a matter of attempting to take over or influence any particular state or national government by participating through democratic processes, or concern for wider economic policies. Even voting is seen as a diversion from what is really necessary, which

---

[11]   Ed Pluth, *Badiou: A Philosophy of the New* (Cambridge: Polity Press, 2010), pp. 164–74.

is engaging in those isolated events where the truth can begin to emerge and that which is radically new might stand a chance of showing itself. It is hard to see how this can be anything other than a withdrawal from mainstream and wider political activity which effectively concedes that any action at that level is not only a waste of time but also a betrayal of the cause. Even though Badiou might present this as a politics of life, as it refuses to collude with current movements that are seen as life-denying and destructive, it seems to me to give too much ground to the latter and to fail to engage when positive change and challenge are still a possibility. Perhaps this is the direct consequence of a pre-autonomous view of human subjectivity which eschews any involvement at a rational level?

Where I do think Badiou has something very positive to offer though is in his notion of fidelity, and this is worthy of further comment. In his book on St Paul and the foundation of universalism,[12] he sets out in greater detail how this notion of fidelity links to his other concerns. Truth consists in declaring an event, when something radically new has entered the equation. Such truth cannot be either structural or axiomatic but is singular, therefore no generality can shape the subject who claims to follow in its wake. Nothing that has gone before can predetermine what now follows, including what is required of the subject who is faithful to the event. With reference to the Christian event as an example of this, Badiou argues that the Christian subject does not pre-exist the event that he or she declares. What does this tell us about the nature of fidelity?

Fidelity to the declaration is crucial, as truth is a process and not an illumination. Three concepts are then required. The first names the subject at the point of declaration, and this can be described as conviction. The second names the subject at the point of his conviction's militant address – this can be appropriately rendered as love. Then, finally, one names the subject according to the force of the displacement conferred upon it through the assumption of the truth's completed character – this could be called hope, or certainty. Each of these means that the subject is subtracted from, or separated from, the state and is nothing whatsoever to do with matters of opinion. Hence fidelity is to be distinguished from what is often portrayed as normal political activity. In many ways it is closer to a faith-based understanding of commitment and conviction, one that argues that being faithful is itself what brings the new person into being, rather than that accepting arguments creates the conviction which is then put into practice. The practice of fidelity is what comes first.

It is not simply a matter of being faithful in the traditional sense, as one is then always left with the question of what one is being faithful to. What is important for Badiou is the idea that one is faithful to the very idea of fidelity, almost irrespective of what one is being faithful to. I am sure that he himself is clear what it is appropriate to give one's commitment to, and questions can be raised about how he justifies which specific events call for fidelity. However, I think

---

[12]   Alain Badiou, *Saint Paul: The Foundation of Universalism* (Stanford: Stanford University Press, 2003), pp. 14–15.

what he is suggesting provides a necessary counter-balance to a rather vacuous pragmatism that steers away from the notion that being committed requires a degree of unconditionality and a willingness to make sacrifices. Faithful presence, I would argue, is something in terms of our relationships with others that is often life-enhancing and life-giving, and makes it clear that there is a cost involved that cannot be measured in narrowly economic terms. It is the fact of being there alongside and being prepared to remain there even when things seem hopeless that is the test of our commitment and a point at which, perhaps as Badiou suggests, we begin to realize what it is to be human. As I will argue in my conclusion, we are engaged in entangled fidelities, though more complex and contradictory than Badiou might be prepared to envisage or entertain.

From Latour to Entangled Fidelities

To recapitulate the problem to be addressed: how does one develop a discourse capable of acknowledging the presence of values and ethical stances before it is so late in the process that they are bound to be ineffective? The argument is that what is required is an understanding of human subjectivity that takes account of more than the rational and autonomous. This means an interpretation that makes space for the pre-autonomous or affective dimension of human being, but that also points beyond autonomy to transformative, creative and emerging possibilities. It has been seen that philosophers such as Derrida, Badiou and Levinas offer glimpses of an alternative discourse, but fail in important respects to provide the whole picture of human subjectivity.

   To construct this wider view the argument turns now to the work of Latour. Having already drawn attention to some of the creative aspects of his approach in other work,[13] I will now focus on one particular paper that neatly summarizes and draws together the key components. Latour advocates a shift of discourse that includes replacing matters of fact with matters of concern, the relationship between subject and object with that between the human and the non-human, a questioning of the traditional distinction between fact and value, and the importance of thinking about things as gatherings rather than facts. In other words, the task is that of assembling or reassembling the various components that go to make up any specific matter of concern and of examining each one in appropriate detail. One of the main dangers and limitations of much scientific and political discourse in relation to ethical concerns is that of short-circuiting the gatherings that need to take place and trying to reach conclusions and established positions much too early in the process. Hence Latour's approach stands a much better chance of showing how values and ethical considerations are always already embedded from an earlier stage. It is best to 'keep the references circulating'.

---

[13]   John Reader, 'Speculative Realism and Public Theology: Explorations', *Political Theology*, 13/2 (Apr 2012): 155–65.

In a chapter written in 2008,[14] Latour examines why it is that environmental issues have failed to make a breakthrough in terms of political discourse and action. So here is a contemporary ethical concern being looked at in some detail. Latour suggests that ecological questions are taken as peculiar to one specific domain of concerns rather than as the core of politics. As a result of this, they are not treated with the same sense of urgency or moral energy as other political issues. The issues somehow fail to enthuse or inspire beyond the select few who have presented them in something like an evangelizing manner. Latour proposes that this is not simply a matter of theory but also of feeling, that the emotions evoked are as yet too narrow to create the levels of anxiety associated with religion, war or famine. So the pre-autonomous dimension has not yet been sufficiently tapped into by the way the debate is normally presented.

There are a number of possible explanations for this which Latour now explicates. One is the way that science itself is popularly viewed. It is supposedly the antidote to the morass of ideology, emotions and values that have held back scientific progress for so long. Therefore it is seen as an emancipation or escape from all that happens at the pre-autonomous level. Science subtracts from and distances itself from all that might motivate or inspire concerted public action in this respect. Yet, Latour argues, there is a paradox here, for science and technology have actually amplified both the scale at which humans and non-humans are connecting with each other, and also the intimacy with which such connections are made. This latter understanding illustrates that we are moving from a superficial to a deeper interpretation of what it is to be 'entangled'. Rather than emancipation, there is a continuous movement towards ever greater levels of attachment between things and people.

As Latour has shown throughout his work in Science Studies, it is the intricate and intimate detail of these attachments that is the reality of how science, politics and other areas of human life become interwoven and connected. Science, technology and what we call nature are more closely related than ever before and yet there is still this paradoxical attempt to tear them apart as if this constituted some form of progress. A further consequence of this that is also damaging to efforts to incorporate the pre-autonomous and ethical dimensions into political debate on environmental issues is that humans and non-humans are treated as if they must be pulled apart and kept in separate worlds. This is exactly the experience that emerged from the foot-and-mouth disease crisis.

What needs to be recognized, by contrast, is that the complexity, confusion and entanglement which invariably occurs as a consequence of the unforeseen effects of human activity is precisely what is to be expected and requires constant monitoring and response. It is the interventions, the wanting things to be different and the caring for all that is happening, that have to be taken up into the political debates and turned into action. As Latour says, however, we seem to lack the appropriate emotions and attitudes which would allow this to flourish. We lack the mental, moral, aesthetic

---

[14] Bruno Latour, '"Its development stupid" or How to Modernize Modernization', in Jim Proctor (ed.), *Postenvironmentalism* (Cambridge, MA: MIT Press, 2008), pp. 1–13.

and emotional resources to follow through on the attachments. At this point in the argument he turns to an unexpected source for a model of how to counter this.

Latour examines the strange connections between mastery, technology and theology. Drawing on the Frankenstein myth, he concludes that the sin involved in the story was not that of the creation of this strange creature, but when the Creator abandoned the creature to itself. So it is this failure to follow through, to keep faith with our creations and attachments which needs to be brought into question. It is not 'technology itself, but the absence of love for the technology we have created, as if we had decided that we were unable to follow through with the education of our own children'.[15] So Latour concludes that what we should be working towards is a politics of things in which humans are entangled, involved, implicated and indeed incarnated. In language that he uses elsewhere, this requires an assembling and reassembling of the human and the non-human which takes into account all the different dimensions of human subjectivity, the pre-autonomous, the autonomous and the transformational.

This suggests fruitful connections with the Christian theological tradition, as to imagine that emancipation from or distancing from creation is an accurate reflection of what the Christian God is about is surely a gross misrepresentation, as this is a God who gets folded into, implicated with and incarnated into his creation. If this is mastery then it is very different from an understanding which presents a detached form of autonomy or power.

All of this is very helpful and provides a different and more effective discourse which can begin to facilitate an understanding of how values, theological ideas and ethical concerns impinge upon and are always implicated in our political decision making and policy formations. Yet I still wonder whether it is enough to create and sustain the passion and commitment required for the necessary action. I discussed entangled fidelities deliberately as I want to suggest that something like the notion of faithfulness and commitment advocated by Badiou is also required in order to motivate and drive forwards political action, especially when things appear hopeless. I also wonder whether Latour says enough about the creativity, non-linearity and the breaking in of the unexpected. So the reassembling needed points towards an entangled fidelity that will remain attached to not only the human but also to that which lies beyond it.

So let us see whether Latour's understanding of human subjectivity really does go far enough. Clearly he is concerned that, rather than talking about subjects and objects in the traditional way, we should talk about humans and non-humans. Although this would appear to have implications for environmental issues, this is not really the purpose of Latour's new discourse. His focus is our understanding of the processes by which 'matters of concern' are gathered, assembled and brought into being. The problem, in his view, is that these processes are pre-empted or short-circuited by the language that we use when we talk about 'social explanations' for what is happening, or bring 'society' in as an explanation for the very things that

---

[15]   Ibid., p. 11.

require further exploration and explanation. We need always to step at least one stage further back in the process of assembling in order to identify through the relations that occur, how some 'actors' are having an effect upon others. It is this that Latour is attempting to articulate when he writes about Actor Network Theory (ANT):

> We don't know yet how all these actors are connected, but we can state as the new default position before the study starts that all the actors we are going to deploy might be associated in such a way that they make others do things. This is not done by transporting a force that would remain the same throughout as some sort of faithful intermediary, but by generating transformations manifested by the many unexpected events triggered in the other mediators that follow them along the line. This is what I dubbed 'the principle of irreduction', and such is the philosophical meaning of ANT: a concatenation of mediators does not trace the same connections and does not require the same type of explanations as a retinue of intermediaries transporting a cause.[16]

This would suggest then that Latour's approach does allow for the creativity and transformation that might be hoped for when it comes to political matters of concern. What it adds to the picture, though, is a question about the role of the human being as subject in such processes and suggests that the individual actor – or, as Latour prefers to describe all participants, both human and non-human, actant – is not in control or command of what happens. Hence the possible connections with the notions of pre-autonomy derived from Derrida, Levinas and Badiou. None of which is to deny that humans do act in such a way as to 'make others do things' based on their motives and deliberate intentions. Rather, it is to re-describe the ways in which things happen, and are transformed, to allow for a greater entanglement and complexity of practice.

One final example from Latour will perhaps make this new assembling even clearer. An image that is often deployed when talking about the relationship between social forces and human agents is that of the puppet and the puppeteer. 'Outside forces' or influences are like the hands of the puppeteer pulling the strings of humans as puppets. Latour argues that the relationship between the two is much more interesting than this.[17] What we need to do is to abandon or dissolve this idea of the outside and replace it with the notion of circulation of plug-ins. While none of the plug-ins have power to determine, they can simply make someone do something. So there is not an outside made up of social forces which then determines an inside who is the puppet or agent. If this were the case, then the more that is added to the outside, the less that the actor on the inside has any say over what is happening. Likewise, if you then want to attribute to the actor some moral or intentional action, or to imagine they are exercising a creative

---

[16] Bruno Latour, *Reassembling the Social: An Introduction to Actor Network Theory* (Oxford: Oxford University Press, 2007), p. 107.

[17] Ibid., p. 214.

or innovative power, one can only do so by cutting some of the strings which supposedly connect the person to the outside or the impersonal forces. This is to misdescribe what is actually taking place. So what is Latour's recommendation?

> The only way to liberate the puppets is for the puppeteer to be a good puppeteer. Similarly, for us, it is not the number of connections that we have to diminish in order to reach at last the sanctuary of the self. On the contrary, as William James so magnificently demonstrated, it is by multiplying the connections with the outside that there is some chance to grasp how the inside is being furnished. You need to subscribe to a lot of subjectifiers to become a subject and you need to download a lot of individualizers to become an individual.[18]

The whole way of setting up the relationship between agent and structure is misconceived. What is wrong with the term 'actor' is not that it is limited to humans all too often but that it always designates a source of initiative or starting point, the extremity of a vector oriented towards some other end. Instead, one actant making another do something is not to be equated with causing or determining, but is the mediating of a relationship. The more attachments or mediations any particular actant has, the better. Emancipation does not therefore mean being made free from bonds but, rather, being 'well-attached'. In language that I have used, it is about being blurred, entangled, bundled up and interconnected. Rather than being distanced and detached, one needs to be (as Levinas might say) in proximity to and a companion to all those other components that go to make up a particular gathering or matter of concern.

What this new approach offers to the debate about creating a credible public discourse for the articulation of ethical concerns and moral values, so essential if there is to be a politics of life in the current climate, is the insight that, instead of detaching or removing from the public square those apparently pre-autonomous dimensions of what it is to be human, they need to be more firmly connected and included in the debates. Without explicit recognition of how these impact upon, and relate to, what we describe as 'autonomous human action', we are operating with an inadequate and inaccurate understanding of human subjectivity. But this is never the end of the process, only a more promising beginning. Once the myriad of connections is acknowledged and permitted into the circulating references that should form the process of truth formulation, it can be seen that fidelity, conviction, commitment, and openness to the novel and unexpected, can be catalysts for change. By reassembling the human in this way and allowing for the entanglements that go to make up matters of concern, one can challenge the mantra that 'there is no alternative' and argue that life is indeed open to new possibilities and imaginings.

---

[18]   Ibid., p. 216.

Chapter 4

Grace Jantzen: Violence, Natality and the Social

Alison Martin

Reading Grace Jantzen's work on natality, one is full of admiration for an intellectual whose project was sadly unable to be fully realized.[1] Grace Jantzen was a committed philosopher whose wide-ranging work responds to issues in the world with some urgency. Indeed, in the introduction to her *Foundations of Violence*, she invokes Marx's famous dictum that the point is to change the world, not simply interpret it.[2] Regardless of the particular historical fortunes experienced by Marxist ideology at a given historical juncture – and it would appear to remain a marginalized political force during this period of a new millennium – the thrust of Marx's analysis remains doggedly persistent, especially at moments when capitalism does indeed threaten to implode.[3] Jantzen attempts to respond to that spirit of Marx. And her analysis also draws upon the structural analogies between Marxism and Christianity, given her emphasis on a historical fall narrative and the inherent eschatological tendencies that thus ensue. That the world is urgently in need of redemption is the oft-repeated refrain that Jantzen repeats once more: instead of cultivating the beauty of creation, Western human culture has developed into one of violence and death.[4]

Whilst her claim for the insistent, endemic universality of the need for cultural redemption paradoxically puts into question the extent to which natality is also an endemic cultural pulse as she claims, her analysis remains a rich legacy for philosophy. Blake stated bitterly that, '[w]isdom is sold in a desolate marketplace where none come to buy', and Jantzen is a figure who peddles the kind of wisdom

---

[1]   Grace Jantzen's (1948–2006) ambitious project – an archaeology of death in Western culture – was curtailed by her own untimely death. The second volume in her prospective project was published posthumously from existing materials and notes as Grace Jantzen, *Violence to Eternity: Death and the Displacement of Beauty*, vol. 2, ed. Jeremy Carette and Morny Joy (London: Routledge, 2008).

[2]   Grace Jantzen, *Foundations of Violence: Death and the Displacement of Beauty*, vol. 1 (London: Routledge, 2004), p. 4.

[3]   Rowan Williams caused some controversy with his own nod to Marx in his article following the 2008 banking crisis. See 'Face It: Marx was partly right about capitalism', *Spectator* (24 September 2008).

[4]   Jantzen, *Foundations*, p. 3.

without which we would surely be left with only the desolation of the market place. Jantzen's analysis of the role of death in Western culture is wise for all that it is over-stated. She provides a sober and considered reflection on the multiple manifestations of death in a culture that has tried to seize hold of it in numerous ways by casting aside its enigma – and it is this enigma that fuels the enduring fascination with death – in order to render it an ontically defined certainty or a determinant symbol in the drama of existence. Whilst Jantzen provides extensive analysis of the prevalence of a cultural obsession with death, especially in thought and writing, it is her own intellectual training and milieu that predisposes her to think through the centrality of death in Western culture: she was an intellectual working on theological texts but with the tools of twentieth-century European thought, driven by major thinkers who posit death as a key concept or cultural phenomenon. Within phenomenology, existentialism and even materialist thought, death became a keystone of cultural analysis, nurturing Jantzen's contention that Western culture has a pathological obsession with death that creates an imbalance compared with the flourishing of natality.[5]

Rendering death an analytical keystone has been, on the one hand, a noble response of twentieth-century European thinkers to the cultural politics of their time. Resisting a sanitized and commodified representation of life in a modern culture,[6] and responding to the reality of the horror of twentieth-century wars which, in terms of death and destruction, surpassed all previous forms of violence, many critical thinkers inevitably came to focus on death. Truth demanded a candid analysis of human consciousness over triumphalist notions of progress, and yet the consequence has been that the resulting philosophy often configured death itself as a cluster concept that can simultaneously represent everything that is repressed, true or constitutive of human being. The inevitability of death as the physical termination of an existence will always press upon human culture because it is a universal that represents an existential and cultural dilemma[7] and, of course, the death of others often represents an unfathomable and irreconcilable loss for those left in their wake.

---

[5]   Ibid., p. 6.

[6]   See Philippe Ariès' seminal study *The Hour of Our Death* (New York: Knopf, 1981), which argues that, in contrast to the way previous centuries have dealt with death as a part of life, death is privatized and rendered invisible in twentieth-century Western culture.

[7]   Jantzen contends, contra Freud, that *Thanatos* is not a universal of human nature but a gendered construct of Western modernity (*Foundations*, p. 6). While that could arguably be the case for Freud's particular construal of *Thanatos*, the phenomenon of death is an inevitable cultural construct that essentially requires some form of cultural processing in all societies. Many analyses of historical literature suggest that it has generally represented an overwhelming fear and irreconcilable loss for individuals. See for example, Jonathon Dollimore, *Death, Desire and Loss in Western Culture* (London: Allen Lane, 1998). These emotions are also inextricably linked to cultural attitudes to ageing, as Simone de Beauvoir demonstrates in her *Old Age*, trans. Patrick O'Brian (Harmondsworth: Penguin, 1972).

Yet on the other hand, a further reason that the concept of death became a keystone of much intellectual culture is simply because so many great thinkers and writers engaged with it so creatively in their work. An obvious and seminal work in this respect is Kojève's *Introduction to the Reading of Hegel*, where sober Hegelian thought is transformed into a dramatic life and death dialectic between the protagonists of lordship and bondage.[8] A whole generation of French intellectuals subsequently felt compelled to position themselves in relation to this narrative, whereby the very constitution of human self-consciousness is determined by a life and death struggle for the recognition of a value that determines who becomes the subject, the same, and who the object, the other.[9] Beauvoir absorbed this philosophy and reproduces it in *The Second Sex* by staging woman as the Other to an imperious masculine consciousness without systematically rethinking its central tenets, despite the tensions they create for her fine and detailed analysis of the lived experience of women.[10] Thinkers such as Levinas, while purporting to demonstrate the prior demands of the ethical over the violence of ontology and its concepts, still presume a Hegelian conflation of violence and history.[11] Irigaray has confronted the violence of death inherent in the structures of recent French thought, but is nevertheless compelled to return to the resources of the Hegelian dialectic in her *To Be Two* as a mode of reconstructing consciousnesses as alterity.[12] The problem of death as limit, or the limit of death, permeates this domain of thought whether it is assimilated or transformed.

An obvious counter model to this notion of human consciousness determined through a struggle to the death is that of family relations, and especially the relations between a mother and child. The latter can be absurdly idealized, and Catholicism in particular has at certain moments rendered it a mythologized cult, and yet it remains a potential symbol of a life-affirming natality that is a counter-model to death and the crucifixion. The European philosophy informing Jantzen's work, however, assumes its problematics not in Christianity as such, but in Nietzsche's presumptive contempt for the value of a Christian God and in Freud's deep suspicion. Life affirmation sidesteps an ethics of good and evil, and the creation of new life is deemed to be always already shot through with death. The structures of the castration complex provided a fecund basis for intellectual analysis and retained the Nietszchean contempt for love. And those structures are

---

[8]   Alexandre Kojève, *Introduction to the Reading of Hegel*, ed. Raymond Queneau (New York: Basic Books, 1969).

[9]   Vincent Descombes, *Modern French Philosophy*, trans. L. Scott-Fox and J.M. Harding (Cambridge: Cambridge University Press, 1980), p. 12.

[10]   Simone de Beauvoir, *The Second Sex*, trans. H.M. Parshley (New York: Vintage Books, 1952).

[11]   Emmanuel Levinas, *Totality and Infinity: An Essay on Exteriority*, trans. Alphonso Lingis (Pittsburgh, PA: Duquesne University Press, 1969).

[12]   Luce Irigaray, *To Be Two*, trans. Monique Rhodes et al. (London: Athlone Press, 2000).

constituted through anxieties about death: paternal authority induces an anxiety syndrome in a little boy who allegedly perceives that his own father might well castrate him if he does not cease to merge with his mother. For those who found this scenario somewhat phantasmagorical, the symbolic was offered to sublimate the threat of castration onto a structural plane where death again becomes a limit. Yet death is a defining concept whether or not limit is determined. A symbiotic immersion in the maternal is defined as a form of death (of individuated being), given its natural, static state of non-differentiation, while differentiation into the realm of culture also relies on death, albeit as its threat. Whichever way it turns, the new life in the child, who may nevertheless have been very desired by its parents, is threatened with or suffused with death: *thanatos*, though in tension with *eros*, prevails. This ostensibly empirically and therapeutically orientated analysis was supported by appropriations of Heidegger, not in terms of a shared philosophical analysis, but in the laying out of death as the domain of primary concern. Thus, for Heidegger, the finitude of human existence renders it a being-towards-death; even at birth, death is *Dasein*'s ownmost potential.[13]

Jantzen thus inherits a discourse of cultural analysis in which death can be the flow of non-differentiation and constructed by individuation; it is stasis, nothing, limit, non-being, in being and/or formed by being; it is possibility and impossibility; it is the paternal and the maternal. In short, it is the ultimate metaphor, or at least it has proved a metaphor of choice. One further reason for this may simply be the spirit of gravity that of course readily attaches itself to death. In a period when philosophy struggles to justify its existence, it must prove its seriousness. Georges Bataille acknowledges this in his introduction to his erotic gem, *Madame Edwarda*: any intellectual will treat death seriously, whereas the erotic is viewed as but a frivolous and momentary fancy.[14] Of course Bataille, the morbid philosopher *par excellence*, manages to fuse death and the erotic in the ecstatic communion of *Madame Edwarda*, where yet another apparent form of death, *la petite mort*, prevails.

Against the backdrop of this assumed gravity and indeed intellectual excitement in relation to death, Jantzen's discussion is measured and calm. Her project is to show that Western culture, broadly defined, has been obsessed with death from its Greco-Roman and Judeo-Christian roots. It is a culture that defines itself through death, simultaneously lauding it in cultural representation while increasingly shielding the public realm from any sight or sound of actual death. Jantzen sees natality, birth and peace as an alternative cultural narrative to this preoccupation, a narrative that needs to be developed but one which already exists in counter-narratives to the over-arching ones that have emphasized death. The notion of beauty, especially a biblical notion of beauty, is one such counter-narrative that has typically been suppressed in the Western symbolic.

---

[13]   Martin Heidegger, *Being and Time*, trans. J. McQuarrie and E. Robinson (New York: HarperCollins, 1962).

[14]   Georges Bataille, *Oeuvres Complètes*, III (Paris: Gallimard, 1971), p. 9.

A cursory reading of Jantzen's work might suggest that she is herself tempted to deny the brutality and significance of death in favour of a celebration of life and its flourishing. Jonathan Dollimore, in his own lengthy investigation of the significance of death and desire in Western culture, demonstrates the persistence of that association and its profundity for individuals.[15] However, to assume that Jantzen is denying the profundity of death would be a misreading; it is the association of death with violence which has been endemically pathological in Western culture, as indeed the titles of her works indicate.[16] She objects to the exaltation of and preoccupation with death to the extent that it is coupled with violence. The cultural transformation she envisages would bring about an acceptance of actual death as a part of life.

The scope of Jantzen's project cannot be underestimated. While she identifies it as a Foucauldian geneaology of death, its overarching intellectual argument is analogous to that of Irigaray in *Speculum*.[17] Irigaray analysed Western texts from Plato on as constitutive of a symbolic that erases the feminine to construct women as men's feminine Other, an erasure that manifests a profound cultural anxiety ensuing from an originary failure on the part of male culture to recognize the feminine. Jantzen similarly identifies a cultural anxiety ostensibly prevalent throughout Western culture that has ensued from suppressed fears arising from a failure to acknowledge the otherness of death, or indeed the other as death, in the form of woman. For Jantzen, whilst the cultural neurosis in relation to death goes back to the infancy of Western culture, it is particularly accentuated by the features of an increasingly violent modernity defined by militarism, technology, capitalism, utilitarianism, colonialism, free market economics and the rise of individualism.[18] Very little is exempt from what she terms 'the death-dealing structures of contemporary life' since the latter are symptoms of this profound neurosis. War is evidently a manifestation of the symptoms but, according to Jantzen, they appear everywhere, from popular films to language and they include, of course, intellectual endeavour (the drive to out-smart one's opponent in analytical philosophy is another symptom).

With respect to locating the causes of the neurosis, Jantzen again pursues a line of argument similar to that of Irigaray. No causes can be given in a summary manner, because the purpose of Jantzen's project (which should have extended to several volumes) is to unearth those causes by listening again to the very foundational texts of Western culture. Hers is not a neutral ear, however, because – as with all hermeneutics – Jantzen listens in accordance with the presuppositions of her question, and hears responses within its parameters. Cultural modalities of death are specifically aligned with Western constructions of masculinity and the

---

[15]   Dollimore, *Death, Desire and Loss in Western Culture.*

[16]   Jantzen, *Foundations*, p. 14.

[17]   Luce Irigaray, *Speculum of the Other Woman*, trans. Gillian C. Gill (Ithaca, NY: Cornell University Press, 1985).

[18]   Jantzen, *Foundations*, p. 3.

preoccupation with death is asserted to be a largely male preoccupation.[19] It is men who have structured the symbolic as an obsessive concern with death and other-worldly longing while simultaneously designating women as death, or as allegedly the cause of men's mortality. Beauvoir developed this analysis in *The Second Sex*, and via psychoanalysis the 'French feminists' have rendered it a cornerstone of critical analysis of Western culture. Jantzen draws upon the latter to define culture as a masculinist linguistic symbolic, only attained at the expense of repressing the desire for unification with the maternal and only maintained by neurotic strategies of control that must silence the maternal body, birth and, according to Jantzen, beauty. Her analysis is not simply another psychoanalysis of key Western texts, however, because she does not reduce all theological concepts to psychoanalytical ones, but it is nevertheless an investigation and analysis of them on a therapeutic model. She aims to bring to consciousness the deep psychic structures that make up our culture, which she believes are so embedded that simply appealing to rationality will not overcome all the repetition compulsions and deathly urges that structure Western desire. A process of listening and careful unpicking is required to bring us to an understanding and realization of our preoccupation with deathly violence, and to expose the suppressed possibilities of natality and beauty. The latter are not explicitly linked to the feminine by Jantzen, but there is a metonymic association.

The therapeutic strategy is a powerful mode of textual analysis, and the call to bring about change through therapeutic interpretation is now familiar in critical thought.[20] However, it has limitations in relation to the social, and Jantzen's assumption that it can lead to hope for the future, for a social transformation orientated towards flourishing, does not accord with the social embeddedness and possibilities which Jantzen herself associates with the notion of natality. Intellectual analysis, and especially therapeutic analysis of texts, does not in itself bring about socio-cultural transformation of the order Jantzen desires. Cultural models, particularly transformative models, require social structures to support them, and forms of political organization and action to realize these. The two strategies are not necessarily mutually exclusive: Frantz Fanon put forward a therapeutic analysis of a violent culture in order to transform its social structures, although the former was envisaged as a springboard to political action in order to create the latter. Rather than remain in the domain of the text, his *The Wretched of the Earth* advocated an actual psychic catharsis of the violence internalized as a result of social structures that explicitly dehumanized colonized peoples.[21] Notoriously, Fanon specifically prescribed violence as a solution to his diagnosis that colonization represents an ongoing violent annihilation of the subjectivity of colonized people. Without being an advocate of violence, Fanon did not believe

---

[19] Ibid., p. 15.

[20] See, for example, Kelly Oliver, *Witnessing* (Minneapolis: University of Minnesota Press, 1981).

[21] Frantz Fanon, *The Wretched of the Earth*, trans. Constance Farrington (London: Penguin, 1963).

that the structural causes of violence could be overcome through therapeutic modes or by turning to peace. He abandoned his post as a psychiatrist trying to heal individuals tortured by the colonial situation in Algeria and literally tortured by French forces during the war of independence because he concluded that only violent socio-political change could cure the whole society of its neurosis. Hence his claim that a colonized individual will only overcome their neurosis by the catharsis of violent liberatory action in the realm of the social.

In keeping with therapeutic models, Fanon deemed appealing to rationality ineffective, and yet for Fanon the limitations of rationality are not restricted to the engagement needed to restructure the unconscious in a therapeutic way. Violence is a socio-political necessity because the colonialist settlers would not cede their power and material advantages; no amount of talking would give the indigenous population the land they wanted. Fanon was engaged in a struggle to overcome socio-economic and political structures, thus his analysis of violence is focused on how to shift those at a particular time in the history of Western colonialism. Given the exigencies of his immediate situation, he gave less attention to the long-term consequences of violent overcoming, and in Jantzen's work we find that necessary in-depth philosophical consideration of the effects of ongoing structures of violence. Nevertheless, Jantzen justifiably refuses to conflate the alleged violence of theoretical conceptualizing in itself with the kind of actual brutality that has been inflicted on people by torture. As she says, philosophy has lost its moorings if it does so.[22] She does not become distracted by the 'violence of the concept', and argues persuasively that if all predication is violent, there is no basis for ethics, and no discrimination between one form of language and another, one ethics and another.[23]

Violence cannot be overcome by linguistics or through the invention of a new language that might somehow sidestep the problem of violence via new modes of articulation.[24] For Jantzen, in fact, violence is not inherent to naming or differentiation: naming is as much an act of recognition and respect as it is a constraining limitation, and differentiation is not only a requirement for ethics, but it imposes itself upon us in the face of given differences. It is the specific interplay of difference, rather than differentiation in itself, from which violence emerges. Akin to the way Beauvoir defines oppression,[25] Jantzen asserts that violence arises from the interplay of difference whereby difference is perceived as threatening and force is exerted to dominate and stifle the potential of others.[26] Fanon's work arises from the effects of that force, in which subject annihilation led to an intra-cultural violence that needed to be turned to its objective cause if anything new was to emerge. Situated in a given historical context (and in fact dying as he

---

[22]   Jantzen, *Violence*, p. 21.

[23]   Ibid., p. 22.

[24]   Ibid., p. 25.

[25]   Simone de Beauvoir, *An Ethics of Ambiguity*, trans. Bernard Frechtman (New York: Citadel Press, 1948).

[26]   Jantzen, *Violence*, p. 20.

wrote), Fanon turned to the exigencies of overcoming that particular violence in the manner it apparently demanded.

In contrast, Jantzen advocates natality as that which can help us turn away from violence and its death-dealing structures. For Jantzen, natality is the condition of being born, it is not a concept or an action but an existential predisposition towards life, one that can provide an alternative to a symbolic of violent death. With respect to death, Jantzen's project is specifically focused on denaturalizing the symbolic function of death, and especially its apparent violence, through historical and social analysis. She links it to the sociological through Pierre Bourdieu's concept of the *habitus* to explain how what is an historically specific violent culture is transmitted as a natural fact.[27] A *habitus* is the life-world of a society which individuals inhabit and in which they internalize the objective social rules and language of their society such that they share an understanding of normative behaviour and subjectively position themselves in relation to that: choices and actions appear natural but are in fact structured by a pre-given common code. The code of the Western *habitus* is necrophilic, according to Jantzen, and it is through the everyday learnt assumptions of its members that necrophilia becomes sedimented as common sense and reproduces itself as such. The need to de-naturalize what can only seem to be the most natural of phenomena is also a motivation for Jantzen to present her analysis as a Foucauldian genealogy: unpicking strategies of naturalization as covert technologies of power.[28] Whilst I have indicated that Jantzen's project owes more to Irigaray than Foucault, she nevertheless succeeds in demonstrating that death and violence have become inextricably linked in our culture in a fashion that is historically specific, not a natural given. To that extent, Jantzen does de-essentialize death. However, when it comes to natality as a counter-narrative, the other to death or the suppressed possibility of a masculine culture that has failed to recognize an originary possibility, Jantzen evokes a notion that is not historicized; it bespeaks a transcendent peace, and appears to propose the realization of some pre-existing harmony.

Compared with mortality, natality is not a concept with a very extensive history, which itself attests to the cultural weight attributed to death. Jantzen acknowledges the seminal contribution of Hannah Arendt, for whom birth is the inauguration of the possibility of beginning, not only for the individual who is thus intrinsically free, but for the creation of humanity, without which there is no beginning.[29] Birth thus instantiates a form of Being, one that is free from absolute determination, in accordance with Augustine's Christian theology, and projects individuals into the politics of appearing to others. Jantzen is also familiar with the work of Adriana Cavarero, who has developed Arendt's thought to challenge the linguistic determinations of post-structuralism by developing a narrative

---

[27]   Ibid., p. 6.

[28]   Ibid, p. 29.

[29]   Hannah Arendt, *The Human Condition* (Chicago: University of Chicago Press, 1958).

notion of the self that is individuated.[30] These philosophers are important because relatively little thought has been explicitly given to the condition of being born and its possibilities. And Jantzen's work is also an important contribution to the development of the concept, not least in the way she debunks the naturalism of 'all men are mortal'.

Yet Jantzen's poetics of natality articulates a notion that is not historicized, and detracts from the sociological embeddedness which she has urged in her analysis of death. Her emphasis is upon a Christian notion of transcendental difference as peace whereby violence is not originary, and maybe beauty is. Without proposing that creation is unambiguous, Jantzen sees the beauty of creation as the missed opportunity of Western culture: in Genesis, when God beheld the created world, it is written that he saw it was *good*, whereas Jantzen traces this word back to the Hebrew *tob*, which can mean good or beautiful.[31] The possibilities of an aesthetic and positive existence are soon bypassed in the Christian West for a world in which good and evil are seemingly pitted against one another in a violent existence that struggles to redeem itself. Yet being born is, for Jantzen, an opening to the possibilities of flourishing in this world, it is in some respects an evocation of Eden; natality is a symbol of hope. Hence she projects the possibility of a social order of natals, a social order reconciled to itself, less dependent upon rational legal doctrine than the notion of flourishing.[32]

Jantzen has no wish to project into the future another mythologized past; her work is concerned with the political realities of violence in this world and she is not ostensibly advocating an other-worldly utopianism. And yet she does expect a form of *healing* to come from natality, a healing that is consequent upon her own intellectual therapy, and from the cultural thinking or even attitude that might thus ensue. She emphasizes that natality entails specifically a form of divine immanence in embodiment, and that as a result we are required to develop a positive attitude to bodies and materiality, in contrast to their denigration in the Judeo-Christian Platonic tradition. From that positive attitude, we would need to concentrate on meeting the needs of those bodies and distribute world resources in accordance with them because we would refute a spirituality that demands salvation of the soul in some other world.[33] In this way, natality allows for hope because justice and liberation are more difficult to bypass, and it is perpetually reiterated hope: each new infant represents new possibilities and the freedom to flourish in new beginnings.

While the state of peace and reconciliation is intrinsically desirable, it is somewhat utopian to suggest that the condition of being born – natality – intrinsically contains the germ of that state. Whereas Jantzen's wisdom cuts across

---

[30] Adriana Cavarero, *In Spite of Plato*, trans. S. Anderlini-D'Onofrio and A. O'Healy (Cambridge: Polity Press, 1995).

[31] Jantzen, *Foundation*, p. 3.

[32] Ibid., p. 36.

[33] Ibid., p. 37.

an excitable intellectual discourse on death and violence with a sober voice, when it comes to natality her own thinking is poetic and speculative, detracting from the socially embedded condition of natality she outlines. I understand natality as a minimalist concept; it represents the absolutely undetermined yet simultaneously absolutely conditioned state of being human; a life that is never pre-given yet is not arbitrary. A newborn child is literally and existentially naked – it cries out for communication, yet the communication it receives is always granular within the history of a *habitus*. Sociologists have also tended to ignore birth, which is the condition of their key concept: socialization. Yet if we accept the socialization thesis and a genealogy of concepts, we must accept that natality is itself both a social phenomenon, and a concept ridden with a certain *pouvoir* (power). Hence I do not believe that turning towards natality will necessarily bring us peace, or even a sense of flourishing. It does bespeak a plenitude of being of which death forms one part. But it does not propose peace on this earth, unless the social conditions are such that peace can be maintained for the socialization of peaceful individuals. For Fanon, the new man had to be created out of a violence necessitated by given social conditions; natality symbolizes the given conditions that may induce peace or that may not. Of course we should want peace and the flourishing of all individuals, but I would argue that rather than assimilating natality to concepts of hope and assertions of newness, we should interpret it as a social condition and give priority to building the social and political structures that will engender the socialization of peace, especially as our actual material resources diminish. I think that beauty may indeed play some part in that: beauty, which has been somewhat ignored by philosophers, theologians and sociologists, may yet be an incitement to action for those who lack faith in universal peace.

SECTION TWO
Life and the Limits of Thinking

Chapter 5

Bodies without Flesh: Overcoming the Soft Gnosticism of Incarnational Theology

John D. Caputo

Woody Allen once said that he did not want to live on in his works, nor did he want to live on in his children; he wanted to live on in his apartment. Therein lies a knotted theological conundrum that I will take up here in a more ponderous way, but without any assurance that I will get much further than has this venerable pundit.

For Life

> Do you think we'll still be around in ten years? he says.

> Do you think we'll still be around? Afterwards? he says. He waits for my response.

> I, in any case, don't think so. He says. But I wish it could happen, I wish I could believe differently he says.[1]

Jacques Derrida and Hélène Cixous are talking about death, about the other side. He says that in the end we die too soon, that life will have been so short. She says, not too soon. This is all the more poignant now that death has since overtaken one of them, the one who wonders if we will still be around in ten years. On her side, she takes the side of life. For her there is but this one side, while death in itself, death as such, does not have or constitute a side. For it is mortality, not death, that achieves a kind of uncanny phenomenality, although nothing is more uncanny than death. Not that death is nothing at all. Death, Heidegger says, is not something *Ausstehendes*, still outstanding, like an unpaid debt, but *Bevorstehendes*, 'impending', or hovering before us, like a spectre. As exposure to the I-know-not-what of death, mortality is a mode of being-in-the-world, of what Heidegger will not condescend to call 'life', *vita mortalis*, mortal life. Mortality

---

[1] Hélène Cixous, 'Promised Belief', in Linda Martín Alcoff and John D. Caputo (eds), *Feminism, Sexuality and the Return of Religion* (Bloomington: Indiana University Press, 2011), p. 147.

belongs on this side and to deal with mortality is to deal with life and to take a stand 'for life', *pour la vie.*

My opening hypothesis is that theology has been spooked by death. In the games played in theology, the card hidden in the deck is death. Death is what the 'trans-' in transcendence (or the 'meta-' in metaphysics) hopes to get beyond. Transcendence means crossing over to the other side. The distinction between time and eternity, the one with teeth in it, is ultimately about the status not of ideal forms or mathematical objects but of our own hides. We are ourselves the subject matter of this distinction. Eternity means 'eternal life', whose reign is among the dead. In high theology, it is the dead who have true life. Philosophy for Plato is practising for death, while, for St Paul, to die is a plus (*kerdos, lucrum,* lucrative), a profit that can made on death (Phil. 1.21–2). But if eternal life spells death, while only the dying are actually alive, then the love of eternal life, Mary Daly complains, is a kind of necrophilia,[2] a curious prescription for curing nihilism.[3]

If mortal life is the life of flesh, then to take a stand for life is to stand for and with flesh. Flesh is always in one way or another the promise/threat of death. Carnal life is life-with-death, life/death, the life of vulnerable flesh, while eternal life is accordingly life without flesh. So my concern throughout will be to flush out the stratagems by which we seek to get beyond flesh, to get to the other side of flesh, which is the other side of life. The ways we find to twist free from our entanglement with flesh is what I mean by 'Gnosticism', which I want to counter with a genuinely carnal or incarnational theology,[4] one that turns on glorious bodies of flesh, one that is for life, for the flesh of life, for the life of flesh.

Consider this primal scene: a celestial being comes down to earth in order to rescue mortals from flesh, to ferry them off to heaven on a cloud from whence the celestial being came, their bodies now re-forged as fleshless fiery things, fit for the heavenly abode.[5] That may be. No one has authorized me to gainsay it. There are robotologists all over North America and Western Europe furiously at work on such a thing, where scientists conduct heated pursuit of post-biological life, seriously working on fitting us out with bodies fit for survival on the other

---

[2]   See Mary Daly, *Gyn/Ecology: The Metaethics of Radical Feminism* (Boston: Beacon Press, 1990), pp. 59–63. Daly associates necrophilia and technology. By 'necrophilia', she means not actually wanting to copulate with a corpse but a will to twist free from life in the flesh and achieve total technological domination of life.

[3]   A view that holds that real life begins at death, that life is really turning white hot only when we are stone cold and rotting in the grave, become the work of worms, has no room to talk about nihilism. It has problems of its own. The apostles of such a view would be well advised to devote more energy to explaining why they are not serving up a kind of metaphysical necrophilia and less time to calling others nihilists.

[4]   I will leave 'incarnation' in lower case, to signify a concept of en-fleshment. I will use upper case only when I mean the Christian doctrine of Incarnation in particular.

[5]   I am not saying that the source of John 1.14 is Gnosticism or metaphysics; it is, as is well known, Proverbs 8–9. I am saying it does not take much to reinscribe it in Gnosticism.

side. The two great contenders for the crown of 'post-humanism' today are contemporary robotologists and Christian eschatologists. Which one will win this race – the Rapture or the Robot (the 'Singularity'[6])? Who knows? All I am saying is that to conduct such business under the name of flesh, instead of another round of Gnosticism, is to give a whole new meaning to the word irony.

Taking Christianity at its Word

Let us take Christianity at its word, its Word made flesh, embracing its claim that it is a religion of the flesh, of 'becoming flesh', a Deleuzianism that almost perfectly translates John 1.14 (*sarke egeneto*), like the German *Fleischwerden*.

I distinguish 'flesh' (*sarx, caro, chair, Fleisch*) from 'body' (*soma, corpus, Leib*). The body means the site of agency, action and movement, organic functions, the 'organon' of the soul, its right hand, so to speak. The body is the body subject of phenomenology, appearing everywhere but incognito in *Being and Time* as being-in-the-world, as the user of tools. The body tends to be hale and whole, male and muscular, white and Western. Flesh by contrast is a seat of passivity and affectivity, of feeling, self-feeling, feeling itself felt, of feeling itself alive; flesh is the site of pleasure and pain, joy and suffering, glory and misery. We pass our days in able-bodied fascination with the world but it does not take much to be drawn back into the flesh. The 'reduction' to the flesh occurs when we are driven to the extremes of pleasure or pain, in sexual ecstasy or torture, pushed to a point where the world itself is suspended and we are reduced to sighing and moaning. Flesh aches with hunger even as flesh is meat (*Fleisch*) that is eaten (a problem for early Christian martyrs).[7] When we die it is flesh that rots (first) and stinks. (Who knows when our ceramic hip replacements will rot?) At death, a body, a *corpus*/corpse, remains to be disposed of, but the flesh has melted away. Dead bodies are bodies without flesh, dead weights.

To be sure, nothing is gained by instituting a new form of dualism between body and flesh. My point is exactly the opposite: living flesh is embodied, and all the living bodies we have ever run into are enfleshed. What I am analysing here is the spectre/dream of a 'body without flesh', a living one, not a corpse, and what event is harboured in that figure. If Paul says that on the whole he would

---

[6]   What the Rapture – made famous in *Left Behind: A Novel of the Earth's Last Days* by Time LaHaye and Jerry B. Jenkins (Colorado Springs: Tyndale House, 1995), which describes the sudden ascension into heaven of the physical bodies of the faithful in some sort of resurrected body – and the singularity (see below, fn. 16) have in common is the detachment of life from its biological basis, either in heavenly bodies of fire and air, or in the electronic downloads of 'consciousness' into robot bodies. This is elaborated below in 'Theology and Robotology'.

[7]   Caroline Walker Bynum, *The Resurrection of the Body in Western Christianity, 200–1336* (New York: Columbia University Press, 1995), ch. 1.

rather have a body without flesh (Phil. 1.24), what is the status of this bond with flesh, its ana-status? Is there, as Jean-Luc Nancy suspects, a deep dissatisfaction with carnality concealed in the Incarnation, a 'real and secret horror of bodies', of carnal corruption?[8] Why would a theology of incarnation require flesh to be visited from on high? Is not flesh already high enough? Why a divine *advent into* flesh instead of the divine *event of* flesh? Is the force of this prefix 'in-' privative, 'in-carnation', as in in-corporeal, in-valid, in-carnal? Or might incarnational theology admit other figures and resources, other more glorious bodies of flesh?

The Heavenly Body

The glorious body incarnational theology is dreaming of is a heavenly body. In Luke, Jesus appears to the assembled disciples who 'thought that they were seeing a ghost (*pneuma*)', urging them to touch and see the wounds in his risen body, 'for a ghost does not have flesh and bones as you see that I have'. Then Jesus took a piece of broiled fish and ate it to allay their doubts (24.36–43), after which he 'was carried up into heaven' (24.50). Left to stand as it is, this narrative implies a functioning digestive tract and consequently the production of waste products, to put it rather circumspectly.[9] Giorgio Agamben is less concerned with being circumspect: what must be excluded from the risen body is defecation.[10] The difference between this side and the other side, immanence and transcendence, is defecation. What is so foolish, ridiculous or amusing about all this? Why not wonder what sort of housing, food supply and waste management system would be required to accommodate Alice's surprising change of size in Wonderland? Are we doing something wrong?

Thomas Aquinas, the Angelic Doctor, proposed a devilishly ingenious way out of this heavenly dilemma.[11] The earth is 'thirsty' for water, so it consumes water

---

[8]   Jean-Luc Nancy, *Corpus*, trans. Richard Rand (New York: Fordham University Press, 2008), p. 45.

[9]   Throughout some 800 pages of exposition and interpretation, N.T. Wright manages to elude this question in *The Resurrection of the Son of God* (Minneapolis: Fortress Press, 2003). After repeating what Luke 24 says, he adds approvingly, 'Luke makes no more effort to explain or justify this extraordinary innovation [the "transphysicality" of the risen body] than do any of the others' (p. 661). That is, neither Wright nor Luke (who is supposed to be a physician!) is willing to touch the subject of what a risen body is doing eating bread or broiled fish. Eight hundred pages of insistence that all of this is to be taken in most realistic terms go hand in hand with a resolute refusal to explain what that could really mean. The latter is declared anathema, denounced as just the sort of griping you hear from the Jesus Seminar (p. 656, fn. 21)!

[10]   Giorgio Agamben, *The Open*, trans. Kevin Attell (Stanford: Stanford University Press, 204), pp. 14 and 18.

[11]   See Thomas Aquinas, *Summa Theologiae*, III q.54, a.2 (in some editions art. 3); cf. I, q.51, a.3 ad 5; online at: http://www.newadvent.org/summa/4054.htm

by absorbing it from defect or need, while the sun is higher than water, and does not 'need' water, and so it consumes water by burning it up or evaporating it. The mortal body is like the earth, it needs food, but the risen body is like the sun, it does not need food, but consumes it by evaporating it. The food is not assimilated by the risen body of Christ (which would create the need for heavenly plumbers) but burnt off. From an historical-critical point of view, Aquinas actually is not all that far off! But with this difference: the resurrected body is not analogous to a heavenly body; it *is* a heavenly body, of the same astral stuff. Of course, as Dale Martin says, there is 'no fixed tradition as to the exact nature of the resurrected body of Jesus' in the New Testament.[12] Luke and John emphasize that resurrection is a resurrection of the flesh; that the hands of Thomas could feel the soft tissues of Jesus' wounded side; that Jesus could eat broiled fish, have breakfast on the shores of the Lake Tiberias and break bread in the inn at Emmaus; and that he was no 'ghost' (*pneuma*). This flatly contradicts the words of Paul in 1 Cor. 15.50, which expressly disallows 'flesh and blood' into the kingdom of God, explicitly precluding the suggestions of the later gospels, verbatim.

Paul distinguished corruptible bodies made of earth and water from heavenly bodies made of the finer materials of fire and air. Paul does not distinguish between body and soul (Plato), or body and mind (Descartes), but a 'gross natural body' (*soma physikon*) and a 'refined body' (*soma pneumatikon*). Human bodies are composed of elements of both: *sarx*, 'flesh', the soft tissues of the body responsible for feeling; *psyche*, a 'soul' (*anima*) responsible for its animate vegetative and sentient life, which it shares with the animals; *pneuma*, 'spirit', responsible for the higher acts of cognitive and intelligent life, which is made up of finest, ethereal materials, out of which the sun, the moon and the stars are made. The natural place of *pneuma* is the heavens; these are 'heavenly bodies' (*somata epourania*). *Sarx* and *psyche* are earth-bound and belong to the sphere of *hyle*, which is commonly translated as 'matter', but signifies the grosser heavier side of matter, while *pneuma* means ether, fire and air, finer, lighter materialities. Thus while we today would say that fire and air belong to the 'material' world, they were not, in Paul's vocabulary, hyletic (*hyle*) or 'natural' (*physikon*, material in the 'gross', narrow sense) like wood or dirt.

At death, the shell of this earthly seed is shattered, breaking up its grosser hyletic materiality and animality, in order to come forth as something entirely pneumatic. Death, for Paul, is not the separation of body and soul, but the separation of the body from flesh. The resurrected body is a body (*soma*), not a gross hyletic animal body but a 'pneumatic body', a refined ethereal body exercising higher intelligent life but not lower biological or zoological life. In the gospels, which mean to tell a story, a more mythic and magical view of the risen body is struck. The narrative structure permits the implausible notion of palpably risen flesh, with risen and incorruptible but quite useless bodily functions like eating and drinking.

---

[12]   Dale Martin, *The Corinthian Body* (New Haven: Yale University Press, 1995), p. 124. The paragraph that follows is a summary of ch. 5.

The authors of these gospels ignore, if indeed they even knew, the way Paul had forestalled those problems in advance. Paul was not trying to tell a story but to undo one. He was worried about ridicule from the Greek philosophers at Corinth. The *hoi polloi* at Corinth would swallow almost anything, but Paul, hearing objections from the educated class, proposed a body made of astral stuff that even the learned members of the ancient world would agree is incorruptible.[13]

Theology and Robotology

No one today can fail to notice the connection between the eschatological risen body and the technological body, between these spectacular scenes in the New Testament and the literature of science-fiction, between the miracles of the New Testament and the miracles of a techno-science rapidly becoming a techno-eschatology. The theological imagination is being progressively realized by bionics and bio-technology. Michel Serres has shown how advanced information technology gradually takes over the classical functions of angelology[14] – of winged flight, instant messaging (*angelos*) and guidance (GPS). 'Miracle' drugs can cure disease; biotechnology can replace organs, make the blind to see, the deaf to hear. But the ultimate target of techno-eschatology is the tree of life itself, the elimination of death, the very aspiration for which earned Adam his walking papers from Eden.

Science today is dreaming of transfiguration, resurrection and ascension. Robotology, biotechnology and theology make common cause centred on the common foe they find in biology, in carnal life. The robotologists are no less resolved than Saint Paul to provide us with light, fast, airy bodies, even if such bodies come at the cost of flesh, of the *bios* of life and its biology, of the *zoe* of life and its zoology. The updated version of 1 Corinthians 15 is being written by contemporary robotologists who want to upload consciousness onto a computer and download it into shiny new long-lasting robots. They desire as much as any Christian to put off corruptibility and to put on incorruptibility, are just as ready to leave this earth for some elsewhere in the skies where they will live on and on in very un-earthly bodies. Whether by science or the Spirit, each is anxious to refit disabled bodies with shiny new able bodies without flesh,[15] fit to survive the trip to the other side and to thrive in the atmosphere of that heavenly city. The robotologists are as serious about this as any Bible thumper in Kansas railing against Darwin or any ravished character in *Left Behind*. They share the same

---

[13]   Ibid., pp. 128–9.

[14]   Michel Serres, *Angels: A Modern Myth*, trans. Francis Cowper (Paris: Flammarion, 1993).

[15]   Sharon Betcher, *Spirit and the Politics of Disablement* (Minneapolis: Fortress Press, 2007).

anxiety about dying before the rapture arrives.[16] The heavenly constellation of Bishop N.T. Wright, John Polkinghorne – a theologian at home in particle physics and resurrection – and Hans Moravec – Carnegie–Mellon roboticist – is written in the stars. Robots and risen bodies, particle physics and Pauline particles, iPhones and angels, announce a future that excites and terrifies us, a future of glorious bodies without flesh.

There is something undeniably amusing about this discussion of hot fast and fiery bodies, bodies that can be found only in dreams or literature or painting or perhaps a digitalized animated film. Every such discussion ends by declaring it is all a mystery, but not without first trading jokes about what sort of body we will have, like the medieval hypothesis that we will all be thirty-somethings. Is there any difference between these bodies to come in theology and robotology? Are we on the right track? Theology cannot be about this. Robotology perhaps, not theology. What then is theology about? I have chosen three leads to follow here, Deleuze's 'A Life', St Athanasius and *Slumdog Millionaire*.

The *beata vita*: Resurrection – Once More from the Top

I treat 'A Life' as a way to redescribe resurrection and a postmodern counterpart to Tertullian's *de resurrectione carnis* (not '*corporis*'), also an early creedal formulation.[17] Deleuze analyses a body dimmed down into a neutral and indifferent life, an uncanny deathly life, a barely living remnant of life, a bare life, neither human nor animal, male nor female, in the suggestive scene described in Dickens' *Our Mutual Friend*. Dickens' literary imagination furnishes the philosophy of immanence with a phenomenological reduction that leads directly back to a resurrection story situated on the plane of immanence.

Having nearly drowned in a river accident, the rogue Mr Riderhood lies comatose on the table surrounded by a doctor and the four men who saved him: 'No one has the least regard for the man … but the spark of life within him is curiously separable from him now, and they have a deep interest in it, probably because it IS life, and they are living and must die'.[18] The man lying there, nothing but 'a flabby lump of mortality', of mortal flesh at the brink of death, presents a

---

[16]   Ray Kurzweil thinks it will be only a short while; the rapture will come in 2045, and he has gone on a diet to make sure he will live that long, advice St Paul never thought to pass along to the Thessalonians who shared their anxiety with him about dying before Jesus returned. See Terry Grossman and Ray Kurzweil, *Fantastic Voyage: Live Long Enough to Live Forever* (Easton, PA: Rodale Press, 2004); and Ray Kurzweil, *The Singularity is Near: When Humans Transcend Biology* (Baltimore: Penguin Books, 2005).

[17]   For a commentary on the 'materialism' of speaking of 'flesh' not 'body', see Bynum, *The Resurrection of the Body*, pp. 34–8.

[18]   This and the following quotations come from *The Oxford Illustrated Dickens* (Oxford: Oxford University Press, 1989), bk Three, ch. III, pp. 443–8.

'solemn' scene: 'If you are gone for good, Rogue, it is very solemn, and if you are coming back, it is hardly less so'. They are bound together by life/death, the five men looking upon a fellow mortal, all the vulnerability of his fragile flesh exposed. The solemnity of flesh, its sacredness, arises from itself, not from the decree of a sovereign, as Agamben would have us think. They are reduced to tears when they think they see a spark of life: 'Neither Riderhood in this world, nor Riderhood in the other, could draw tears from them; but a striving human soul between the two can do it easily'. The rogue's daughter, Pleasant Riderhood, is surprised to find her curmudgeonly father the object of such solicitation: 'Also some vague idea that the old evil is drowned out of him, and that if he should happily come back to resume his occupation of the empty form that lies upon the bed, his spirit will be altered'. But then: 'The low, bad unimpressible face is coming up from the depths of the river, or what other depths, to the surface again. As he grows warm, the doctor and the four men cool'. The spark of life was deeply interesting while it was in abeyance but no longer, now that the same surly Mr Riderhood is back, the old father, unimproved. Ungrateful to the men who saved him, unaltered, undeconstructed, he takes his departure out of the ring in which he has had that little turn-up with Death.

Riderhood squandered a chance for rebirth and resurrection. Resurrection means a true repetition, not of the same but of the different, not of a prior actuality but of a virtuality or event, the production of something new. 'A life' – mere life, *vita tantum* – is a cluster of virtualities, events and singularities simmering beneath the body. Fate had unexpectedly given Mr Riderhood another role of the dice, another chance to re-enter the world an altered spirit. But Riderhood refused to be saved, declining the invitation that the cosmos, in its infinite generosity, had extended to him to come out of that tomb a new man, a new being. Here is a Lazarus story where Lazarus, called by the Lord to come forth, unhappily declines the invitation.

In this story, the pure immanence of life to and in itself constitutes what Deleuze calls 'complete bliss', the 'blessed life', the *beata vita*, which is a point in which Agamben has a special interest.[19] The blessed life, Deleuze says, is a 'spirituality of the body' – a phrase not so far from Paul's *soma pneumatikon* – the pure spiritual *flow* of life without organic striation,[20] the unimpeded *breath* or spirit of life. The blessed life *is* life, which is the occasion of this solemnity – 'because it IS life', Dickens says – raised up to a salutary, saving level of intensity. On the plane of immanence, the blessed life and the biological life, theology and biology, converge. As Agamben says, the fundamental category of the coming philosophy

[19] Gilles Deleuze, *Pure Immanence: Essays on A Life*, trans. John Rajchman and Anne Boyman (New York: Zone Books, 2001), p. 27; see the valuable commentary in Giorgio Agamben, *Potentialities*, trans. Daniel Heller-Roazen (Stanford: Stanford University Press, 1999), pp. 220–39.

[20] Gilles Deleuze, *Francis Bacon: The Logic of Sensation*, trans. Daniel Smith (Minneapolis: University of Minnesota Press, 2003), p. 41.

is life,[21] the 'spark of life', the immanent activity where agent and patient coincide. That is what we mean by 'flesh' and what Spinoza called 'beatitude', the joy that is taken in life itself, the joy of feeling alive. Augustine was beset by the dilemma that the *beata vita* is something we cannot *not* desire, even as we cannot but disagree about what makes for a happy life. But I treat that dilemma as an axiom governing the dynamics of life and desire, because on the plane of immanence, as in the New Testament, what is genuinely universal is singularity, while the various essentialist universals, the categories or generalities of *quidditas*, of 'what-ness', are bullies, pseudo-universals trying to intimidate us. The only thing that is repeated perfectly, 'univocally', throughout the cosmos is difference, the way every snowflake is singularly itself, a point that both Duns Scotus and contemporary particle physics apply to everything.

Bodies of Glory

Do not mistake my intentions. I am not trying to drum the Christian Resurrection and Incarnation out of theology. Far from it. I am speaking throughout for life, for flesh, and trying to find the flesh in incarnation and to replay resurrection in such a way as to persuade its glorious bodies to remain on earth. I am trying to see in *anastasis* (resurrection) a way of standing up for life, for the body and the earth, of rising up into glory, but without the aerodynamics, without the Gnostic urge to twist free from earth and flesh and stand on the other side. I am seeking an earthy Jesus and an equally earthy resurrection to go along with it. I regard speculative forays into the heavenly body, from St Paul to Polkinghorne, as a category mistake. Fiery airy bodies are not what incarnation and resurrection are all about. If they are, I predict the robotologists will win the race with the Second Coming.

The stroke of genius of Christian theology is that it means to be a theology of the becoming-flesh of God, which is the Christian answer to the great Nietzschean critique. But as incarnation is risky business, to say the least, requiring interpretation, I propose here a commentary by way of two kinds of glorious bodies, bodies which glow with Deleuzian doxological intensity, which I propose as alternates to – and glosses upon – the glorious bodies without flesh of sky high theology. From glory to glory (2 Cor. 3.18). The first of these proposals is trying to bring about heaven on earth, while the other is trying to avoid hell on earth.

The first glorious body goes back to a view of Incarnation common in Eastern Christianity and earlier Western Christianity as a story of *theopoesis* and *theosis* (Athanasius and Gregory Nazianzus).[22] 'God became man so that man can become God', Athanasius famously said.[23] What I like about the Athanasian figure is the

---

[21]   Agamben, *Potentialities*, p. 220.

[22]   *Theopoiesis*, 'deification', and *theosis*, 'divinization', refer to the supernatural transformation of human life by the grace of Christ, making it God-like.

[23]   Athanasius, *On the Incarnation*, 54:3, *Patrologia Graeca*, 25:192B.

double course it charts: *both* the becoming-flesh of the divine (but not because the divine was not flesh to begin) *and* the becoming-divine of flesh (but not because flesh was not divine to begin). My Athanasius, you see, lands on a Deleuzian plane, or has a Deleuzian tilt brought out by Peter Hallward who criticizes instead of congratulating Deleuze for having a deeply theophanic side that reminds us of John Scotus Eriugena.[24] The becoming-flesh of the divine is one side whose other side is the becoming-divine of the flesh, but both sides belong on the same side, this side; both sides are 'for life'. Incarnation means both at once, both *ab initio*, from the beginning, or, as Heidegger might say, *gleichursprünglich*, 'equiprimordial'. A divine so entangled with the flesh tethers the body to the earth, blocking off the aerodynamics, while opening the earth to the heavens. Here is a way to find heaven on earth and to treat incarnation and *anastasis* as songs to the earth. These are indeed heavenly bodies, in the sense of the 'heavens' as sources of life, not 'heaven' as a place to go after death. Now the primal scene means that the celestial being comes down to earth the way the sun or rain come from heaven, making life grow and glow with glory.

In these terms the Gospel renderings of the resurrection are more for life than 1 Corinthians. By retaining the full flush of flesh in their stories, by describing, *per impossibile*, risen flesh, their effect is to prevent the risen body from flying off to heaven.[25] At the very least, we should say they insinuate a more earthly event, a kind of Deleuzian intensity, ascension as intension, which is why Deleuze often feels perfectly free to speak of bodies of 'glory'. The Gospels invite us to rethink the risen body as heaven-on-earth, as the heavenly glory of the flesh itself, as the glory of the world, of the only world we know. They graft the resurrected body on to lovely earthly scenes, an evening meal in an inn (part of whose charm is being tired), fresh fish frying on a morning lake (which requires hunger), suggesting the *reficerium*, the 'refreshment', which the early theologians attributed to resurrection. But if eating by a lake, then why not sex by a lake? Why not lovers entangled in carnal embrace who have been known to exclaim, 'this is glorious', 'this is heaven', 'over the moon', 'glory be to God!' And if this is not heaven, then to hell with heaven. Such heavenly exclamations, such heavenly ejaculations! What doxological glory to link (this might not survive the copy-editor) erection and resurrection.

But St Paul, who had his doubts about flesh and bodies in heat, is not to be excluded from this picture. For Paul, too, is for life, the Paul who said we are already reborn with baptism, for we were once dead under the law, held captive in a kingdom of death, but now live in Christ. That means resurrected life does

---

[24]   Peter Hallward, *Out of this World: Deleuze and the Philosophy of Creation* (London: Verso, 2006).

[25]   As Bynum, *The Resurrection of the Body*, p. 26, points out, the second-century theologians insisted upon a *resurrectio carnis* precisely as a counter to Gnosticism. I am not denying their good intentions. I am just saying that as a coherent concept, resurrected flesh has no legs.

not require fiery airy bodies; it has already begun in the flesh that is flush with the life of Christ (Romans 6–8), of grace and the new creation, while no longer living according to the 'flesh' of sin. That is the Paul upon whom Žižek and Badiou famously seize to launch a critique of the rule of death in market capitalism, which is killing off the life of everything from love and politics to religion and sports.[26] The profit motive (*lucrum*) corrupts everything. We can make a profit on anything – from prostitution to pictures of the Pope to death itself, trading in our own vulnerable bodies of flesh for the lucre of everlasting treasure. But in my view it is fragile flesh that constitutes life's treasure, life's fragile absolute, and it is there that our heart should be. Flesh is the site of a genuine life that breaks the rule of death, of the not quite dead or undead lives we lead, the site of a genuine mortal life, not a living death.

So this first glorious body turns on erotic intensities, on finding heaven on earth, and it has nothing to do with the cosmo-theological glorious body of 1 Cor. 15. The Gospel narratives are not an inspired Google map to heaven but a song to the glory of the earth.

Slumdog Millionaires

The second glorious body has to do not with the glory of *jouissance* (pleasure, enjoyment) but with the glory of justice. It arises, or rises up, not in erotic intensity but in response to the intensity of the misery and cruelty of our mortal condition. It is intent on avoiding hell on earth, which is the other side of finding heaven on earth.

The body of flesh par excellence in the Scriptures, the body which is almost all flesh, is the crucified body of Jesus. This is a very dangerous body. A recent study has shown that the crucified body amazingly is nowhere to be found in Christian art before the tenth century. It appears first during the Carolingian empire.[27] This body, exploited by Mel Gibson and inspiring so much anti-Semitic fervour,[28] has blood on its hands. It was enlisted in the support of a theology of Anselmian atonement – shedding infinite blood to pay off infinite debt. It was further enlisted in a redescription of the Eucharist as a ritual repetition of the 'sacrifice' of the body of Christ, which refocused the theology of the Eucharist away from the repetition of the first glorious body, the resurrected body, toward the second body, the mutilated body of Jesus, which makes the Mass the daily

---

[26] See Alain Badiou, *Saint Paul: The Foundation of Universalism* (Stanford: Stanford University Press, 2003), and Slavoj Žižek and John Milbank, ed. Creston Davis, *The Monstrosity of Christ: Paradox or Dialectic* (Cambridge, MA: MIT Press, 2009). See also John D. Caputo and Linda Martín Alcoff (eds), *St. Paul among the Philosophers* (Bloomington: Indiana University Press, 2009).

[27] Rita Nakashima Brock and Rebecca Ann Parker, *Saving Paradise: How Christianity Traded Love of the World for Crucifixion and Empire* (Boston: Beacon Press, 2008).

[28] *The Passion of Christ* (2004), Director: Mel Gibson.

repetition of shedding blood, the daily torture of the body of Jesus. It was finally enlisted in the army where it became an emblem of Christian soldiers, of being willing to die for Christ who died for us, which really meant being willing to kill for Christ in the Crusades.[29] This is a very dangerous body to glorify because we risk thereby glorifying violence and a God who is appeased by violence. But, as Foucault said, I am not claiming everything is bad, I am conceding that everything is dangerous.[30]

For over and against the danger of glorifying violence, this body also harbours what Johann Baptist Metz calls the 'dangerous memory of suffering', the *memoria passionis*.[31] The bodies of the 'poor' and of the 'sinners' to whom Jesus ministered are, as William Herzog has shown, desperate and destitute beyond what these words normally suggest. They led short, miserable lives under the heels of a cruel occupation.[32] They were the 'slumdogs' of the day. So when Agamben observes that it is defecation that divides mortals from the bodies of the blessed, we recall in *Slumdog Millionaire* Jamal plunging into the cesspool, into a sea of defecation, a figure of the earthy pungency of flesh and mortality.[33] If the poor were sinners, they were first sinned against, driven to theft and collaboration by the unrelenting cruelty of the occupying Roman army. Like the horrible scene where the children are intentionally blinded to make them more pathetic beggars. It is thus to slumdogs everywhere that Jesus brings good news, among whose bodies his own sacred body circulates, and among whom his own crucified body is finally to be numbered.

These people never win a million dollars, are not rescued from their desperate plight, and end their lives in misery, destitution and a degrading death. The harshness of reality in fact intruded into this film when the young actors, chosen from among 'real' slumdogs, after picking up their Academy Awards were about to be returned to these very slums from whence they came. At this point Hollywood and the Indian government, overwhelmed with embarrassment, intervened upon this repetition of the same, the repetition of this shame. The slumdogs, the real, concrete and incarnate ones, lead ruined lives, damaged beyond repair. By the time help arrives, if it ever arrives, they are already blind or dead. There is nothing we can do to help the dead. They are not going to come back to life.

---

[29]   It was also integral to a deeply grim and other-worldly version of Christianity which treats the body as a menace to eternal salvation deserving only discipline and denial.

[30]   Michel Foucault, 'On the Genealogy of Ethics', in Hubert L Dreyfus and Paul Rabinow (eds), *Michel Foucault: Beyond Structuralism and Hermeneutics*, 2nd edn (Chicago: University of Chicago Press, 1983), pp. 231–2.

[31]   Johann Baptist Metz, *Faith in History and Society*, trans. D. Smith (New York: Crossroad, 1980), pp. 109–15.

[32]   William Herzon, *Parables as Subversive Speech* (Louisville: Westminster John Knox Press, 1994), pp. 63–6. My thanks to Craig Keen for this reference. See my exchange with Prof. Keen in Eric R. Serverance (ed.), *I More Than Others: Responses to Evil and Suffering* (Newcastle upon Tyne: Cambridge Scholars Publishing, 2010), pp. 6–34.

[33]   *Slumdog Millionnaire* (2008), Director: Danny Boyle.

Unless they do, as indeed they do in a theology of resurrection which comes to the rescue of shattered flesh. Not, alas, in the nick of time, but too late, after time, after it is too late for time. Too late, much too late, does resurrection love the living body. Just as John contrives to have Jesus show up too late (intentionally) in Bethany, which allowed Lazarus to die and in turn allowed Jesus to put on a display of divine power.

Here the danger is that the high theology of Christian orthodoxy will fly off to heaven and leave the rest of us to face the worst. Here it loses its nerve and loses the thread of God's entanglement with flesh, of the double becoming, both the becoming flesh of the divine and the becoming divine of the flesh. It displaces the crucified body of Jesus, disentangling the mystical body of Christ from the crucified flesh of Jesus, with the disentangling of the rest of us from flesh to follow. Now the coming of the celestial being into flesh offers relief, sublation and redemption from flesh. Analogy, which turns on the same tripartite structure as *Aufhebung* (affirmation, negation and eminence), provides relief from flesh, a way to burn off flesh and ascend the ladder of being with elevated astral bodies. Life, but *not* incarnate life, but bodies *eminentiore modo*, bodies in a higher way, bodies without flesh. Theology becomes astral-ology by way of *analogia*, *anastasis*, *Aufhebung*. Their earthly bodies redeemed for fleshless bodies of glory, the slumdogs become millionaires after all, which is the lucrativeness of death.

The Weakness of the Flesh and the Weakness of God

Again, I am not trying to scuttle incarnational thinking but to identify its desire, to feel around for the glorious bodies it affirms. If thinking is not affirmation, and if affirmation is not the affirmation of life, if it is not 'for life', then it is worth nothing, or less than nothing because it is for the other side of life. *Denken* is *Danken*, Heidegger quips in Greco-German; 'to think is to thank'. Thinking means saying 'yes', 'amen'. *Viens, oui, oui*, Derrida would say in Franco-Hebrew, 'Come, yes, yes'. A double 'yes'. First of all, flesh itself is what we are, 'yes', all the way down, so that if flesh is burned off then all that is left of us is ash and cinder, which is the anomaly of necrophilia, of attributing pure life to those mouldering in their graves. Secondly, flesh itself is of itself something saving, 'yes', not something needing to be saved; flesh is hallow of itself, not in need of being hallowed. 'Yes, yes'.

Flesh is healed by flesh, as the wounds of time are healed by giving more time, and life is healed not by giving death but giving more life. Give flesh time to heal; do not rush off. To seek to be healed of our mortality is to seek to be healed of life. Mortality means vitality. Mortality is first and foremost a form of life not of death. Vitality and mortality are the same, like the evening star and the morning star. Life is sculpted by mortality the way a statue is etched by its limits. The beauty of life includes the patina of our mortality, which is part of the beauty of the post-mortem conversation Cixous has with Derrida.

Remember the earthy ending of the story of Job. He was given fourteen thousand sheep, six thousand camels, one thousand yoke of oxen, one thousand donkeys, seven sons and three daughters, and to live for one hundred and forty years and to see four generations. Then he died, 'old and full of days' (Job 42.10–17). There is no mention of a fiery airy body. When your conception of family or community is powerful enough, you see rebirth in the coming generations. Immortality is for individuals; it plants the seed of individualism, in technology, in theology and in politics, which is dangerous, not always bad.

Flesh itself is more interior to me than I am to myself, the most *heimlich* ('secret') of all, while death is the very definition of the *unheimlich* ('the uncanny'). But death is not the enemy, not a devil, but a creature. Theology, too easily spooked by these uncanny companions, flesh and death, too easily disconcerted and unsettled, sends forth shiny astral bodies to do battle with these spectres and drive them off. All-Saints Day is conjured up to trump All-Spooks Day, Hallow'een, but it never quite closes the gap between the two.

That is why in a theology that says 'yes' to flesh, that does not distance itself from flesh, it makes perfect sense to speak of 'disabled God' (Nancy Eiesland), or a 'mortal God' (Derrida), of 'the body of God' (Sallie McFague) or of a 'suffering God' (Metz), or of the 'weakness of God' (Saint Paul).[34] Disability, disease and death itself are part of the way that the multiple forms of life are etched and not, as Augustine thought, a lasting punishment for a fateful exercise of bad judgement by two children in Eden who never existed. Life is not lived within the lines and it cannot be thought of in terms of straight and crooked. Disease, disability and death are not scandals requiring the urgent attention of theodicy. They are part of life's mutations and multiplications, its twists and turns and folds, its harshness and risk. They constitute the creative instability by which life, breaking up its regularities, is enabled to move on. If individuals did not die, life would be brought to a dead stand still.

Thinking about God as absolute perfect rectitude makes everything bent look scandalous and dark, suspicious and sinister, sinful and left-handed, which is why the best that Augustine could come up with when he considered disabled bodies was to call it the 'residue of Eden'.[35] God is not the name of the perfect constellation of all possible perfection, but of an event of provocation, solicitation, invitation, which calls to us at the limits of joy and grief. God is not an unlimited being but the God of limit situations. God is not an ideal of being but the ordeal of an event astir within being, an impatience within the world that pushes the world beyond itself, beyond the horizons of foreseeability, making being restless with promise/risk. God is not a pure act but a pure impulse, not pure perfection but a pure provocation, not

---

[34] See Nancy L. Eiesland, *The Disabled God* (Nashville: Abingdon, 1994); Jacques Derrida, *Rogues: Two Essays on Reason*, trans. Pascale-Anne Brault and Michael Naas (Stanford: Stanford University Press, 2005), pp. 15–67; Sallie McFague, *The Body of God* (Minneapolis: Fortress Press, 1993); Metz, *Faith in History and Society*; and 1 Cor. 1.25.

[35] Betcher, *Spirit and the Politics of Disablement*, pp. vii–xiii.

a being but an event, the name of an event whose name I do not know, the name of a secret, of the secret sources and resources of life. God is not the God 'almighty' of strong theology but the subjunctive 'might' of weak theology.

Bodies of Glory and the Flesh of Christianity

Theology must take every precaution not to be spooked by death, not to allow its salutary indignation at injustice to trick it into cutting a desperate deal with life. It must not be panicked into concluding that if life and justice are only to be had at the cost of flesh, then so be it. But then what about the slumdogs? What of all the nameless and innumerable dead whose lives were short and brutal, whose deaths were cruel and unjust, all those who have and will have lived and died as slumdogs and never become millionaires? What justice is there for them?

But where is it written that justice is always served? Justice is a solicitation not an assurance, a promise not always filled, a hope always vulnerable and at risk (like flesh itself). Nothing is guaranteed. *Slumdog Millionaire*, we recall, is about a quiz show in which the correct answer to the question, how did an uneducated slumdog know the answer to all those questions, is not that he cheated, was lucky or knowledgeable, but 'it is written', fate. But fate too is just more strong theology, like predestination. On that account, the fate of all the others is heartless and unhappy, so why bother? Justice is written in the Scriptures but the Scriptures are words of prophecy, prayer and promise, not books of fate. Words are spirits and solicitations where what happens in the flesh depends on the response, the witness. Nothing ensures that they will be fulfilled. The name of God harbours the event of a promise/risk of justice, of messianic peace. That promise is a weak force, a call, but without an army to back it up. It is incumbent upon us to respond, to make the truth come true, to do the truth, to bring about the Kingdom of God in the flesh. That we may or may not do. The memory of the crucified flesh of Jesus does not mean there is magic coming from the sky to do it for us. It is a figure of solidarity with the slumdogs, and it solicits us to fill up what is lacking in this body.

The bodies that glow with glory minister to the misery of the slumdogs. They are the people of the impossible, people who make the impossible happen, people driven by faith in the impossible. They *incarnate* the truth, inscribe the truth in their flesh, *in memoria passionis*. They make up not a mystical church but what a Catholic priest who serves the slums of North Philadelphia calls the 'working church',[36] where the tent of God is pitched among the shanties of the slumdogs.

---

[36] See Craig Keen, 'The Resurrection of the Body: The Liturgy of Martyrdom and the Hallowing of the Flesh', *Wesleyan Theological Journal*, 40/1 (2005): 172–207; 'Working out the Body and Blood of Christ on the Eight Day of Creation: Toward a Martyr-Ecclesiology', (unpublished); and John D. Caputo, *What Would Jesus Deconstruct: The Good News of Postmodernism for the Church* (Grand Rapids: Baker Academic, 2007), ch. 6, 'The Working Church: Notes on the Future', pp. 117 ff.

Whatever you did for the least of mine you did for me. There we find Christianity
in the flesh. My idea is not to find the essence of Christianity but its flesh. It
is precisely the working church that marks the difference between theology and
robotology. The church is interested in making justice flow like water over the
land, whereas robotology is interested in longevity. Robotology wants *us* to live
forever, whereas theology wants justice to live forever. Theology has nothing to do
with having hot, fast and fiery bodies – that is for robotology not theology – or with
investing earthly flesh in the lucrative funds of fleshlessness – that is economics
not grace. Theological truth is *theopraxis*; *theopoesis* is doing the truth. The name
of God is the name of a deed. Indeed, in what classical theology calls *resignatio ad
infernum* (resignation to or even preference for hell, see Rom. 9.1–3), these lovers
of the impossible are measured by the immeasurable, by the impossible itself. If
the love of God, which means the service of the slumdogs, required it, the saints
would prefer *per impossibile* to be separated from the love of God, to go to hell
rather than to go to heaven. To avoid having hell on earth, to bring a little more
heaven to this living hell, they would go to hell themselves. So we have come full
circle: instead of purchasing eternal life by death, these saints purchase a better life
in time by eternal death!

These people are indeed 'saints', but there is nothing in the power of a church
that can sanctify them. It is they who sanctify the church, not the church who
sanctifies them. The church does not sanctify flesh, thank you very much, but
the service of the flesh lends the church such sanctity as it can tolerate.[37] Without
these people, there is no church – the church is a call, not a fact – and no excuse
for religion and all the violence religion brings down on our lives. The miracle,
the grace, the sanctity, the intensity, the glow of these glorious bodies lies in doing
the impossible, in the becoming-flesh of justice, the becoming-flesh of the event
harboured in the name of God.

* * *

Do you think we'll still be around in ten years? he says.

We might. 'If God wills', his mother used to say. But for him the name of God
names not the God 'almighty' of strong theology but the divinely subjunctive
'might' of the weakness of God, the 'perhaps' that stirs restlessly in the provocation
of God. Like her, he is after all, 'for life'.

---

[37]   As Dostoevsky points out so memorably in 'The Legend of the Grand Inquisitor',
the last thing the Church wants is to have its work interfered with by having Jesus return in
the flesh. Jesus is dead and from here on in what you get is the Church. Fyodor Dostoevsky,
'The Legend of the Grand Inquisitor', *The Brothers Karamazov*, trans. Constance Garnett,
available online at http://www.bigeye.com/broskara.htm

From World to Life: Wittgenstein's Social Vitalism and the Possibility of Philosophy

Neil Turnbull

Introduction: Repositioning Wittgenstein?

Overall, how are we to evaluate the significance of Ludwig Wittgenstein's philosophical endeavours? In the last analysis, what more can be said about the canonical status of his contribution to twentieth-century philosophy? Some contemporary philosophers may wonder whether these are still important and/ or interesting questions; especially in the current period, when the philosophical scene seems to be dominated by the ideas of techno-vitalists, postmodern Jewish philosopher-mystics and Maoist defenders of the 'revolutionary theology' of St Paul. In this radically altered intellectual context, where a number of varieties of metaphysics have reappeared to reshape philosophical agendas, must not we conclude that Wittgenstein's philosophy is now little more than a historical curiosity; merely a footnote to post-structuralism and the work of a philosopher who, although influential in giving impetus to the so-called 'linguistic turn', fared rather badly during the apogee of a new and often 'theologically inspired' metaphysical awakening that began in earnest at the end of the last century? As a consequence, many may think that it is now time to 'forget Wittgenstein'. As one recent commentator has suggested:

> I think that in a century's time – if humanity survives that long and still goes
> in for philosophical debate – there will be great deal of head scratching among
> philosophers as to why one of their number, Ludwig Wittgenstein, exerted such
> a massive influence on so many thinkers of an earlier generation.[1]

In what follows, I will suggest that any such assessment of Wittgenstein's status vis-à-vis the contemporary philosophical canon needs to be contested. More specifically, I will endeavour to show that Wittgenstein's therapeutic 'anti-philosophy' – that is often claimed to have attempted to 'analytically work through', with a view to 'dissolving', philosophical problems by means of an *übersicht* (overview) of

---

[1] Christopher Norris, 'The Limits of Whose Language? Wittgenstein on Logic, Mathematics and Science', in *Language, Logic and Epistemology: A Modal Realist Approach* (London: Palgrave Macmillan, 2004), p. 66.

the logic or grammar of ordinary language – in fact situates him at the heart of contemporary debates about the philosophical significance of life. The philosophy of the later Wittgenstein in particular, I will suggest – and contra Alain Badiou[2] – is much more than a contemporary sophism, in that it offers some very strong quasi-metaphysical assertions about the nature of life as well as suggesting appropriate contemporary philosophical responses to it. As such, I will suggest that Wittgenstein provides us with a conception of philosophy centred upon a distinctive strategy that might be usefully termed 'social vitalism'. This is a strategy that attempts to facilitate philosophy's return to classical philosophical concerns with how to 'live rightly' via a new understanding of a broadly metaphysical significance of 'life as it is ordinarily lived' by individual speaking persons operating collectively within specific historical contexts. In this way, Wittgenstein provides us with a philosophical opening that requires the philosopher to pay close attention to the complex relationship that 'necessarily' exists between 'thinking', 'speaking' and 'living an ordinary life'. As such, he exposes many of modern philosophy's most cherished questions, especially those pertaining to the nature of the subject and its epistemological relationship to 'the world', as symptoms of 'life gone awry'.

Thus, overall, I want to claim that, contrary to current orthodoxy in Wittgensteinian scholarship, for Wittgenstein it is not *language* that ought to be the main concern of the philosopher but the 'language-relatedness' of *life*. As the later Wittgenstein put it: 'Language, I should like to say, relates to *a way of living*'.[3] The entire question of historical significance of Wittgenstein's philosophy is how we are to unpack this claim. For what, in Wittgenstein's view, is a 'way of living' and what exactly is its relationship to language and ultimately to philosophical discourse itself?[4] Moreover, what are the wider philosophical implications of this quasi-metaphysical claim, a claim that makes the activity of living the first principle of all philosophizing? In the light of this, and contrary to the received interpretation of his work that views him as an anti-metaphysical philosopher of broadly Kantian provenance,[5] I will suggest that his famous focus

---

[2]   Alain Badiou, *Wittgenstein's Anti-Philosophy* (London: Verso, 2011).

[3]   Ludwig Wittgenstein, *Remarks on the Foundation of Mathematics* (Oxford: Blackwell 1998), p. 335; my emphases.

[4]   For the later Wittgenstein, existence, in the philosophical sense of the term, *is* life; and existence, as life, is always ordinary. Moreover, for him, life as ordinary is also always something that, in part, *belongs to someone in particular*. However, there is an acute unresolved tension in the thought of the later Wittgenstein, in that he seems unclear about whether life is *essentially* constituted by collective human actions and reactions or whether life is always, in the last instance, a phenomenon that belongs to some individual or other. More specifically, the question of the relationship between the individual and social 'levels' of life seems to be left unresolved in his later work – and this is why there is as yet no agreement as to the wider *political* significance of his ideas.

[5]   Typically, Wittgenstein has been conceived as a philosopher for whom the traditional Kantian question of the cognitive limits to human understanding is rearticulated in terms

on the philosophical significance of the 'meaning of the word' is only an artifice, and a preface, to a much more interesting philosophical project that strives to heal the modern fracturing of the lived world; its radical separation from both personal collective living, advocated and in some cases instigated by a number of modern philosophical traditions.[6] In this way, Wittgenstein, especially in his later incarnations, is much more 'Goethean-Spenglerian' in philosophical orientation than Kantian, in that like Goethe he suggests that it is only through the lived deed that we can discern the dynamic unity of life (what philosophers formerly understood as the 'unity of spirit and matter'). Such a claim may risk *auto da fé* at the hands of a 'Wittgensteinian magisterium' bent as it seems on maintaining Wittgenstein's analytic philosophical credentials.[7] However, I believe that it is

---

of the underlying grammar of language (games). Thus, much contemporary work on Wittgenstein has assumed that he was operating within an inherited framework of Kantian transcendentalism. As should be familiar, one of the key problematics of Kantian philosophy is the question of the ontological and epistemological status of 'the transcendental object'. More specifically, Kant's account of the nature of reality and our knowledge of it presupposed the existence of agents and objects that cannot be experientially known and thus are beyond the bounds of meaningful cognition. These transcendental objects/subjects help us to discern both the nature and the significance of what has been given to us via experience (see John Finlay, *Kant and the Transcendental Object: A Hermeneutic Study* [Oxford: Clarendon Press, 1981], p. 5). Wittgenstein is often viewed as arguing for the impossibility of any philosophical articulation of the transcendental object, as to do so would require a radical transgression of the limits of our language. However, his focus on life – an 'object' that is always and at the same time a kind of 'subject' – suggests that his thought moves beyond Kantianism in many respects, closer to Hegel than Kant we might say.

[6] Overall, then, I will claim that Wittgenstein is both more accurately and more usefully conceived as a philosopher who attempted to liberate conceptuality from what he believed to be centuries of bad philosophy-induced confusion, by relocating philosophical reflection on the familiar ground of the linguistic complexities, multiplicities and ambiguities that are always expressions of modes of life as it is 'historically lived' by 'living human beings'. This is not to say, however, that Wittgenstein was a pantheistic venerator of life – as the force or spirit of nature – as Wittgenstein's approach to vitalism is somewhat less metaphysically committed than this (his conception of life, although metaphysical in the sense of playing the role of an absolute, is much closer to the Christian ideal of life as 'common life'). Wittgenstein's vitalism is based upon a conception that combines ideas of human life, meaningful human practice and an understanding of the ethics of philosophy into a single coherent vision. In this way, his is a vitalism that is fundamentally *humanist*, because in his view only of a human being can we say that it has sensations, is conscious, is a locus of moral significance, and thus, in any ordinary sense, is 'living a life'. See Ludwig Wittgenstein, *The Philosophical Investigations* (Oxford: Blackwell, 1953), §281.

[7] See Severin Shroeder, *Wittgenstein* (Cambridge: Polity Press, 2006). In fine, and despite the philosophical misgivings of analytic philosophers – largely because they want to maintain that Wittgenstein is a philosophical anti-realist who paved the way for the 'assertion-conditional semantics' of the Dummett school of analytic philosophy – even a cursory inspection of his work shows that Wittgenstein's philosophy was an important and

crucial to bring out this dimension of Wittgenstein's thinking as his work has much to say to us today in an age when life has not only become a definitive, if highly politicized, *zeitgeist* concept but when it is often assumed that life is necessarily a naturalistic and biological phenomenon and thus of no concern of the philosopher.[8]

In the discussion that follows I will outline the position of 'life' within the work of both the early and the later Wittgenstein. I will show that, although an appreciation of the philosophical sense and significance of this term seems to be central to both of these periods in his philosophical development, we can chart something of an evolution in Wittgenstein's conception of life – from a conception of a life as a 'problematizing perspective' that needs to be 'empirically enworlded' if its problems are to be genuinely answered in the early work, to an understanding of life in the later work as a basic quasi-ontological and ontologizing condition that needs to be 'deworlded' and immunized against the enworlding habits of the philosopher if we are to understand it and act within it in appropriate ways.

It must be acknowledged, right from the start, that in this context attempts to foreground the idea of life in relation to Wittgenstein's later philosophy have (to some extent) already been attempted before.[9] However, these philosophical reflections have led to the conclusion that Wittgenstein's later philosophy was either a species of philosophical naturalism – *à la* Hume – or a self-reflexive inquiry into the role of philosophical reflection in relation to his *own life*.[10] Although insightful as initial moves, it is easy to point out that Wittgenstein's arguments at the very least imply and often directly state that 'nature' as such is not a particularly useful term in the context of his overall philosophical goals.[11] Also, the idea that his view of life is essentially 'autobiographical' cuts against the radical *externalism* – one might even say the existential and pragmatic *realism* – of his overall philosophical

---

innovative variation on the *Lebensphilosophical* theme that dominated philosophy in the early decades of the twentieth century (see Neil Turnbull, 'Wittgenstein's *Leben*: Language, Philosophy and the Authority of the Everyday' in Peter Candler and Conor Cunningham (eds), *Belief and Metaphysics* [Canterbury: SCM Press, 2008], pp. 384–92).

[8]   Wittgenstein in effect warns us off such an easy 'default Aristotelianism' in this respect by showing us that life is more 'ethically redolent' than this, especially in comparison to the truncated naturalistic version of life at large in contemporary philosophical debates.

[9]   See David Bolton, 'Life-form and Idealism', in Godfrey Vesey (ed.), *Idealism Past and Present* (Cambridge: Cambridge University Press, 1984), pp. 269–84; and Stanley Cavell, 'Notes and Afterthoughts on the Opening of Wittgenstein's *Investigations*', in H. Hans Sluga and D.G. Stern (eds), *The Cambridge Companion to Wittgenstein* (Cambridge: Cambridge University Press, 1991), pp. 261–95.

[10]   See also Nelson Garver, *This Complicated form of Life: Essays on Wittgenstein* (New York: Open Court, 1994) and Peter Hacker, *Wittgenstein: On Human Nature* (London: Weidenfeld and Nicolson, 1997).

[11]   Ludwig Wittgenstein, *Culture and Value* (Oxford: Blackwell, 1980), pp. 1e, 57e, 192 and 356.

approach.[12] Therefore, as the following should underline, in the philosophy of the later Wittgenstein in particular, it is clear that 'life' signifies neither a naturalistic substratum nor a metaphysical order of causality. Nor does it refer to Wittgenstein's own first-person phenomenological experiences. This is because, for Wittgenstein, it is a concept that is fundamentally and ultimately *primordial*, denoting 'the totality of what there is', the 'material' for all of the meaning-making practices required of historical subjects.[13] Indeed, following on from this, we can say that at the most general level of analysis 'life', for the later Wittgenstein, is simply the historical contextualizing element within which we recognize ourselves and our practices as possessing both sense and significance. In this vein, I want to suggest that Wittgenstein's philosophy operates in the conceptual space between vitalism in the strict sense and social holism. One of the key questions for Wittgensteinian scholarship today is how recognition of this impacts upon how we read Wittgenstein in the context of the intellectual history of twentieth-century philosophy.[14]

Preparing the New Ground: The Significance of Life in Wittgenstein's Philosophy

Clearly, any such repositioning of Wittgenstein's philosophy must also involve substantially more than a banal restatement of familiar arguments for the centrality of 'forms of life' – *Lebensformen* – to the overall *telos* ('end') of his

---

[12]   This is because in Wittgenstein's view nature, if it is a viable philosophical concept at all, is more Goethean than Humean. More specifically, in his view, it is not that human thought and behaviour are conditioned by an underlying nature, but rather that nature, more typically understood by the later Wittgenstein as *life*, in all its existential richness and complexity is simply the primordial setting that allows us to recognize the meaning and significance of everything that we do. In this way, what appears to be natural to us is simply a set of historically constituted actions and reactions – it is our specific *form* of life.

[13]   In this way, Wittgenstein attempts to circumvent the old Kantian distinction between the empirical and the transcendental (see Jonathan Lear, 'Transcendental Anthropology', in Philip Pettit and John McDowell (eds), *Subject, Thought and Context* [Oxford: Oxford University Press, 1986], pp. 267–98). Life, for him, is the basis of human reason yet it itself defies rationalist systematization. Life transcends such categories: it is both a simple if problematic given, yet the condition of possibility for all thought and action.

[14]   Wittgenstein is well aware that life can take a myriad of different forms and has many different modes of expression. This is clearly shown in his anthropological technique that exposes as futile any attempt to give life an essentialist interpretation. However, for the later Wittgenstein in particular, every mode of expression of life can only count as such if we, in our form of life, discern its lived and liveable qualities – that is, if it can be seen as an example of 'living a life'. One of the most difficult and barely articulated questions underlying Wittgenstein's later philosophy is how the human being recognizes something 'as a life', or as one of life's elements, and not, say, as robot replication and/or simulation of life. For Wittgenstein here the issue always turns on the vital immediacy and complexity of the former.

later philosophy.[15] For to view Wittgenstein as a social vitalist solely because he recognized the centrality of forms of life to our meaning-making practices would be to claim little of any significance. This is largely because this expression has become a staple 'term of art' in much contemporary philosophical and sociological discourse; where it is often claimed that it is merely a philosophical synonym for 'culture' – leading many to (mistakenly) position the later Wittgenstein as a kind of proto cultural theorist, whose critique of metaphysics was in fact a quasi-sociological plea for a new hermeneutical 'social science of meaning' – grounded in the results of ethnographic research concerned with uncovering the transcendental socio-cultural conditions of possibility for human interpretative practices.[16] Therefore, in any attempt to make anything more of the philosophical import of this term, a reinterpretation of its meaning and significance is clearly required; especially if this is to be basis for a significant intellectual repositioning of Wittgenstein's work. This I attempt below, but what should be emphasized at this point is that any attempt to 'sociologize' Wittgenstein is something that would clearly have been anathema to him, as he was no supporter of the modern scientific attempt to *theorize* human life at all.[17] In my view, the essential point to be made in relation to Wittgenstein's philosophy is that forms of life are much more than mere social frameworks or cultural contexts but are what Wittgenstein says they are: *forms* of *life* – that is, ways in which life, whatever 'life' means in this context, is *informed*; given shape, direction and ultimately purpose.

---

[15]   See Norman Malcolm, 'Wittgenstein and Idealism', in Vesey, *Idealism Past and Present*, pp. 249–67.

[16]   See Harry Collins and Trevor Pinch, *Frames of Meaning: The Social Construction of Extraordinary Science* (London: Routledge and Kegan Paul, 1982); and David Bloor, *Wittgenstein: A Social Theory of Knowledge* (London: Macmillan, 1984).

[17]   See Jacques Bouveresse, 'The Darkness of this Time: Wittgenstein and the Modern World', in A. Phillips Griffiths (ed.), *Wittgenstein: Centenary Essays* (Cambridge: Cambridge University Press, 1991), pp. 11–40. Also, this claim should involve much more than a recognition of the later Wittgenstein as a kind of 'radical externalist' and quasi-behaviourist critic of the epistemic significance of private inner experience – see also Norman Malcolm, *Problems of Mind: Descartes to Wittgenstein* (London: George Allen and Unwin, 1972) – for whom life is understood as a set of behavioural responses to environmental stimuli. For to view Wittgenstein in this way is to view him as a positivist critic of the epistemological priority of subjectivity and the foundational significance of inner life more generally – something that, in my view, is very wide of the mark. For Wittgenstein was not opposed to inwardness as such as long as we do not view it as the primary basis and beginning of meaning. For him, inner life is simply one manifestation of *unsere Leben* – our life – and as such it has no special epistemological or ontological status. For, although life for the later Wittgenstein is clearly something that transcends subjectivity, it remains for him a phenomenon deeply tied up with forms of engaged selfhood. The self is profoundly implicated in life, as I am always one (for me highly significant) element within it.

Tractarian Vitalism – Life as Perspective and as Problem

Clearly, the above claim requires a good deal of exegetical support if it is to amount to anything more than a crude speculative intuition. Thankfully, the textual evidence is manifold and cuts across the entire corpus of Wittgenstein's work – both early and late. Although the philosophical problem of life is more central to the later work, in my view the best place to begin examining this claim is via an interpretation of the so-called 'Schopenhauerian sections' of *The Tractatus*; sections that, as many have pointed out, are profoundly existential and suggest that the early Wittgenstein's notorious logicism was simply a first premise in a more significant ethical and ultimately quasi-vitalist philosophical argument.[18] In this text Wittgenstein's focus is as much on the philosophical 'problematic of life' as it is on the more familiar philosophical issue of the logical basis of linguistic meaning. For example, it is in these sections that Wittgenstein writes of the philosopher's concern with the 'events of life', 'the riddle of life' and 'the problems of life', and these notions seem to possess a fundamental *ethical* significance for him (as can be seen in his preface to this text and also in the way that he that dismissed later positivist claims on it).[19] However, what, we must ask, does Wittgenstein mean by 'life' in these terse aphorisms? It is tempting to read his early conception of life 'transcendentally', as a variation on the *Schopenhaurean* notion of *Wille Sum Leben* ('will to live') translated into the abstract conceptualism of the Frege/Russell philosophical universe.[20] However, although this suggestion is helpful in its own way, a global reading of *The Tractatus* suggests that the early Wittgenstein is attempting something much more distinctive here: specifically, an examination of the relation of 'ordinary life issues' – such as epistemological doubt and the philosophical desire for transcendence – to the metaphysical problem of the world; specifically to *The Tractatus*' metaphysics of logical atomism, a metaphysics that he believes allows us to understand life therapeutically as it is in actuality; devoid of 'pseudo-intellectual problems' and 'riddles'. In this way, for the early Wittgenstein, life becomes conceived as *a point of view* that often suffers from a profound misrecognition of how things actually are; a misrecognition that can, in the last analysis, only be corrected by 'enworlding' it; in his case, by bringing it under the aegis of *logic and empirical facticity*. This, in his view, requires what might be termed a 'self-effacing attitude to life', for in *The Tractatus* the argument seems to be that if the problems of life are to be 'resolved' then it is necessary to overcome the philosophy-induced separation between the self, the world and life. More specifically, for the early Wittgenstein it is only once we recognize 'that there is no such thing as the subject that thinks or entertains

---

[18]   Ludwig Wittgenstein, *The Tractatus Logico-Philosophicus* (London: Routledge and Kegan Paul, 1922), 6.4 ff. Also see Martin Stokhof, *The World and Life as One: Ethics and Ontology in Wittgenstein's Early Thought* (Stanford: Stanford University Press, 2002).

[19]   See (respectively) Wittgenstein, *Tractatus*, 6.4311, 6.4312 and 6.521.

[20]   See Johann Glock, 'Wittgenstein and Reason', in J.C. Klagge (ed.), *Wittgenstein: Biography and Philosophy* (Cambridge: Cambridge University Press, 2001), pp. 195–220.

ideas' that we will begin to understand that life is not 'our life', is not a predicate of subject, in anything but a transcendental sense.[21] In fact, *The Tractatus* claims that the correct conception of life is one of a depersonalized empirical *world*; only when life is conceived in this way will the perspective and its associated 'problems of life' disappear in the world and life becoming conceived as 'one'.[22] Here, we can see that for the early Wittgenstein 'life' as we ordinarily conceive it must be eliminated in favour of a logically circumscribed idea of worldhood. In the round, we can say that the early Wittgenstein advocates a new unity of self, world and life to the extent we can say that the overall goal of *The Tractatus* is to 'reconnect' life to the logic of the empirical world in such a way that we, as thinking beings, accept the logic and contingency of the world as our fate.

This argument is easy to defend once we concentrate on how the early Wittgenstein approached the philosophical problem of 'worldhood'. Fortunately, the early Wittgenstein defines this term explicitly. As is well known, in *The Tractatus* the world is viewed as the 'totality of facts' in logical space – each fact being a logical picture of the worldly actuality that it purports to represent (specifically, for him it is a representation of a concatenation of 'objects' whose *form* symbolic representation mirrors logically).[23] For the early Wittgenstein, then, the world is essentially a phenomenon of logic and its content is essentially phenomenal in character.[24] More specifically, the world, for the early Wittgenstein, is always a composite 'logical picture': a grand logical conjunction/disjunction of 'all the facts', each of which is a logical micro-picture of the substantial objective reality that it mirrors.[25] Put simply, for the early Wittgenstein the world is a logical macro picture constituted by all the logical micro pictures that happen to be objectively the case at any particular moment.[26] We might say, therefore, that for the early

---

[21]   Wittgenstein, *Tractatus*, 5.631.

[22]   Ibid., 5.621.

[23]   See ibid., 1.13. The 'Tractarian world' is not comprised of things but of logical relations between signs and the substance of the world (as is well known, a 'Tractarian fact' is when sign/proposition and its object(s) stand in a corresponding picturing relation with the objects that comprise the substance of the world).

[24]   See Pasquale Frascolla, *Understanding Wittgenstein's Tractatus* (London: Routledge, 2000), p. 204.

[25]   However, importantly, for the early Wittgenstein the picturing relationship between 'sign' and 'object', that is the logical possibility for 'worldliness' as such, 'can only be shown'; it cannot be said as, for him, 'propositions show the logical form of reality', they cannot logically state it (see Wittgenstein, *Tractatus*, 4.121) – to the extent that, essentially, the 'Tractarian world' is a logico-aesthetic phenomenon whose elementary structure is revealed via a precise philosophical articulation of the pictorial form of the proposition. The question of the perspective that allows us to view the world as showing its sense is left unclear in *The Tractatus*, given that 'showing' is itself not something amenable to a logical analysis.

[26]   In this way, for the early Wittgenstein philosophical logic *shows* how the world has sense, and therefore the philosopher, who attempts to account for the sense of the world, is not *in the world* as such but is someone who attempts to transgress the limits of the logic

Wittgenstein, in the world there are only philosophically unproblematic facts; but that certain facts can *appear* to be problematic when viewed from a certain vantage point, in this case from the vantage point of 'misconceived life' – a life conceived as a phenomenon of worldly subjectivity, where life is viewed as a subjective phenomenon taking place within the world. What he is suggesting here is that when we view the facts in this way (from the perspective of life conceived as a 'special fact' that exists within the world), the facts themselves can appear to be radically insufficient and there may seem to be more to be said than can legitimately be said. For the early Wittgenstein, such problems appear when the subject of life, in viewing its own life as something to be understood 'as comprised of other facts', albeit ones deeper and more significant than 'mere facts', misconceives itself as something possessing a problematic *existence within the world*. However, this is to misunderstand the precise nature of the relationship between life, self and world in his view – a relationship that is in reality one of *identity*.[27] As such, for the early Wittgenstein, the solution to the 'riddle of life', the question of why there is anything at all, whether it means anything and so on, is only obtained via the philosopher showing the logical mistake involved in viewing life as something that takes place *within the world*. For him, life is in truth rather like the subject itself a *limit* of the world: a mysticism inducing transcendental co-extensive with the world itself that can only be *shown* and not explicitly *stated*. In this way the everyday conception of life is rejected; the idea that life is something that happens to us and something to which we respond with a point of view is denied and its status as a distinct vantage point undermined by a series of transcendental arguments concerning the possibility of symbolic representational meaning.

For the early Wittgenstein, then, it seems that life can often go awry in viewing itself as a problematic point of view pertaining to an unknown facticity; to a site of quasi-empirical questioning and issue-raising through which we view the pseudo-problems of life in scientific terms (that is, where we conceive of, say, the question 'What is life?' hypothetically). However, as he states: 'We feel that even when all *possible* scientific questions be answered, the problems of life remain completely untouched. Of course then there are no questions left, and this is itself the answer. The solution to the riddle of life lies in the vanishing of the problem'.[28] The 'philosophical problem of life', the early Wittgenstein seems to say, only exists through life's misconception of itself, specifically because of a widespread belief that there are meaningful problems that remain after all the factual problems have been addressed. However, in his view the urge to problematize and interrogate our lives more than is logically necessary vanishes once the authentic work of philosophy has shown that the 'world is all that is the

---

and in so doing take thought 'out of this world'. How, then, can philosophers, as necessarily world-bound creatures, say anything significant at all? Why does philosophy exist at all? This is another question that is left hanging in Wittgenstein's philosophy.

[27]   See, for example, Wittgenstein, *Tractatus*, 5.64 ff.

[28]   Ibid., 6.52, 6.521.

case'.[29] Therefore, in an important sense for the early Wittgenstein, the problems of life are cured by rearticulating them in terms of the facticity of worldhood: by bringing the problems of life into a new harmony with the empirical logic of the symbolic word. As he claimed in his early preparatory notebooks, to live happily means to live in *agreement with the world*.[30] Life, however, cannot be more than the world in his view. As such, life – like the subject – is the vanishing point of Tractarian metaphysics.

In sum, the early Wittgenstein tries to show that life is not really a problem at all and is only a problem from the point of view of its own misrecognition, through its placing of itself in the wrong philosophical category (in the 'empirical' rather than 'the transcendental'). Life, here, is thus a perspective that can lead us to believe, erroneously, that there is more to life than the facts of world. The perspective of life attempts to take thought outside the temporalized categories of worldly contingency by refusing to be satisfied with our worldly condition, and the early Wittgenstein's overall aim in *The Tractatus* is to show how the perspective of life through its affinity with the idea of infinitude creates strictly pathological philosophical problems to which an appreciation of the finitude of the world *as facticity* is the cure.[31] The 'point of view of life' is, then, something that creates the

---

[29]   Ibid., 1.

[30]   Ludwig Wittgenstein, *Notebooks: 1914–18* (Chicago: University of Chicago Press, 1984), §75; my emphases. This is one of the most difficult aspects of *The Tractatus* to understand – for if the world 'is all that is the case', how can there be another position from which to view the world 'as a whole'? That is, from where does philosophy gain its intellectual traction here and how does the misrecognizing perspective of life emerge? Of course, paradoxically, Wittgenstein at the end of *The Tractatus* finally dismisses the perspective of the philosopher as an illusion. However, given all that he states in this text, such a conclusion is far from satisfactory. Somewhat speculatively, a more useful way of conceiving this matter is to view philosophy as a problem that emerges from within the perspective of life, showing to some extent that there remains an 'autonomy of life' vis-à-vis the facticity of the world in the work of the early Wittgenstein. Thus in the last analysis the early Wittgenstein, I think, does not want to dismiss life in the name of 'positivist clarity', at least not quite. This is because in his view life presents itself as a space where the question of value (and the experience of the mystical) appears, albeit with a mistaken tendency to view these dimensions in terms of facts. However, we might say that, without the perspective of life, for the early Wittgenstein there could no appreciation of a value as 'that which is higher' than the facticity of the world. Thus, in this context, life is conceived as a transcendental vantage point through which the world appears as world; that is, as something 'ethical'. The world thus is not sufficient, ethically, for the early Wittgenstein; but the perspective of life must not be viewed as *anything* in ontological terms. In this way the question of the significance of life remains the insubstantial apparition that haunts the entire Tractarian project.

[31]   Here, we can see the claim that the world is always 'my world' (Wittgenstein, *Tractatus*, 5.63). This reveals an important aspect of Wittgenstein's early philosophy: the 'intimate' relation that exists between world-life-self. How do we understand this relation, especially the relation between life and world? One way, is to see the early Wittgenstein as claiming an identity of life and world – and that as the world is always 'mine' so too

need for strictly *philosophical* resolutions to the intellectual pseudo-problems that its misconception of itself seems to generate.[32]

Therefore, we might say here that the philosopher for the early Wittgenstein is a logico-vitalist under-labourer: clearing the conceptual ground in order to make life *liveable* again by showing that the world and life are necessarily one, that all that living human beings can legitimately take into account is the facts of the world.[33] The traumatic encounter with life's philosophical riddles, that suggest that life can deliver deeper forms of insight than mere mundane propositional content, is 'finally overcome' by means of a logical analysis of language: an analysis that proves that, at the level of authentic meaning, the sum total of facts *is* the world and that as a worldly creature the inquiring human being must be content with this.[34] This is why Wittgenstein claims that in answering the riddles of life we show 'how little is achieved when these problems are solved' – as all they leave us is an understanding of the basic surface facticity of the world that was rather obvious to most all along.[35] Thus we might say that *The Tractatus* is simply a prolegomenon to the real task of philosophy proper – that is, the task of living a life according to a new categorical imperative: to 'say nothing except what can be said'. This is the early Wittgenstein's *positivist therapeutics*: where attention to third person, logically circumscribed, worldly facticity shows that the problems of life are pseudo-problems (to the extent that after they are resolved we are unable to exactly say what constituted their sense).[36]

---

is life (see ibid., 5.62). We are tempted to claim that for the early Wittgenstein life always belongs to the subject. Life, we might say, in *The Tractatus* is the basic property of the metaphysical subject (and not 'consciousness' or 'thought' or even 'language'). Put bluntly, we could conclude, for the early Wittgenstein, life always stands in relation to a particular 'subjectivity' and that relation is one of 'possession'. Here Wittgenstein connects his philosophy to ordinary conceptualizations of life – life as expressed in the exclamations of 'It's my life! Leave me alone!'

[32]   However, such problems are both profound and important because they touch on what is essential to being human (the desire for transcendence, something that cannot be articulated but only acknowledged).

[33]   Even though the demand for transcendence has to be respected, albeit in a reverential silence: showing that there is a profound if tacit affinity that exists between positivism and vitalism.

[34]   Wittgenstein, *Tractatus*, 2.063.

[35]   Ibid., 4.

[36]   See ibid., 6.521. In one sense, Wittgenstein's claims in *The Tractatus* reveal the submerged 'modernist ethics' underlying contemporary analytic philosophy. For the early Wittgenstein, the 'clarity and timeless certainty' of logical analysis dispel the puzzlement that comes from ordinary living and thus, in his view, logic offers us new secure basis for worldly action, a new form of life. However, we must ask why the later Wittgenstein abandoned this logicist ethic and adopted a radically alternative form of philosophical modernism that is much more recognizably vitalist. Clearly, the answer resides in dissatisfaction with the Tractarian idea of the unity of life as a source of puzzlement.

Social Vitalism in *The Philosophical Investigations*: Life, 'the Weave' and Language as Life's Form

However, for the later Wittgenstein, matters are very much the other way around in that it is the cognitive certainty and self-evidence of *life*, conceived here as human ways of acting, reacting and interacting in familiar historical settings, that now dispels the intellectual puzzlement derived from misleading notions generated by general philosophical conceptions of the nature of the *world* (and in this regard it must be pointed out that he *really does* cease to be an analytic philosopher).[37] Here, life is simply what is given – it is what typically cannot 'enter one's head', the tacit dimension that we forget but cannot go beyond in all of our cognitions. Moreover, in the later work, the sense of propositions is no longer empirical in the strict sense because propositions are now no longer logically verified but determined by instants in what the later Wittgenstein refers to as 'the flow of life'.[38] More generally, for the later Wittgenstein, language is viewed as a phenomenon not of logic but of life. In his view, language is what ensures that there is a *form of life* as a specific context; and thus in the later work he replaces the idea of *logical form* with the idea of *life-forms* that guarantee any proposition's meaningfulness. As such, for the later Wittgenstein, language does not 'need' to refer to the world at all as it carries little in the way of logic-metaphysical baggage, but rather works as an instrument that aids human beings in the tasks of living by providing life with both form and direction (largely through its ability to generate a sense of generality and futurity). In fact, the term 'world' largely drops out of view in the later work.[39] Here, logico-philosophical riddles about reference, about how words refer to things and so forth, are seen as the result of the pseudo-philosophical problem of worldhood: specifically, the problem of how the concepts 'proposition, language, thought, world stand in line one behind the other, each equivalent to each'.[40] In this way, the main focus in the later work is on the way in which the main element of worldhood in his early philosophy, 'the picture', can mislead us into thinking that the world *must* have a particular essential structure or form.[41] We might say that, for the later Wittgenstein, the world is still constituted by the logical power of pictures, although now these pictures no longer function as the 'hook up' to reality (life) but, rather, are centrally involved in the creation of philosophical illusions.[42] Specifically, pictures in the

---

[37]   See Wittgenstein, *Culture and Value*, p. 4e.

[38]   Ludwig Wittgenstein, *Philosophical Remarks* (Oxford: Blackwell, 1975), pp. 80–1.

[39]   However, we can still detect a conception of worldhood in the later work through his recognition of the role of 'pictures' in the learning of language and the fixing and suggesting of particular senses of particular propositions (see Wittgenstein, *Investigations*, §352).

[40]   Wittgenstein, *Investigations*, §96.

[41]   Ibid., §115.

[42]   There is clearly a submerged Platonism to the later Wittgenstein's philosophy here, in that he offers a critique of the philosophical illusions associated with the *aesthetization* of meaning where pictures are seen to provide a model of truth.

later work are now reconceived as potential sources of radical dysfunction that 'hold us captive' by generating philosophical problems that can only be resolved once it is recognized that *im Leben* ('in life') there are many different ways in which the sense of a proposition can be fixed, many different pictures of the world and that it is the complexity and multiplicity of the forms of living that are any system of representation's fundamental practical origin and support.[43]

Clearly, in opposition to his earlier philosophical conception of worldhood, 'life' in Wittgenstein's later work is no longer conceived as a vantage point without ontological reference to anything of ontological substance, but is, rather, reconceived in terms of a fundamental social ontology: specifically, as a complex of actions 'weaved' into meaningful patterns by the institution of human language. This is a conception that recognizes that understanding the significance of forms of life will always be a complex affair that defies the essentializing categorizations of the enworlding philosopher.[44] Here, life becomes conceived as the primordial connection(s) upon which language acts as a means for reweaving life into meaning in order to ensure that life functions as a higher exponent of the wider process of social-ordination (here we can see why Wittgenstein had a certain sympathy for the ethics of Marxism). Thus, in his view, what language presupposes is

> not what one man is doing *now*, an individual action, but the whole hurly-burly of human actions, the background against which we see any action.
>
> Seeing life as a weave, this pattern ... is not always complete and varied in a multiplicity of ways. But we, in our conceptual world, keep on seeing it the same, recurring with variations. This is how our concepts take it. For concepts are not for use on a single occasion. And one pattern in the weave, is interwoven with many others.[45]

We can say that, for the later Wittgenstein, it is only when a particular phenomenon is surrounded by certain 'ordinary manifestations of life' woven into a distinctive pattern that we can begin to recognize anything for 'what it is'. Only by being receptive to recurring patterns in the weave of life are we thus able to ultimately name them and articulate them.[46] More generally, after Wittgenstein we might say that it is only when we grasp a concept's *vital function* – that is, apprehend its

---

[43] In this way, in *The Investigations* pictures no longer express logical form, rather they become 'a trap' that we can only emancipate ourselves from by means of a better philosophical appreciation of life.

[44] Wittgenstein, *Investigations*, §74.

[45] Ludwig Wittgenstein, *Zettel* (Oxford: Blackwell, 1981), pp. 567–9.

[46] See ibid., p. 534. For Wittgenstein, the priority of life to thought in this sense can be seen in the way that a child learns what things both are and mean. According to Wittgenstein a child will, for example, learn to fetch a book before he or she knows what a book is. Being able to recognize and understand that life contains 'books' is a lived activity that is beyond 'true' and 'false'. See Ludwig Wittgenstein, *On Certainty* (Oxford: Blackwell, 1969), p. 476.

connection to, and role within, the general articulation of a particular manifestation of life – that we are able to appreciate its meaning. In this way, for the later Wittgenstein, in order to conceive of something as something, to *predicate*, we must be able to discern a particular weave in the complex perhaps even chaotic flow of things and events that comprise life, in this case as it is ordinarily lived. These weaves cross and criss-cross with other weaves – and we may mistake one weave for another in our ordinary ways of speaking and acting (this is the origin of many philosophical problems in the later Wittgenstein's view). These living patterns are nothing mysterious however – as, for him, life is simply the totality of actions and reactions that constitutes our human life at any historical juncture. Thus, for the later Wittgenstein, the meaning of a word is not only its use, its role in a particular language game, but the difference that it makes to life, especially its ability to order life through its powers of generalization. As such, in his view, although human life is always a *specific* array of activities, at the same time it contains within itself an ordering agent, what we might term 'a linguistic subject', that allows it to be conceived in terms of *universalities*. In this way, in the later work 'life' takes the place of the mysterious 'Tractarian object' and logic is supplanted by the idea of the rule-governed 'language game' – the famous *Sprachspiel* that people often define in terms of ordinary forms of social interaction (this they certainly are, but they are not only this). More generally, when his oeuvre is understood in this way, in *The Tractatus* 'logic pervades the world' but in the later work it is the rule-governed nature of language that 'permeates our *life*'.[47]

Therefore, for the later Wittgenstein, it is a focus on the immediacy of life as that which is simply but 'problematically' given to all speakers and hearers whose goal is to linguistically 'inform it' that allows Wittgenstein to alleviate what he now recognizes to be the vexing philosophical problems associated with the metaphysics of worldhood (particularly questions pertaining to the nature of truth, knowledge, meaning and the like). For the later Wittgenstein, these philosophical problems must be reconceived as problems of life, problems that are now understood to be practical problems with practical solutions. By means of a powerful dialectical reversal, in the later works the phenomenon of 'the world' understood as a logically ordered unity is seen as the problem to which a philosophical conception of *life* – as a pre-ordered given – is the solution. Indeed, in the later works an understanding of the practical realities of life is proposed as the answer to the philosophical 'riddle of the world' and the site for the emergence of authentic meaning is now understood to be the ordinary moments in the ebbs and flows, the mysterious weaving patterns, of life. Thus in the later work, we see that the 'identity of world and life' is retained, but now this requires that the philosopher facilitate *the practical disappearance of the world as a point of view*. Here, the world and life remain 'one', but only as a result of a recognition that

---

[47]   See Wittgenstein, *Tractatus*, 5.61 and Ludwig Wittgenstein, *Last Writings on the Philosophy of Psychology: Volume 2, The Inner and the Outer* (Oxford: Blackwell, 1992), p. 72e.

the logical pictures generated by the idea of worldhood are now understood as an attempt to squeeze the complexity of life into intellectually constricting a priori worldly schemes and limits (as if into shoes that are 'too tight').[48]

Having said this, Wittgenstein's conception of language acknowledges its status as a collectivist solution to the 'problem of life' (now no longer conceived as an existential or a religious problem, as a point of view on the world, as it was in the early work, but as a problem of finding a *way of doing*, of finding a way to achieve collective practical goals). Thus, in Wittgenstein's later philosophy, the relationship between language and life becomes the basis for a *social vitalism* that is at the same time a form of metaphysical realism. Here, language is viewed as 'self-informing life' and life is conceived as the totality of lived actions and reactions thus suitably informed. This can be discerned in the famous opening sections of *The Philosophical Investigations*, where Wittgenstein elaborates on a conception of a form of life, a generic representation of 'our modern form of life' as socially co-ordinated activity – that is, where speaking a language is viewed as a tool, an instrument of social coordination and an essential aspect of collective human *living*.[49] In this passage, the basis of our forms of life is the social deed and it is these that constitute the basis of all our contemporary language games. This is why, in the opening sections of *The Investigations*, Wittgenstein explicitly states that to imagine a language is to 'imagine a form of life'.[50] Thus, for the later Wittgenstein, life can take many forms, but the only life that we can *understand* as life (even if we can recognize other phenomena as life) is 'our life' – the life of our personal, familial, societal existence. Only this form of life can count as life for 'us' – 'we', the historical collectivity that has informed our lived situation as a form of life within which 'we' can live and understand ourselves, our projects and our lives.

Here, as Pierre Hadot has observed, we can see the similarity between Wittgenstein and Neoplatonist philosophers like Plotinus – a philosopher for whom life is a 'formative, simple and immediate activity, irreducible to all our analyses'.[51] The parallels with ancient philosophy *as way of life* are, more generally, highly instructive here: as when life is understood to have a philosophical priority over the world, philosophical work must be reconceived as a kind of ethical activity

---

[48]   Wittgenstein, *Culture and Value*, p. 41e.

[49]   Wittgenstein, *Investigations*, §23.

[50]   Wittgenstein, *Investigations*, §19. In the later work, life has the ability to 'show' itself a context guaranteeing the meaningfulness of an assertion simply and directly, and in so doing show that such and such a state of affairs do in fact obtain (see ibid., §284; Wittgenstein, *On Certainty*, p. 7). Life, we might say, is that which underlies and guarantees the sense of every assertion and is what is shown and shows itself in each and every claim on how the world is. Moreover, another difference between the early and the later work seems to be equally clear here, in that 'forms of life' are now understood to have the same philosophical status of 'the mystical' in *The Tractatus*.

[51]   See Pierre Hadot, *Plotinus or Simplicity of Vision* (Chicago: University of Chicago Press, 1998), p. 41.

that supports forms of reconciliation with life through the attainment of what the ancients termed *ataraxia* ('tranquillity') – where our thoughts no longer try to get beyond life in a way that causes us unnecessary cognitive perplexity. This, in fact, was the later Wittgenstein's overall aim – to develop a philosophy 'that brings peace' by returning the philosopher 'to life'.[52]

In general, life is reconceived metaphysically, as the 'immanent–transcendent' non-deterministic condition of possibility for linguistic meaning in Wittgenstein's later work. However, for him there is no special metaphysical discourse that can fully articulate it – and he tries to persuade us that we can only *look* and *notice* that we are already 'in it'; always acting 'within it' as living human beings. For the later Wittgenstein, recognition of this will deliver the wisdom that modern philosophy, in its attempt to rationalistically and postivistically 'enworld' life from the position of the subject, has overlooked. As such the later Wittgenstein exhorts us to grasp the fact that philosophy itself, if it is to become part of life, must function as something that pertains to this immediate context of lived activity. This is exactly what Wittgenstein tries to achieve, to translate the metaphysical aims of classical philosophy into an intellectual *activity* (this is why he often referred to the 'business of philosophy', a mode of philosophy that could appropriately inform our lives).[53] In so doing, what the later Wittgenstein effectively 'achieved' was the removal of life from the sphere of the 'philosophically criticisable' in his 'demonstration' that philosophical reflection on the deeper theoretical significance of life can only engender *apraxia*. Therefore, in the later works, philosophy not only

---

[52]   Wittgenstein, *Investigations*, §133.

[53]   It is tempting at this point to claim that Wittgenstein is attributing an 'educational function' to life here. We might wrongly conclude that Wittgenstein is claiming that 'life shows' because life 'teaches us' as it is the site of a basic experience through which the world is made present to us in a decisive way. More specifically, we might think that Wittgenstein thinks that life gives rise to a certain *Bildung* (self-cultivation), to a form of semantic and possibly existential formation in relation to the basic experientially-grounded universals that are necessary conditions of assertability – to the extent that life becomes the context for truths that emerge simply from the basic fact of living. This existential-phenomenological interpretation of the relationship between life and meaning is not the correct one here, however. Although there is clearly something of this thesis' 'anti-intellectualist atmosphere' in Wittgenstein's later work, it is easy to demonstrate by a simple exegesis that Wittgenstein was not a philosopher who wanted to 'plumb the depths' of life as *Existenz*, but was someone who wanted to argue that life shows its significance directly and simply – like logic – without further ado. Again the parallels with *The Tractatus* are striking here, for he claims that at the end of our philosophical analyses it becomes clear that there is no separation between life and world, human action and the world as 'phenomenon'. In fact, for the later Wittgenstein, 'life's showing', the simple revelation of the world of ordinary practical things appearing 'problematically before us', is the context of our 'ordinary doings and sayings'. Life, for him, is thus in many ways the most obvious of all 'things' – so obvious in fact that in forgetting it we look for metaphysical explanations that explain the things and events in terms of an impersonal world.

becomes a form of therapy that reminds us that worldhood can have no semantic, epistemological or ontological priority over life, but also the basis for a new way of understanding ourselves founded upon a philosophical reflection of the relationship between thought, personal life and ultimately the life of the collective as a whole. In this way, Wittgenstein's conception of life is essentially normative in that he asks: 'Given that life *is* the true world, a world from which we as living beings cannot separate ourselves, how then *ought* we to speak, think and act?' *His* answer is that we can only act *conventionally* because to act *im Leben* presupposes that we acknowledge the authority of the informing power and affectivity of linguistic conventions; the rules of our language games that allow us to organize life into meaningful activities. This is because, for the later Wittgenstein, philosophy cannot say any more than life already shows 'us' through the ways that we ordinarily inform it, and it is for this reason that philosophy must 'leave everything as it is'. Language and life, again here echoing the approach of *The Tractatus*, reside in a kind of mystical pre-established harmony. However, it is by no means clear that this answer is the only answer possible here, as new conventions – new concepts – can always be invented. Life can be weaved differently. This is the great lacuna in Wittgenstein's philosophy, the relationship between language and creativity: a relationship that he believed would be forever a closed book to us.[54]

Therefore, for the later Wittgenstein, 'in life' the style of thinking associated with philosophy, especially modern philosophy with its attempt to speak for the theoretical outlook of the natural sciences, simply has 'no purchase' and a focus on the lived aspects of practical life – of living – is the most appropriate response to all forms of 'idle philosophical speculation'. For the later Wittgenstein, as soon as thought becomes divorced from life and rearticulated into a theoretical discourse via a metaphysics of world-representation, then we no longer recognize things for what they are and, as a consequence, life is rendered strange, *unheimlich*. As such, to call life into philosophical question is to immediately remove both the context through which we can see how things stand and the basis through which mental activity becomes 'thinking' about things that *really count*.[55] For the later Wittgenstein asks, what significance can philosophical questions possess if they fail to relate in some way to the events and practical decisions that we have to make

---

[54]   However, Wittgenstein's imaginary 'us' that provides the basis for his conventionalist critique of 'philosophical excess' is not the only possibility here, and we can imagine, as the later Wittgenstein often does, another 'we' that weaves the patterns of life in terms of new forms, in terms of a different language.

[55]   In this way, life becomes a metaphysical object in the world – full of riddles and problems. 'What is life?' 'Who am I?' 'Where am I?' Here we are tempted to find a general theoretical answer to these questions – via cognitive science perhaps. Wittgenstein's response is rather different. Wittgenstein asks us to stand back and look at the ordinary comings and goings that surround us, to see the world as alive in comparison to the inert, dead articulations of the modern theoretician. Then we will see language as a phenomenon of life, and all forms of worlding as attempts to place a useful order on this domain.

in our lives? In his view, meaningful forms of questioning are always phenomena that take place *within life*; they are practically significant events where what might be termed the 'social vitality' of the question shows itself directly. The forms of questioning conditioned by our metaphysical pictures of the world, pictures that freeze-frame life into 'essential structures', carry no such vital significance in his view – and thus it is not clear that they can be deemed to imply anything that we can, *im Leben*, call an 'answer' (and may in fact, from this vantage point, be 'unanswerable'). They are, for him, simply examples of 'language idling' and thus pointless living. In the spirit of the later Wittgenstein, we might say that *in life* we question only because questions relate to both the context for, and the consequences of, real lived events. In his view, what we simply cannot do is question the 'forms that life takes' – the basis for the language games that we do in fact use because they are 'contextualizing shapes' within which modes of questioning emerge as significant activities in their own right. Importantly, there is no informing linguistic 'event of philosophy' *in life* for the later Wittgenstein because there can be no 'form of philosophical life', no recognizable way of acting, of informing and co-ordinating life according to the way in which philosophy, especially modern philosophy, raises its questions. Thus, after Wittgenstein, we must ask, how could one actually *live* as a philosopher when philosophy *questions* the status of life, its own life, as the ground of existence? Moreover, this forces us to ask, what does the life of the philosopher look like today? Philosophy, as the 'question of the question of life', is in this way, for him, simply a question too far to the extent that the only way to be a philosopher now is to cure ourselves of the urge to philosophize in this manner and find a way of doing philosophy that *matters* in relation to our personal and collective lives. The later Wittgenstein did not believe that such a philosophy is now possible – but here his work remains, to say the least, unconvincing.

Conclusion: Wittgenstein and the *Phronesis* of Quotidian Life

In sum, life, for the later Wittgenstein, is that about which there can be no question. And in this way it is the answer to all those questions that present themselves as 'ultimate': that is, to questions that masquerade as 'larger than life'.

Life is what is given to language, and language returns this as the gift of form (here we can catch a glimpse of Wittgenstein's Spinozism). However, as language is a collective phenomenon, the informing here always takes place between individuals and is thus game-like according to the later Wittgenstein. Nevertheless such 'games' always act upon something other than themselves – life (Wittgenstein was *not* a linguistic idealist, except perhaps in the absolute sense).[56] For the later Wittgenstein, language, we might say, turns life into a game (a game between both people and things), but it is the job of the philosopher is to discern whether the

---

[56]   That is, in the sense that the real metaphysical subject is more than the individual mind – in his case 'life'.

correct game in any particular situation is in fact being played, that is, whether life is being informed in the right way.[57] Thus, for the later Wittgenstein, the old Aristotelian distinction between matter and form becomes re-socialized as the distinction between life and game, and the job of the philosopher is not to contemplate form but to socialize our consciousness in ways appropriate to our tasks.[58] Thus Wittgenstein's later philosophy recognizes that thought only has sense and significance in relation to much wider socially useful and socially instituted activities. 'Our life' is now a life of collective activity and so thought itself must connect and inform this 'reality', it must become part of the social game. More theologically, philosophy, we might say, the intellectual discourse of the pagan master, can have little part to play in a society where life has largely become the life of the Judeo-Christian slave: the life of *collective doing*. In our modern form of life, where language largely functions in order to assist 'the practical deed', everything happens as part of a wider lived context that is no longer under the aegis of any one individual because it is now widely co-ordinated as a *system of work*, and we respond to it in the ways that we ordinarily do – by 'questioning', 'counting', 'obeying instructions' and so on. We cannot question why we make these kinds of response; there is simply nothing 'beyond them', they are simply 'what we do' and any question as to why we do such things cannot really provide satisfying answers, because the only possible meaningful answer to such questions is that these activities are simply 'our form of life as it is currently lived'. Thus there is, *pace* Heidegger, no special extraordinary question, no position for the question to celebrate itself as 'the piety of thought' for the later Wittgenstein. *Im Leben*, a question is, simply, a particular kind of human action, one weave in the pattern of life. In the end, what the later Wittgenstein seems to be suggesting is that the nature of meaning and thereby the possibility of engaging in activities with real practical significance requires us to 'forget about the world', at least as a philosophical problem (as it is something that in his view is in reality little more than a linguistic goldfish bowl). In this way, in claiming that life has a certain priority over and above worldly facticity, Wittgenstein can be seen not only as a modern version of the classical sceptic and cynic, as more perceptive analytic

---

[57] Perhaps we can say that life takes the position of the 'transcendental subject' in the philosophy of the later Wittgenstein and that his attempt to view life as the quasi-transcendental basis of meaning is simply an attempt to ground idealism in a philosophical idiom that makes its point more readily understandable to an age where subjectivity is becoming rapidly 'scientized'.

[58] Moreover, this way of viewing things situates Wittgenstein's philosophy beyond the paradigmatic strictures of the analytic tradition in important respects. Moreover, as language is for him essentially a 'rule-governed' game, it is thus fundamentally a *normative* ordering principle with respect to life. Overall, we might say that life, for Wittgenstein, is normative to the extent that it is *informed* by language (and this is why Wittgenstein believed that ethics and aesthetics were essentially the same). Thus, for him, language is the ontology of the ethical.

philosophers such as Kripke have already suggested,[59] but, at the same time, a quintessentially *modern* philosopher who combines these classical insights with a philosophical Romanticism that connects life to 'language' and ultimately to modern forms of 'work'.

In the last analysis, Wittgenstein's objection to metaphysics is not so much that it is in a positivist vein 'meaningless', but simply that it is that about which there can be no question, because a discourse on metaphysics can only ever amount to a description of life as it is *informed* by particular communities of language users. Metaphysics, we might say, is simply the attempt to believe that once all the problems of life have been answered, theoretical problems still remain. But in his view, once we can live, we no longer need metaphysical supports for what we do. Therefore, for the later Wittgenstein, returning philosophy to 'life' portends a 'post-theoretical mode' of philosophy that, in liberating us from illusions, in this case the illusions of modern subjectivity, teaches us *how to live* – how to respond, in language, to the events of life in appropriate ways – by asking us what 'we' *would actually do and say* in such and such a situation where a philosophical problem seems to present itself as real and pressing. For the later Wittgenstein, it is the confidence to act within forms of life – to live – that should be the goal of all our philosophical endeavours: confidence that philosophical forms of questioning seem in his view to sap.

Interestingly, Wittgenstein returns to some of the anti-Platonic themes of the ancient world here. More specifically, Wittgenstein can be seen to be continuing the philosophical task first set by Epicurus, who observed that the contemplation of nature must have a real human consequence if it is to be counted as significant. Thus he proposes that 'we must not suppose that any object is to be gained from the knowledge of the phenomenon of the sky … than peace of mind and a sure confidence'.[60] For Wittgenstein as well, to view 'the sky' as a 'phenomenon of life' (and not of philosophy and its excrescence modern science) is to liberate us from the desire to attain a particular kind of abstract philosophical knowledge of it.[61] Thus, in response to the Cartesian problem of subjectivity, Wittgenstein implores us to look at the sky and say to ourselves 'how blue it is' – if we do, all metaphysical riddles and sceptical doubts will immediately disappear. In this way, Wittgenstein supplements traditional forms of philosophical sensibility with an everyday *phronesis* ('practical wisdom') that begins and ends with an appreciation of what might be termed the 'ordinary recognition of life', a life that is the lived basis of all our *useful actions*. Moreover, as a result, in his view, as life becomes the first principle of philosophizing, the philosopher must learn to look; to *see life* and only

---

[59]   See Saul Kripke, *Wittgenstein on Rules and Private Language* (Oxford: Blackwell, 1984).

[60]   See Pierre Hadot, *Philosophy as a Way of Life* (Oxford: Oxford University Press, 1995), p. 266.

[61]   Wittgenstein, *Investigations*, §275.

then to think.[62] Only then can we begin the long road back to the philosophical insights lost in the passage to modern subject-centred ways of doing philosophy. For Wittgenstein, it seems, the modern quest for knowledge of the world 'as world' has involved a 'flight from life'. As such, philosophy must now be reconceived as a vitalist *anamnesis* that *reminds* us that life is always and already there before us, in front of our eyes as the unassuming context within which all forms of worldiness – that is, all ideas of truth, certainty and existence – receive their ultimate significance and proper measure. For the later Wittgenstein, philosophy can make this return if, and only if, it redefines itself as a distinctive kind of practical life-oriented *expertise* that should be acquired by all those who truly desire to understand their own lives. The implication (not drawn by Wittgenstein) here is that if philosophy is to be significant today, then it too must become *lebensform* – a move that would require a return to philosophy's anti-Platonic classical *telos*. For Wittgenstein, however, this is not possible as philosophy can have no relation to life – although, as with *The Tractatus*, here his own practice again seems to contradict his *philosophical* orientation. This, of course, is one of the most significant problems associated with Wittgenstein's philosophy, but when read in vitalist terms, the 'return of philosophy to life' is not really its rejection at all but rather its *refounding*, albeit within a space of problems now radically transformed by the theoretical endeavours of scientific modernity (for 'our life' is no longer that of the age of Epicurus). In this way, Wittgenstein's anti-philosophy was simply a propaedeutic to a new mode of philosophizing, one where we recognize that the role of the philosopher is to speak *for our* life and how we should inform it and live it.

---

[62]   See Judith Genova, *Wittgenstein: A Way of Seeing* (London: Routledge, 1995). In this context we can see the influence of the philosophical therapeutics that was implicit within twentieth-century positivism. For the positivists, it was *vision* that, in good modernist ways, liberated thought from the dead hand of tradition.

Chapter 7

'A Weariness of the Flesh': Towards a Theology of Boredom and Fatigue

Kenneth Jason Wardley

Introduction

It may seem odd – perverse even – to include an essay on boredom and fatigue in a book subtitled the 'affirmation of life'. And yet they are part of our everyday lives:[1] fatigue, as Jean-Louis Chrétien has suggested, is one of the fundamental phenomena of existence, implicating not only a person's work and body, but their temporality, death, meaning and being.[2] And while English-speaking commentators may contend that the word 'boredom' is an invention of the nineteenth century (a product of either the Enlightenment or Romanticism), they also acknowledge that the French *ennui* 'in all its metaphysical dignity' originated in the twelfth century.[3]

French studies of boredom are certainly more elegiac, perhaps because they associate boredom with depression[4] – what the poet Baudelaire called 'the planes of *Ennui*, vacant and profound'. At the start of the twentieth century French philosophy exhibited a divided and dialectical character: a philosophy of life on the one hand, a philosophy of the concept on the other. At stake, Alain Badiou suggests, was the human subject as a 'living organism' and 'creator of concepts' with both its 'interior, animal, organic life' and 'capacity for creativity and abstraction' under scrutiny.[5] As Badiou observes, this 'relationship between body and idea, or life and concept, formulated around the question of the subject, thus structures the whole development' of twentieth-century French philosophy.[6]

---

[1] Jean-Yves Lacoste, *Présence et parousie* (Genève: Ad Solem, 2006), p. 317.

[2] Jean-Louis Chrétien, *De La Fatigue* (Paris: Les Éditions de Minuit, 1996).

[3] Patricia Meyer Spacks, *Boredom: The Literary History of a State of Mind* (Chicago: University of Chicago Press, 1995), pp. 9 and 14.

[4] Peter Toohey, *Boredom: A Lively History* (New Haven: Yale University Press, 2011), p. 201. Cf. Bernard Granger and Georges Charbonneau (eds), *Phenomenologie des sentiments corporels: II – Fatigue, lassitude, ennui* (Puteaux: Le cercle herméneutique, 2003). My thanks here to Agnes Chalier.

[5] Alain Badiou, 'The Adventure of French Philosophy', *New Left Review*, 35 (2005): 69.

[6] Ibid., p. 69.

Indeed, Jean-Luc Marion argues that the supernatural boredom which 'turns the spiritual away from the good ... away from charity'[7] also 'undoes being from its very beingness' and 'abolishes the very name of being'.[8] Conversely, rather than this disengagement of ontological difference, Emmanuel Levinas observed that fatigue is 'not a cancellation of one's contract with being'[9] but the opportunity for an 'interrogation of being'.[10] Instead, understood as 'some lapse or diminishment in our capacity to go on',[11] fatigue is probably our most common form of experience, one which happens so frequently and closely to humanity that it can often escape proper reflection and understanding.

Such familiarity, I suggest, has though, until recently, bred philosophical neglect, while in theology the very idea that God might be something we are tired of – or even bored by – seems blasphemous. Indeed, as the phenomenologist and theologian Jean-Yves Lacoste notes, in the history of ideas what was usually referred to as wisdom was in fact the 'life of the mind' or the 'vitality of the spirit'. By contrast, Lacoste continues, fatigue is often defined as *failure*, a closing off of ourselves from the world.[12] Theological claims that the God to whom humanity prays is tirelessly[13] concerned with the world come to naught if I am so bored that I cannot pray well, or if I am so tired that I cannot pray at all.

This chapter will thus follow two impulses: Lacoste's suggestion that philosophy and theology should speak about boredom and about fatigue, just as they do about anguish or joy, and the Swiss theologian Karl Barth's contention that theological anthropology and philosophy of religion are incoherent without them. Above all, it will try and offer a tentative answer to the question of what it means to pray when one is tired or bored. To this end, I shall begin by examining some of the traditional theological and philosophical readings of fatigue and boredom (beginning with Jewish and Christian scripture), before turning specifically to Martin Heidegger and Giorgio Agamben, and finally to recent phenomenological accounts, drawing from them some suggestions for a possible theology of boredom and fatigue.

---

[7]   Jean-Luc Marion, *God Without Being*, trans. Thomas A. Carlson (Chicago: University of Chicago Press, 1991), p. 135.

[8]   Ibid., p. 120.

[9]   Emmanuel Levinas, *Existence and Existents*, trans. Alphonso Lingis (Pittsburgh: Duquesne University Press, 2001), p. 25.

[10]   Chrétien, *De La Fatigue*, p. 12.

[11]   Jeffrey Bloechl, 'The Difficulty of Being: A Partial Reading of E. Lévinas, *De l'existence à l'existant*', *European Journal of Psychotherapy, Counselling and Health*, 7:1–2 (2005): 78.

[12]   Lacoste, *Présence et parousie*, p. 311.

[13]   Cf. Hans Urs von Balthasar, 'On unceasing prayer', trans. William Morlock, *Communio*, 4/2 (1977): 99–113.

The Theological Status of Fatigue and Boredom

Both Thomas Aquinas[14] and the desert fathers understood the dangers of apathy (*accidia*), or a lack of interest in spiritual matters. But while the author of Ecclesiastes offered a warning to every theologian that 'of making books there is no end, and much study is a weariness of the flesh' (12.12), the biblical witness is for the most part silent on the topic of boredom,[15] with the prophet Isaiah (40.28–31) typifying scriptural attitudes to fatigue. The Gospels at least offer some solace for weary souls (and theologians a space for contemplation and investigation[16]) revealing that even the incarnate God was himself tired from his journey (John 4.6). Elsewhere the Gospels record a specific type of boredom, arising from a jadedness born of excess and repetition (or what Svendsen terms the 'boredom of satiety'[17]): is this what befalls the disciples in Mark 14.32–42 as Christ prays in the Garden of Gethsemane?

As scriptural commentary, Lo Spagna's painting of *The Agony in the Garden* (1500–05) certainly gives that impression: it depicts three drowsy disciples, their heads resting on their forearms (a position which Toohey considers 'a sign of boredom'[18]). Now, the disciples ought not to be bored and sleepy – they ought to be 'full of attention and prayerful devotion. But they have had enough of their Easter service and this terrible garden. Their dereliction … is expressed as boredom with the travails of their Saviour',[19] and Toohey applauds Lo Spagna's genius in adding 'this boredom to the usual depiction' of the sleepy disciples in Gethsemane.

Now, as evocative as this is, it is probably an exegetical stretch. More damning is an incident from the career of the Apostle Paul (who commands us to pray unceasingly in 1 Thessalonians) in which we learn that a young man, Eutychus, sank 'into a deep sleep as Paul talked on and on' until, 'sound asleep, he fell to the ground from the third storey … dead' (Acts 20.7–12). This, one might suggest, is the first recorded incident in the history of the Christian church in which a member of the congregation is bored to death by the preaching; a cautionary tale of a preacher who drones on until the service becomes an all-nighter and 'vespers

---

[14]   *Summa Theologica* II/2, q.35, art.4, 'Reply to objection 3'. Cited in Michael L. Raposa, *Boredom and the Religious Imagination* (Charlottesville: University Press of Virginia, 1999), p. 177.

[15]   Although Proverbs 31.27 describes an ideal wife as one who 'avoids the bread of idleness'.

[16]   Chrétien, *De La Fatigue*, p. 13.

[17]   Lars Svendsen, *A Philosophy of Boredom*, trans. John Irons (London: Reaktion, 2005), p. 41.

[18]   Toohey, *Boredom*, p. 13.

[19]   Ibid., p. 13.

has turned into a lock-in'.[20] No wonder then, that it is usually passed over by embarrassed biblical commentators.[21]

Echoing the author of Ecclesiastes, in his commentary on Paul's *Letter to the Romans*, Karl Barth talked about the flourishing business of sin with 'the publication of books such as the one I am now writing'.[22] For Barth, writing in the wake of World War I, 'the signature of modern man' seemed to consist 'simply and unfortunately in his utter weariness and boredom … man is bored with himself'.[23] Modern man, Barth avers, 'can no longer work up any interest in himself, or give himself to the stimuli and disillusionments of seeking and self-transcendence'. He thus reacts 'neither positively nor negatively to his experience, however intense' and is incapable 'of the joys of faith or of the fierceness of atheistic defiance. Everything has become a burden to him. He has attained only to the indifference which lets things take their course'. For Barth such lethargy was 'a pressing reality' in post-war Europe; the 'fateful question' was whether Europe would succeed 'in shaking [it] off'.[24]

His study of human phenomena in part leads Barth to the rejection of the existential thought that characterized his early theology[25]: here 'the religious interpretation of human life obviously reaches its limit'. Boredom is immanence in 'its purest form'.[26] Yet the assertion that human life is related to transcendence

> presupposes that man is interested in himself, that he is not weary of himself but in search of his true self … [I]s it fair to take account of the enthusiasm which is able either to affirm or to deny the mystery suggested, but to ignore the lethargy

---

[20]   Anna Carter Florence, 'A Prodigal Preaching Story and Bored-to-Death Youth', *Theology Today*, 64/2 (2007): 238.

[21]   Those that do normally skip to Eutychus' resurrection, glossing over the fact that Paul was at least partly culpable. One of the few references to this incident notes, archly, that '[i]f this was not his first and his only sermon at Troas, it was certainly his last'; Alexander Whyte, *Bible Characters: Stephen to Timothy* (Edinburgh: Oliphant, Anderson and Ferrier, 1901), p. 43.

[22]   Karl Barth, *The Epistle to the Romans*, trans. Edwyn C. Hoskyns (London: Oxford University Press, 1933), p. 174.

[23]   Karl Barth, trans. Harold Knight et al., *Church Dogmatics* III/2 (Edinburgh: T&T Clark, 1960), p. 117.

[24]   Ibid.

[25]   Cf. Stephen H. Webb, *Re-Figuring Theology: The Rhetoric of Karl Barth* (Albany: State University of New York Press, 1991), p. 153. However, the French 'theology of work' which emerged in the 1950s amounted to little more than a 'theology of pious consciousness' that ignored pressing socio-ethical problems; the papal encyclical *Laborem exercens* recognized only that man rest in order to 'prepare himself, becoming more and more what in the will of God he ought to be'; *On Human Work* (Washington: United States Catholic Conference, 1981), p. 25. See Lothar Roos, 'On a theology and ethics of work', trans. Albert K. Wimmer, *Communio*, 11/2 (1984): 100–19.

[26]   Svendsen, *Philosophy of Boredom*, p. 47.

which may also be a reaction in this situation, leaving out of account the tired and indifferent man, as though there could be no place for him too, and for him precisely, in a coherent anthropology?[27]

And not just existentialist philosophy; systematic theology itself, Barth suggested, was 'the turning over of a sick man in his bed for the sake of change'.[28] What one generation found interesting will likely bore the next;[29] as Stephen Webb notes, theology, 'because it must speak from the emptiness of human life, is always seeking something new to say, a newness that Barth suggests can only barely cover up its profound *ennui*'.[30] Even the relatively mundane activity of weekly preaching falters: 'The people do not need us to help them with the paraphernalia [appurtenances] of their daily life', writes Barth,[31] thus exposing the embarrassing conceptual myopia behind Schleiermacher's definition of religion as a 'taste for the infinite' or a 'feeling of ultimate dependence' (*Gefühl schlechthinniger Abhängigkeit*) which has plagued the philosophy of religion ever since.

The Temporality of Boredom

Similar sentiments were echoed by Edmund Husserl, writing in 1936 that

> the exclusiveness with which the total world-view of modern man, in the second half of the nineteenth century, let itself be determined by the positive sciences and be blinded by the "prosperity" they produced, meant an indifferent turning-away from the questions which are decisive for a genuine humanity.[32]

Barth's comments were directed in part at Husserl's pupil, Martin Heidegger. While the phenomenological analysis which Heidegger had offered in *Being and Time* had centred on anxiety, in his winter semester 1929–30 lecture course it was replaced by boredom as the basic mood of *Dasein*. Boredom here means literally a

---

27   Barth continues: 'Is not this unfairness a further indication that it is not quite correct to maintain that the frontier situation is laden with transcendence or that this is genuine transcendence? Is it not a further indication of the highly problematical nature of the main principle of this philosophy?' *Church Dogmatics* III/2, pp. 117–18.

28   Karl Barth, *The Word of God and the Word of Man*, trans. Douglas Horton (London: Oxford University Press, 1928), p. 184.

29   Jacques Ellul identified boredom – 'gloomy, dull, and joyless' – as one of the defining perversions of modern social life; *Violence: Reflections from a Christian Perspective*, trans. Cecilia Gaul Kings (London: SCM Press, 1970), p. 121.

30   Webb, *Re-Figuring Theology*, p. 134.

31   Barth, *The Word of God and the Word of Man*, p. 187.

32   Edmund Husserl, *The Crisis of European Sciences and Transcendental Phenomenology*, trans. David Carr (Evanston: Northwestern University Press, 1970), pp. 5–6.

'long while' (*Langeweile*) and, Heidegger asks, 'Who is not acquainted with it in the most varied forms and disguises in which it arises, in the way it often befalls us only for a moment, the way it torments and depresses us for longer periods too'.[33]

This German term conveys the temporal aspect of the experience, one in which 'the imagination is crucified';[34] if time does become intolerably 'long' for *Dasein*[35] then it tries to drive that time and its boring character away with petty distractions. *Dasein* simply does not wish to experience a 'long time':

> Such boredom is still distant when it is only this book or that play, that business or this idleness, that drags on and on. It irrupts when "one is bored". Profound boredom, drifting here and there in the abysses of our existence like a muffling fog, removes all things and human beings and oneself along with them into a remarkable indifference. This boredom manifests beings as a whole.[36]

Heidegger asks, how might 'we escape this boredom, in which we find, as we ourselves say, that *time* becomes drawn out, becomes long?' His response is simply 'by at all times making an effort, whether consciously or unconsciously, to pass the time, by welcoming highly important and essential preoccupations for the sole reason that they take up our time'.[37] Heidegger, like Kierkegaard and Pascal, considered boredom to be a fundamental human 'attunement'[38] with 'profound metaphysical, if not explicitly religious, significance'.[39] These attunements are not 'merely subjectively coloured experiences or epiphenomenal manifestations of psychological life' but fundamental modes of being, 'ways of *Dasein* in which *Dasein* becomes manifest to itself'.[40] Such powerful habits of feeling shape our perceptions of the world, and Heidegger was concerned with finding a way to make our boredom 'resonate' rather than allowing it only to

---

[33]   Martin Heidegger, *The Fundamental Concepts of Metaphysics: World, Finitude, Solitude*, trans. William McNeill and Nicholas Walker (Bloomington: Indiana University Press, 1995), p. 79.

[34]   Raposa, *Boredom and the Religious Imagination*, p. 40.

[35]   As Agamben observes, Heidegger's *locus classicus* is that of waiting on a railway platform. Giorgio Agamben, *The Open: Man and Animal*, trans. Kevin Attell (Stanford: Stanford University Press, 2004), p. 63; Heidegger, *Fundamental Concepts of Metaphysics*, p. 101.

[36]   'No matter how fragmented our everyday existence may appear to be, however, it always deals with beings in a unity of the "whole," if only in a shadowy way. Even and precisely when we are not actually busy with things or ourselves, this "as a whole" comes over us – for example, in authentic boredom'. Martin Heidegger, 'What is Metaphysics?' in *Pathmarks*, ed. William McNeill (Cambridge: Cambridge University Press, 1998), p. 87.

[37]   Heidegger, *Fundamental Concepts of Metaphysics*, p. 78.

[38]   Ibid., pp. 77–9.

[39]   Raposa, *Boredom and the Religious Imagination*, p. 54.

[40]   Heidegger, *Fundamental Concepts of Metaphysics*, p. 238.

manifest itself '*wherever* we create a diversion from boredom for ourselves'.[41] This boredom is rooted in an experience of emptiness – what Raposa calls the 'emptiness of each passing moment, as well as that of the object that confronts us and of the situation that binds us'.[42] This overpowering feeling, that in boredom 'we are *bound* precisely by – nothing',[43] that is, 'not bound by time but by the emptiness of *this* time',[44] becomes clearer in Heidegger's intensification of boredom as more than simply being 'bored by' a particular object or activity. Anxiety and boredom constitute a state of mind that is both a kind of calmness and an uneasiness that 'leaves us hanging, because it induces the slipping away of beings as a whole'.[45] 'Profound boredom' as a state of detachment and indifference provides a 'vehicle of transcendence'[46] beyond specific circumstances and particular beings, one which 'manifests being as a whole'. This reading of boredom as a state in which we might be open to the demand of Being has been challenged by Jean-Luc Marion, who points out that it is more likely that it is a state in which we are unable to say anything at all, in which every call or claim (including that of Being itself) is disqualified: 'boredom does not evaluate, does not affirm, does not love'.[47] Indeed, the only other possibility of such revelation, Heidegger concedes, is 'the joy we feel in the presence of the Dasein … of a human being whom we love'.[48]

The Bored Animal

One should then ask the question of whether boredom is 'affect' or 'affect-lessness'. These preoccupations testify to 'being-left-empty as the essential experience of boredom',[49] and Giorgio Agamben's own reading of Heidegger (developing the notion of 'profound boredom', *tiefe Langeweile*) assigns it the privileged role of 'metaphysical operator'[50] in the anthropological 'machine' which

---

[41]   Ibid., p. 90.

[42]   Raposa, *Boredom and the Religious Imagination*, p. 55.

[43]   Heidegger, *Fundamental Concepts of Metaphysics*, p. 97.

[44]   Raposa, *Boredom and the Religious Imagination*, p. 55.

[45]   Heidegger, 'What is Metaphysics?', p. 88.

[46]   Ibid., p. 57.

[47]   Jean-Luc Marion, *Reduction and Givenness*, trans. Thomas A. Carlson (Evanston: Northwestern University Press, 1998), p. 190. For an incisive critical discussion of Marion, see Joeri Schrijvers, *Ontotheological Turnings: The Decentering of the Modern Subject in Recent French Pheneomenology* (Albany: State University of New York Press, 2011), pp. 159–78.

[48]   Heidegger, 'What is Metaphysics?', p. 87.

[49]   Agamben, *The Open*, p. 64.

[50]   Ibid., p. 68.

produces – and thereby separates – humanity from animality.[51] Boredom is the keynote of 'anthropogenesis, the becoming Da-sein of living man'[52] suspending its animal captivation with its habitual stimuli (what Agamben calls the 'carriers of significance which constitute its environment'[53]). 'Dasein', concludes Agamben, 'is simply an animal that has learned to become bored'.[54] What separates us from the animals is our awareness of tedium, both the tedium of having nothing particular to occupy us, and the tediousness of what does, and which might enable us, however briefly, to forget how much we are restrained by our habits. Boredom exposes 'the unexpected proximity of Dasein and the animal':[55] both are 'open to a closedness ... totally delivered over to something that obstinately refuses itself'[56]; nonetheless this non-relation ultimately leads to an estrangement from our environment.[57] And yet this anthropology remains incoherent: disaffection is not simply the absence of affection. It has an object: people are disaffected *with* something or *by* something; in this sense, as we shall note later on, it has the same structure as fatigue. While Agamben's 'weak messianicity' articulates an 'ontology of potentiality', fatigue – to which we now turn – remains a neglected theme of Agamben's post human bio-politics.[58]

The Phenomenology of Fatigue

Chrétien's thesis is simple: 'ever since we came into the world we have always found (or lost) ourselves in this familiar but immemorial ordeal'.[59] We are tested by fatigue, in one or other of its many forms, every day. Fatigue is a constant

---

[51]   In *Animal Boredom: Towards an Empirical Approach of Animal Subjectivity* (Leiden, 1993), François Wemelsfelder offers an account from the perspective of physical sciences (although one still drawing upon Heidegger and Merleau-Ponty), suggesting that animals and humans participate in a common pre-reflective environment (*Umwelt*).

[52]   Agamben, *The Open*, p. 68.

[53]   Ibid., p. 41.

[54]   '[I]t has awakened *from* its own captivation *to* its own captivation. This awakening of the living being to its own being-captivated, this anxious and resolute opening to a not-open, is the human'; ibid., p. 70.

[55]   Ibid., p. 65.

[56]   'In boredom, Dasein can be riveted to beings that refuse themselves in their totality because it is constitutively "delivered up" [*überantwortet*] to its own proper being," factically "thrown" and "lost" in the world of its concern ... *In becoming bored, Dasein is delivered over* (ausgeliefert) *to something that refuses itself, exactly as the animal, in its captivation, is exposed* (hinausgesetzt) *in something unrevealed*'. Ibid., p. 65.

[57]   The 'jewel ... at the center of the human world ... is nothing but animal captivation'; ibid., p. 68.

[58]   *Homo Sacer*, *The Open* and *Means without End* make no references to fatigue.

[59]   Chrétien, *De La Fatigue*, p. 9.

part of the fabric of human lives and accompanies all of its activities: exhaustion represents an extreme form of fatigue, intelligible only according to that tiredness of which one has prior experience. It is, therefore, a sign of solidarity, the condition of our living and our humanity; experienced (*donné*) as both indivisible and yet infinitely varied: 'even if philosophical analysis[60] could distinguish (or even resist) the fatigue of the body and lassitude of the soul, that is not for us the beginning of the fatigue … which weighs upon our actions, our feet and our faces, nor the sheer physical effort that plunges us into some stupor or bewilderment'.[61]

Since fatigue thus lies in the background of every activity, it is there in idleness too (one can get tired of doing nothing – 'each act has its own fatigue'). Chrétien's genealogical investigation asks whether it is always the *same* tiredness, or does it have a history, even a destiny? Is the history of fatigue, in fact, not the history of the body? It is one of the most humane, common and enduring experiences; intimate, unspectacular and unobjectifiable, present at the heart of each human life, affecting both body and soul. But, according to Lacoste, the marks of fatigue upon the body remind us that it is also a self. And with this in mind, one can understand the philosophical meaning of fatigue. Whenever someone says that they are tired they do not mean that their body is tired,[62] or that certain physical-chemical processes have tired them: they mean that, above all, fatigue has an egological reality. Now, this does not mean that animals are never tired, nor does it suggest that they have an ego; it simply reminds us that once again consciousness and the body are inseparable.[63] Indeed, for Lacoste, dreamless sleep reveals the irreducible animality of human life.[64]

Boredom and Life

Phenomenology maintains that 'things are endowed with meaning and value only through the comportment adopted toward them and in accordance with how

---

[60] Lacoste himself describes the task of the philosopher as 'that of an ascetic … but this work has nothing to do with that of the manual worker or servant'; Lacoste, *Présence et parousie*, p. 310.

[61] Chrétien, *De La Fatigue*, p. 9.

[62] Of course one might 'challenge the impression that being must be either actively engaged in what Levinas calls "effort" or else in some state of deceleration or decline. This division seems to overlook the humble experience of *leisure*, of being at one's ease'; Bloechl, 'The Difficulty of Being', p. 85. Cf. Jean-Yves Lacoste, *Le monde et l'absence d'œuvre* (Paris: Presses Universitaires de France, 2000), pp. 18–21.

[63] Jean-Yves Lacoste, *Etre-en-Danger* (Paris: Editions du Cerf, 2011), p. 243.

[64] Ibid., p. 132.

such things appear to the subject'.[65] One should ask then what the significance of boredom and fatigue is.

Merleau-Ponty who, like Husserl, understood the importance of embodiment,[66] contended that attentiveness was crucial to consciousness.[67] On the other hand, in examining our affective lives, Lacoste wishes to preserve the 'formal plurality' in which the world appears including inattentiveness, disappointment and boredom. Like Gethsemane, there should be no time for boredom: the *desideratum* (longing) for God supersedes the sort of temporary 'micro-eschatology'[68] of peace or the rest that Levinas found somewhat ridiculous.[69] Nonetheless, this play between rest and restlessness is one of our most commonplace experiences.

In his own analysis of the affective life, Lacoste states unequivocally that 'the experience of fatigue ... is not pathological: a tired person is not a sick person (even if the distinction is often not that clear)'.[70] Often '[f]atigue is defined as failure', when I cannot read or pay attention to whatever I am supposed to be listening to. Fatigue can be described in terms of opening and closing: openness, because it is 'my exposure to certain things or events in the world which tires me', closure, because it is 'the refusal of that opening that is called fatigue'. One of the purest examples of fatigue, offered by Lacoste, is the desire to sleep:

> if not for fatigue I would be dead to the world ... In such a case, *I* would be tired. But the world would be only incidental for exhaustion ... [nevertheless] it is the same world which appears to me in my tired state as in ... my rested or relaxed state.[71]

---

[65]   Jean-Luc Petit, 'Constitution by movement: Husserl in light of recent neurobiological findings', in Jean Petitot (ed.), *Naturalizing Phenomenology: Issues in Contemporary Phenomenology and Cognitive Science* (Stanford, CA: Stanford University Press, 1999), p. 221.

[66]   Our bodies are 'given as the constant bearer of the center of orientation'; Edmund Husserl, *Ideas Pertaining to a Pure Phenomenology and to a Phenomenological Philosophy: Second Book: Studies in the Phenomenology of Constitution*, (Collected Works, vol. 3) trans. Richard Rojcewicz and André Schuwer (Dordrecht: Kluwer Academic, 1989), p. 70.

[67]   Maurice Merleau-Ponty, *Phenomenology of Perception*, trans. C. Smith (London: Routledge, 2002), p. 30.

[68]   Lacoste (here borrowing a term from Richard Kearney), *Etre-en-Danger*, p. 283. See Richard Kearney, 'Epiphanies of the Everyday: Toward a Micro-Eschatology', in John Panteleimon Manoussakis (ed.), *After God: Richard Kearney and the Religious Turn in Continental Philosophy* (New York: Fordham University Press, 2006), pp. 3–20.

[69]   'Mortality renders senseless any concern that the ego would have for its existence and its destiny ... nothing is more comical than the concern that a being has for an existence that it could not save from its destruction'. Emmanuel Levinas, *Otherwise than Being*, trans. Alphonso Lingis (Pittsburgh: Duquesne University Press, 2002), pp. 128–9.

[70]   Lacoste, *Présence et parousie*, p. 310.

[71]   Ibid., p. 311.

Fatigue and boredom thereby reveal the incipient structuralism of daily life; fatigue has directionality:

> I am of course tired of this or that, of having read the *Critique of Pure Reason* or having had too long a hike,[72] but the tiring thing (or tiring action) has the remarkable phenomenological property of affecting every other occurrence. The *Critique of Pure Reason* tires me. But during the act when it tires me (and, of course, in that act alone – I will always be able to do something different and allow the world to appear to me differently), it is the whole world, in its totality – and this is the important point – which tires me.[73]

It is axiomatic that '[t]he experience of fatigue is the daily bread of prayer': the spiritual life represents a costly break in our *being-in-the-world*. So is fatigue simply 'a reclamation of man' by the secular world? Lacoste admits that we might easily believe that – after all, it is not necessary for us to be tired to discover that prayer is difficult. The place which defines us does not necessarily include any *ad esse Deum*, any being towards God, but it does unfold as corporeality, as flesh and spirit, and this corporeity is characterized as a closure on itself as much as by its openness to the world. This closure might be the autonomy (*adséité*) of the transcendental ego or it may be the strain of the pray-er (*orant*) battling with their 'thoughts', the *logismoi* of the ascetic tradition. Whichever it is, it is important that we can name this 'heaviness' or 'embarrassment'[74] and the two experiences – of prayer and of fatigue – 'should be linked … in order to better illumine this relationship'.[75] In other words: 'We must learn to pray in times of fatigue … It is especially important – and it is this point that we should emphasize – to learn that it is in time of fatigue that we really pray'.[76]

Fatigue characterizes the dispossession of the self when subjectivity is bracketed out in and by the world. And yet, fatigue presents obstacles: 'The heavy gestures of he who is not master of his own body. The voice that stumbles over its words. And other mundane realities. But there is more. It follows that the body is too tired to pray "well".'[77]

---

[72]   Lacoste may here be making an implicit reference to Jean-Paul Sartre's own discussion in *Being and Nothingness: An Essay On Phenomenological Ontology*, trans. Hazel E. Barnes (London: Methuen, 1986), pp. 454–5.

[73]   Lacoste, *Présence et parousie*, p. 311.

[74]   Ibid., p. 316.

[75]   'By "prayer", we understand a way of life/existence (if we take "life/existence" within its current Kierkegaardian meaning), or more-than-existence (if we take "life" in the sense of Heideggerian analytic), being before God, *esse coram Deo*'; ibid., p. 314.

[76]   Ibid., p. 316.

[77]   Ibid., p. 315.

Nihilism and Affection

For Friedrich Nietzsche, such fatigue and exhaustion were the chief exports and essential characteristics of the Christian faith,[78] so much so that the highest goal of Europeans was 'wakefulness itself'.[79] The 'will-to-power' thus represented an epistemological principle whereby Nietzsche intended to 'construct a philosophy consistent with the extraordinary openness he felt was available to man',[80] in opposition to the 'transcendental nihilistic fatigue' of which Christianity was merely the most radical form.[81]

But, contends Levinas, the subject cannot be described merely on the basis of intentionality, freedom and will; it has to be described on 'the basis of the passivity of time'.[82] The patience of ageing is 'not a position taken with regard to one's death, but a lassitude, a passive exposure to being which is not assumed ... that peculiar "being too much" which is also a failing but in a deficiency in which the *conatus* [impulse] is not relaxed'. Moreover, the non-repose or restlessness of the ethical concern implicit in 'being for another' is 'better than rest' and 'bears witness to the Good'.[83] However, Lacoste reminds us that since nothing is given to us without first being reduced to that which we can receive of that gift, then being is constantly in danger: 'A human being is flesh and body, and this duality puts it in danger of being treated merely as a body: for instance, the surgeon is only concerned with a body, the flesh being somehow anesthetized – he would operate on an animal in the same way'.[84] Thus, as well as letting things appear, 'we can also allow [them] to disappear. Reduced to an object by distractions, the work of art disappears. Reduced to a body, the anesthetized flesh disappears. Our being-at-rest disappears when we find ourselves without a place in the world'.[85] Nihilism – in its reduction of truth[86] to the will-to-power – diminishes the importance of place. Lacoste invites us to rethink our humanity by refiguring place, and how our comportment as 'liturgical beings' – beings before God[87] – might exceed our being in the world.

The simple thesis behind Henri de Lubac's *Surnaturel* was that Enlightenment modernity was the product of a neoscholastic theology which overlooked

---

[78]   Chrétien, *De La Fatigue*, p. 137.

[79]   Friedrich W. Nietzsche, *Beyond Good and Evil: Prelude to a Philosophy of the Future*, trans. J. Norman (Cambridge: Cambridge University Press, 2002), p. 4.

[80]   Arthur C. Danto, *Nietzsche as Philosopher* (New York: Macmillan, 1965), p. 12.

[81]   Chrétien, *De La Fatigue*, pp. 136–8.

[82]   Levinas, *Otherwise than Being*, p. 53.

[83]   Ibid., p. 54.

[84]   Lacoste, *Etre-en-Danger*, p. 7.

[85]   Ibid., p. 316.

[86]   Being-at-rest, Lacoste suggests, conveys one of 'the truths of the world'. *Présence et parousie*, p. 316.

[87]   Ibid., p. 314.

humanity's natural desire for God, leading to 'a conception of grace as something so totally extraneous and alien to human nature that anything and everything natural and human was downgraded and demeaned'.[88] That meant that human nature – including reason, feeling and the body – became 'temptingly easy to denigrate'.[89] Lacoste concedes that the concept of 'pure nature' probably 'died from the rebuttal inflicted upon it by Lubac'.[90] But does that mean that it became merely a chapter in the history of theological nonsense with nothing to tell us? According to Lacoste, the history of modern philosophy will, in fact, turn out to be nothing more than the history of philosophers' inability 'to grasp an object (the humanity of mankind[91]) that "natural reason" is, in principle, sufficient to grasp'.[92] The idea of a pure nature – with all its attendant epistemological implications – is a modern hypothesis, a product of the division of theology and philosophy into 'separate bodies'.

Lacoste's own phenomenological analysis is interested in the margins of language, what he calls 'the pre-discursive gift of the world to the self'.[93] This priority of the affective-corporeal dimension involves a privileging of the corporeal and topological register of experience as offering possibilities of human freedom that precede and exceed the merely conceptual or discursive. This represents a freedom from ontotheological language, a freedom in which human subjectivity is revealed as much at the level of passive syntheses such as disappointment or frustration as the perceptive life of which they are a part. These affections may overwhelm our perceptive life: when something appears to us, it is given to be both seen and felt (sensory *hulè* and intentional *morphé*) and the joy of seeing (or feeling) is all part of the composition of that experience. That something affects us, which means that it is *present* to us. Yet, while we are enjoying its presence, tiredness overcomes us – that something is still there and is still perceived, but it is no longer *present*. And nothing is more common, Lacoste suggests, 'than to allow oneself to invest in a presence, only to let that which was present to then absent itself'.[94]

This affective flux not only recalls Heidegger's emphasis on the pre-reflective dimension of existence but is, in part, reminiscent of Lubac's own claim that our minds rest on a certain 'anticipation', or *prolepsis*[95] that there is a truth 'which is

---

[88]   Fergus Kerr, *Twentieth-Century Catholic Theologians: From Neoscholasticism to Nuptial Mysticism* (Oxford: Blackwell, 2007), p. 74.

[89]   Kerr, *Catholic Theologians*, pp. 74–5.

[90]   Lacoste, *Le monde et l'absence d'œuvre*, p. 26.

[91]   The 'strangest of beings', one whose 'strangeness is that of a pure enigma' and yet sustains 'a cognitive discourse … about what we are here and now'; Ibid., p. 45.

[92]   Ibid., p. 32.

[93]   Lacoste, *Présence et parousie*, p. 117.

[94]   Lacoste, *Etre-en-Danger*, p. 51.

[95]   'God must be present to the mind before any explicit reasoning or objective concept is possible … he must be secretly affirmed and thought'. Henri de Lubac, *The Discovery of God*, trans. Alexander Dru (London: Darton, Longman & Todd, 1960), p. 58.

lived before it is known, perceived with certainty before being subjected to the discipline of proofs and the control of concepts – because it is connatural to us'.[96] And, as Levinas observes, 'human labor and effort presuppose a commitment in which we already involved'.[97] But while the non-appearing divine may be perceptible through an affective act of mediation,[98] the *orant* still risks boredom. Regardless of any proleptic, eschatology reminds us that God (or the Absolute) cannot easily be brought to mind in prayer, which may be destined only to be frustrated. Lacoste wishes simply to articulate 'a possibility of a beyond-the-world in which nothing could be reduced to an object, in which flesh could be bracketed out to the benefit of the body, a world beyond, therefore, in which being would not be being-in-danger. Such eschatology is a possibility, and thus not necessarily wishful thinking'.[99]

Boredom thus provides a measure of how liturgical experience is, above all, a non-experience (one that undermines conventional accounts of 'religious experience' since Schleiermacher) that cannot be prescribed, rooted in something besides the intentionality of consciousness. Despite the claims of certain theological texts,[100] Lacoste maintains it is impossible to apprehend God via an act of the will or the intellect, here recalling Schelling and Kierkegaard, philosophers who transgressed the border between philosophical and theological reason in favour of a rationality that bypassed the opposition of natural and the supernatural in the interest of a vision of human freedom. But while philosophy can be concerned with human happiness, it does not follow that it possesses the necessary conditions for beatitude; although most claim to understand 'well-being', Lacoste notes wryly that philosophies such as logical positivism do not present themselves as lifestyles.[101] And it remains fascinated by happiness even when this 'well-being' no longer has a divine warrant once philosophy asserts – following Nietzsche – that God is dead. As an example of this 'right to the philosophical life', Lacoste suggests Heidegger's notion of 'serenity'[102] in which human beings enjoy everything that is their due, untroubled by anything that might exceed their 'ontological requirements'. This existential logic is thus one of satiety: humanity's desire can be filled because it lives in an intelligible world. And because it wants to achieve those goals it has given itself the power to do so;

---

[96] Ibid., p. 59.

[97] Levinas, *Existence and Existents*, p. 19.

[98] The idea of God 'prior to our concepts, although beyond our grasp without their help, and prior to all our argumentation, in spite of being logically unjustifiable without them … is the inspiration, the motive power and justification of them all'; Lubac, *Discovery of God*, p. 43.

[99] Lacoste, *Etre-en-Danger*, p. 8.

[100] Lacoste, *Le monde et l'absence d'œuvre*, p. 33.

[101] '[N]or do they claim for the philosopher the privilege of living life itself'; ibid., p. 33.

[102] Ibid., p. 44.

the figure of the will which creates that power has its own name: the will-to-power, in reality a closed human experience.

This will-to-power was an 'all inclusive principle for Nietzsche',[103] encompassing ontology, axiology, anthropology and epistemology. So, does the split between philosophy and theology (with its concomitant theory of 'pure nature') leave humanity 'helpless before the disturbing reality of nihilism'?[104] Although he never discussed human nature, Heidegger outlined the conditions for a possible happiness on a godforsaken earth. And, Lacoste continues, it was a quote from Nietzsche's *Zarathustra* which provided the inspiration for his essay 'What is thinking?'.[105] Thinking should oppose the growth of that Nietzschean desert. But what is thinking? For Heidegger it involved tracing the links between thinking, building and living, between thinking and our physical contact with the country lanes along which we (if not necessarily Sartre[106]) walk. But such things do not engender hope.[107] And, for Lacoste, the Hegelian 'God' died because it deprived humanity of hope.

What is at stake in Nietzsche is, Lacoste suggests, a direct consequence of Hegelian eschatology. While Nietzsche cared little for either Hegel or his 'Swabian piety',[108] the affirmation of the 'eternal return of the same' is his response to Hegelian idealism. Following the death of God,

> life wants to survive, and survive through the work of a will to power to create new values. But … the work of the will to power is an endless task: at a time without end and without purpose, eternal and folded in on itself. The will to power can never pronounce its last word. It can never lead itself to a final experience. It must assert itself with joy.[109]

Although it offers us a future, the truth of its being resides in the present – the will-to-power is founded on neither promise nor hope. Moreover, eschatologies which survive the death of God cannot resist the endless claims of the will-to-power.[110] This absolute future has its own name: the advent of the *Übermensch*, an

---

[103] Ammar Zeifa, 'Le Nihilisme et l'Épuisement: Heidegger ou Nietzsche' in Granger and Charbonneau, *Phénoménologie des sentiments corporels*, p. 128.

[104] Lacoste, *Le monde et l'absence d'œuvre*, p. 34.

[105] 'The desert grows: woe him who harbours deserts!' Friedrich Nietzsche, *Thus Spoke Zarathustra*, ed. Adrian Del Caro and Robert B. Pippin (Cambridge: Cambridge University Press, 2006), p. 252.

[106] See fn. 72 above.

[107] Lacoste, *Le monde et l'absence d'œuvre*, p. 42.

[108] Lacoste reminds us of Nietzsche's disdain for Hegel's *gothische Himmelstürmerei*. Friedrich Nietzsche, *Nachgelassene Fragmente: Frühjahr bis Herbst 1884* (Nietzsche Werke VII/2), ed. Giorgio Colli and Mazzino Montinari (Berlin: De Gruyter, 1974), p. 251.

[109] Lacoste, *Le monde et l'absence d'œuvre*, p. 41.

[110] Ibid., p. 43.

early attempt to overcome metaphysics – that is, to overcome humanity (*dépasser l'homme*[111]) as a metaphyscial animal. And history has made us understandably cautious about that so-called 'eschatology'.

Christian theology is, on the other hand, defined by its refusal of any quantifiable eschatology. Every other end, however enviable and respectable it might be, cannot claim anything more than the status of a 'penultimate end': 'Nothing that the world is home to is eschatologically *simpliciter*'.[112] And because de Lubac never pretended to describe 'the current conditions of this existence', the theologoumenon he rehabilitated leaves the Heideggerian hermeneutics of facticity intact. Is, Lacoste asks, the longing for the *eschaton* – understood as consciousness-of-desire – really an eschatological event? Is the fate of the *desideratum* to pass incognito among the conditions – such as boredom and fatigue – that being-in-the-world dictates to experience?

As someone associated with the post-metaphysical 'theological turn' in phenomenology, Lacoste is unlikely to assign, as Agamben does, any one thing the status of a metaphysical operator; he wishes simply to preserve the 'formal plurality'[113] in which the world appears. Here phenomena (particularly 'irregular' ones such as religious phenomena) are either dissolved or subsumed under metaphysical categories; the doctrine of pure reason, in its level of abstraction and iterability, ultimately reduces humanity to the level of the herd, without a place in the world and susceptible to domination by the will-to-power. In the experience of fatigue, in fact, 'one must trace a link from myself to the world or abandon any attempt at explanation'[114] and we 'must therefore speak of the world and about fatigue, just as we talk about a world of anguish or joy'.[115] Christianity, which negotiated the apparent scandal posed by the non-realization of its *eschaton*, 'has precisely the ability to teach humanity how to exist without drama ... in an accomplished history, devoid of ontophanic and ontopoetic promises'.[116] This existence is typically characterized as vigil.

---

[111]   On this and the relationship between the so-called 'new atheism' and natural beatitude see Rémi Brague, *Les ancres dans le Ciel: L'infrastructure métaphysique* (Paris: Éditions du Seuil, 2011), pp. 77 and 110.

[112]   'Only those realities of which the kingdom of God provides the conceptual figure, and for which the resurrection of the flesh (with its corollary in the "beatific vision") provides the hermeneutic principle'; Lacoste, *Le monde et l'absence d'œuvre*, p. 35.

[113]   'The world always appears to us in the formal plurality of worlds, among them the world of fatigue'; Lacoste, *Présence et parousie*, p. 312.

[114]   Ibid., p. 311.

[115]   Ibid., p. 312.

[116]   Able to 'cope without investing new messianic hopes in the future'; Lacoste, *Le monde et l'absence d'œuvre*, p. 38.

Vigil and Sleep

Although Nietzsche counselled 'wakefulness',[117] vigil usually has a specific religious significance. A self-declared follower of John of the Cross,[118] Lacoste draws upon an important liturgical register of 'night and vigil'.[119] Human beings live by day and by night. Although sleep, 'from which the freedom and the intentional acts of consciousness are absent, is not a part of life where we manifest who we are', this 'lesser mode of existence during the hours we devote to purely physiological operations is nevertheless essential to what we are'.[120] Only angels ignore sleep – Lacoste reminds us that the Aramaic name for angel is '"one who keeps vigil" ["*veilleur*"]'.[121] But vigil is not our perpetual mode of consciousness: keeping vigil; and sleep, as being-*less* and as indicative of being-*less* in general, reminds us that we are not masters of ourselves: '"life," in this case, has power over "existence"'. What, then, asks Lacoste, makes someone forego sleep so as to gain time for the vigil? It is a question of the victorious protest of 'existence' against 'life'. Life precedes our existence in the world.[122]

The animal can suffer sleepless nights or stay awake simply because it is hungry or afraid (and human beings can certainly remain awake for the same reasons). But, notes Lacoste, there would no sense in saying that an animal is capable of keeping vigil:

> keeping vigil cannot be the object of an obligation; it is something that can only be the object of a *desideratum*. The philosophical importance of the question should not make us forget that we do not necessarily invest ourselves in the vigil

---

[117] William Desmond notes the paradoxical 'hypnotizing effect … marvellous to behold' that Nietzsche has had on 'some of the better minds of the last century', charming us 'with the belief that at last we are waking up and no longer asleep in the nightmares of the millennia'; William Desmond, *Is There A Sabbath For Thought? Between Religion and Philosophy* (New York: Fordham University Press, 2005), p. 204.

[118] Jean-Yves Lacoste, 'Perception, Transcendence and the Experience of God', trans. Aaron Patrick Riches, in Conor Cunningham and Peter Candler (eds), *Transcendence and Phenomenology* (London: SCM Press, 2007) p. 14.

[119] Cf. The 'saved night' in Agamben, *The Open*, p. 82.

[120] Jean-Yves Lacoste, *Experience and the Absolute: Disputed Questions on the Humanity of Man*, trans. Mark Rafferty-Skehan (New York: Fordham University Press, 2004), p. 78.

[121] Lacoste wishes to determine the 'affirmative practice represented by the liturgy' by specifying 'a new register' in which its symbolic place lies: 'in the night and the vigil'; ibid., p. 78. He continues: '[O]ne might be justified in affirming that the attention that he devotes to and his expectation of God symbolically assume the nocturnal character of the vigil in which, every ethical duty having been honored, man gives to the Absolute the time (and thus the being) which he might otherwise have given to sleep'.

[122] Lacoste, *Présence et parousie*, p. 163.

for the most laudable reasons: though we see nothing but futility in his actions, the reveler [*fêtard*] also keeps vigil.[123]

In struggling to 'exist' a little longer 'the time of vigil is truly our time ... time which we gain at the expense of ... pure biological necessities'; that is, beyond the ontological satisfaction of serenity. And although we are not accountable to any authority for this time, even our rest has a political dimension:

> To deliberately deprive me of sleep, or of the sleep necessary to my good health, would be tantamount to abuse; I have the right to expect that the state or the company, except in cases of emergency, leave me sufficient time to sleep. The act of keeping vigil appears to us then as the purest form of the self positing itself, as the epitome of an affirmation of our freedom.[124]

In its decentring of human subjectivity, liturgical time is diverted time (a time of inoperativity, time 'given over'). Boredom, *pace* Heidegger, reveals that this time can also be experienced as wasted time: impatience reappears, wishing to put an end to this *temps mort*, this dead time (to devote it, Lacoste notes sardonically, to 'an indisputably more "interesting" activity, such as theological work'[125]). The bored consciousness wastes its time. It might compensate for this wasted time and transform the dialogue it would like to establish with God into a soliloquy and thereby retake possession of this time.[126] This phenomenology of the liturgy suggests that boredom might be a principal mood of nocturnal experience. Can man become bored with facing God? As provocative as that may seem, the answer must be yes. It would 'be contradictory for man to be completely eschatologically satisfied with the Absolute'.[127] The nocturnal nonexperience is, however, not eschatological and by 'precariously distancing himself from history, the man who prays signifies and anticipates the accomplishment of this history'.[128]

Since God is 'always greater' (*Deus semper maior*) and resists conceptualization, the act of 'making oneself present' that inaugurates liturgy cannot help being affected by the distance which remains between God (or the Absolute) and whoever prays. Liturgical experience is by no means ecstatic.[129] As Lacoste argues,

---

[123]   Lacoste, *Experience and the Absolute*, p. 79.

[124]   'Once our inevitable allocation of work, whose distribution is necessary, foreseeable and commonplace, has been completed, and proves that we remain in possession of a fundamental right: that of proving, by the content we give to our vigil (which we can spend doing philosophy, writing poetry, or praying – and many other things besides), the surplus of meaning we give to our humanity'; ibid., p. 79.

[125]   Ibid., p. 149.

[126]   Ibid., pp. 148–9.

[127]   Ibid., p. 148.

[128]   Ibid., p. 78.

[129]   Ibid., p. 26.

'[i]nexperience has no hold over knowledge' and actually permits its rationality – that of Schelling and Kierkegaard – to unfold 'while contradistinguishing itself as clearly as possible from religious emotionalism'.[130] Nonetheless, it does exert a hold over the present, which is therefore not structured primarily by the impatient expectation of some promised *parousia*, or an earthly satisfaction which it has promised itself. Instead, as a work of an *ascesis* (of making oneself present and waiting), one might well understand that this time can be one of *theologically profound boredom*.[131]

Conclusion: The Eschatological Consummation of Fatigue

Theological reflection upon boredom and fatigue represents a call to impurity:[132] an end, perhaps, to the distinctions between faith and reason, mind and body, and the debate over an elusive 'pure nature'. It is also recognition of a certain porosity between theology and philosophy, at least in the continental tradition.

It is also an affirmation of life: in contradistinction to Agamben, these are not the non-states prior to some unspecified captivation scheduled to be overcome in the post-human condition – they are basic and constant conditions of humanity. Subjected to proper philosophical and theological reflection, boredom and fatigue may offer a reparative to the reduction of humanity to animality, to nothing more than a herd mentality at risk of being dominated by the will-to-power. For phenomenology, the human form is the foundation of the world's meaning; for theology, the embodiment of God (in the Incarnation) is the basis of the moral and physical integrity of those bodies, whose meaning resides in their being in the image of Christ.[133] Lacoste's own post-Heideggerian analysis suggests that – as Barth suggested – boredom is theologically constitutive of any coherent anthropology.

In his recent enquiry into God and Being, George Pattison makes the suggestion that possibility represents 'a kind of trace of non-being within Being, the index of a given entity's mutability and corruptibility and, since possibility is a feature of the sublunary world in general, a marker of the world's falling-short of true Being'.[134] Thus conceived, the phenomenological attention that boredom and nihility receive is due to their capacity to reveal the negative potential of possibility. Unlike his

---

[130]   Ibid., p. 148.

[131]   Fatigue demonstrates that 'the logic of work is not the most human of logics'; Lacoste, *Présence et parousie*, p. 320.

[132]   Cf. Espen Dahl's comments on Radical Orthodoxy in *Phenomenology and the Holy: Religious Experience After Husserl* (London: SCM Press, 2010), pp. 266–8.

[133]   Cf. Stephen H. Webb, *Jesus Christ, Eternal God: Heavenly Flesh and the Metaphysics of Matter* (Oxford: Oxford University Press, 2011).

[134]   George Pattison, *God and Being: An Enquiry* (Oxford: Oxford University Press, 2011), p. 295.

friend Jean-Luc Marion – who remains a philosopher of experience, and therefore closer to Maurice Blanchot (who writes, like Marion, of an excess of experience) – Lacoste treats religious phenomena as (potentially) *inexperienced*: 'It is not necessary for a presence to be total for it to delight us ... it can happen that anyone or anything that delighted us yesterday bores us today (as the angels themselves, according to Origen, were capable of being bored by the presence of God)'.[135]

This not only remains truer to the day-to-day experiences of so many believers (phenomenologically speaking there is no difference between a congregation after a church service than before; indeed, as Lacoste has shown, the most profound mood of liturgy is probably boredom), but it allows (liturgical) revelation more room than what has already been specified by phenomenology. Michel Henry (another philosopher for whom life was pre-eminent) and Lacoste both agree that humanity is not fully explicable in terms of worldliness, and wish to construe the human being as one that exceeds the strictures of Being-in-the-world. However, unlike Henry, Lacoste insists that flesh and blood humanity never is completely free from the strictures of Being-in-the-world. Here rest and sleep are more than physical necessities; however provisional or marginal,[136] they represent micro-eschatologies of the kingdom or a fleeting 'taste'[137] of happiness to come, brief pauses in a life of vigil.

---

[135]   Jean-Yves Lacoste, 'The Phenomenality of Anticipation', trans. Ronald Mendoza-De Jesús and Neal DeRoo, in Neal DeRoo and John Panteleimon Manoussakis (eds), *Phenomenology and Eschatology: Not Yet in the Now* (Farnham: Ashgate, 2009), p. 26.

[136]   Lacoste, *Présence et parousie*, p. 320.

[137]   Lacoste, *Le monde et l'absence d'œuvre*, p. 22.

SECTION THREE
Life and Spirituality

Chapter 8

The Spirituality of Human Life

Lorenz Moises J. Festin

Introduction

As a reality made up of multifarious aspects, human life requires a holistic perspective to make sense thereof. Although the fundamental significance of life in its various forms has to do with biological existence, there is a comprehensive approach to understanding human life that could lead to a better appreciation of its various dimensions, including human spirituality.

There are three parts to this chapter. In the first, I discuss how life is essentially an unfolding. Here I employ Aristotle's general interpretation of life as an actualization of a potentiality, in relation to which his notion of *ergon* ('function') and *energeia* ('activity') proves to be decisive. Aristotle argues that the main reason for the variety of life forms is the diversity of principles that stand behind it. And in this regard one can see the importance of using the instrument of analogy in understanding human life in relation to the other life forms because the former diverges radically from the latter. The second part then focuses on the purposiveness of life. Here the concept of *eudaimonia* or 'happiness' enters in and is interpreted as human being's ultimate good. Very often this ultimate good is understood purely as an end to be pursued, and human life is likewise treated simply as a purposive task. My interpretation, on the other hand, exploits the significance of the Greek words. I maintain that a better and more coherent approach to the problem of *eudaimonia* would be to see it as an actualization of human potentiality, which is best illustrated by the affinity between the two aforementioned Greek terms.

The last part tackles the transcendental element in human life. While human life and the end to which it directs itself consist in the actualization of human being's characteristic task, one must not take for granted that human existence has the tendency to go beyond its capacity and the mere realization thereof. And although Aristotle writes only of a divine element in human being, Thomas Aquinas on that basis already conceptualizes a more spiritual and otherworldly understanding of human ends. I conclude by pointing out that human life is ultimately spiritual both in its foundation and object. Following Aristotle's line of reasoning, I will argue that, on the basis of its potentials, human being has a spiritual life and that it can develop a spirituality that tends towards a life beyond biological and perceptual existence. My main contention here is that human reason is not just a human capacity among many others, but one that opens human being up to a possibility that allows it to pursue a deeper spiritual life.

Human Life as Actualization

Aristotle's insights about human life have their roots in his interest in biology. As a biologist, the Stagirite is not unacquainted with what distinguishes a living thing from that which is non-living. Aristotle's conceptualization of life can thus be said to be firmly grounded in everyday experience. A living thing, in its most basic sense, is understood as something capable of initiating an activity by itself. In *De anima* for instance, Aristotle writes: 'Of natural bodies some have life, others not; by life we mean self-nutrition and growth and decay'.[1] Again, shortly after that, he reiterates the same argument by saying: 'We resume our inquiry from a fresh starting-point by calling attention to the fact that what has a soul in it differs from what has not in that the former displays life'.[2]

It is in view of this capacity for auto-activity that Aristotle differentiates among the various life forms and for that matter among the different types of souls, which account for the diversity of life exhibited by living things. Animal life is to be distinguished from plant life in that the former manifests other forms of auto-activity not present in the latter, which means that a distinction must likewise be made between an animal soul and the soul of a plant, for by soul is meant the principle that accounts for the activities that a living thing displays. Aristotle accordingly proposes that we understand life not in one singular sense. For example, he writes: 'Now this word ["life"] has more than one sense, and provided any one alone of these is found in a thing we say that a thing is living – viz. thinking or perception or local movement and rest, or movement in the sense of nutrition, decay and growth'.[3]

For Aristotle, life is associated with the performance of certain activities, included among which are the exclusively human acts of thinking and perception. But what Aristotle regards as fundamental to 'life' is the activity manifested by the most basic among living things. This means that anything alive or living must at least have the power of self-nutrition. From the Stagirite's perspective, this is the basic requirement for a thing to be considered as having life. And plants have precisely this capacity. Still, insofar as this is just the most basic type of life, one must acknowledge that there are other forms which are far more complex. Aristotle writes:

---

[1]   Aristotle, *De anima* 412a13–14. The English translation of all the Aristotelian texts cited in this chapter is from Jonathan Barnes (ed.), *The Complete Works of Aristotle: The Revised Oxford Translation* (Princeton: Princeton University Press, 1984).

[2]   Aristotle, *De anima* 413a21–3.

[3]   Ibid., 413a23–5.

> This [i.e. the capacity for self-nutrition] is the originative power the possession of which leads us to speak of things as *living* at all, but it is the possession of sensation that leads us for the first time to speak of living things as *animals*; for even those beings which possess no power for local movement but do possess the power of sensation we call animals and not merely living things.[4]

The manner in which Aristotle differentiates animal life from plant life can also clarify the novelty and difference human life bears in comparison with both animal and plant life. Considering that life, as Aristotle has pointed out, is not to be understood simplistically in one singular sense, we must not then treat life in human being as totally the same as the other forms thereof. But neither is it to be viewed as totally different from them.

The reality of life as found in human being can hardly be reduced to the activities found in plants, such as self-nutrition, growth and decay, or to the other activities displayed by animals, such as sensation and local movement. Human being manifests activities other than these, including thinking, reflection and reasoning. And yet, human life can neither be regarded as something totally heterogeneous to the more basic forms of life. After all, human life in itself involves also those activities exhibited by plants and animals. More specifically, the capacity for self-nutrition is so basic in every living thing that it always forms part of any type of life, which is exactly what prompted Aristotle to say that the other capacities of living things necessarily presuppose it. Thus, he states: 'The power of self-nutrition can be separated from the other powers mentioned, but not they from it – in mortal beings at least. The fact is obvious in plants, for it is the only psychic power they possess'.[5]

All this suggests that, in relation to other forms of life, the life of human being ought to be understood analogically. That means that while there are similarities that can be detected between human life and other life forms, one must not ignore the great differences that exist between them. There are, of course, certain elements in subhuman life forms which can help in making sense of human life. But the latter transcends the former significantly, in that it displays capacities which defy comparison with the potentialities present in subhuman beings. This should caution us then against understanding human capacities and activities such as thinking and reflection exclusively according to the structure or auto-activities of life in its most basic form.

Analogy is one instrument Aristotle frequently employs in his writings, comparing heterogeneous things despite their fundamental diversity. Still, it is on account of this diversity that, in such a comparison, one must consider not so much the similarities as the differences. And this is where we encounter the importance and usefulness of analogy. For in analogy, similarities between two essentially divergent things are sought and established, in order to gain some insight into the

---

[4]   Ibid., 413b1–3.

[5]   Ibid., 413a31–3.

lesser known thing by employing the other and more known thing as illustration. Such is what Aristotle in fact does in comparing plants and animals; he sees some resemblance and equivalence between them. Consider for instance the analogy he makes between these two different forms of life. He writes: 'The parts of plants in spite of their extreme simplicity are organs; e.g. the leaf serves to shelter the pericarp, the pericarp to shelter the fruit, while the roots of plants are analogous to the mouth of the animals, both serving for the absorption of food'.[6]

In view of all this, we can ask, in what way can human life be understood? And, how can we employ analogy better to appreciate the implications for human life? One basic point about Aristotle's insight about life is the principle in which it is rooted. And this is what he means by the soul. The soul is what accounts for what a living thing can actualize. The activities of a living entity are actualizations of its capacities, and these are determined by the kind of soul it possesses. Accordingly, Aristotle regards the soul as the first actuality a living entity receives, for it defines the sort of thing it is. But there is a further actualization that takes place, and this is when the living thing displays in its activities the potentialities that its soul enables it to possess. Aristotle states: 'It is obvious that the soul is an actuality like knowledge; for both sleeping and waking presuppose the existence of soul, and of these waking corresponds to reflecting, sleeping to knowledge possessed but not employed, and knowledge of something is temporally prior'.[7]

The soul is the basis of the very activities displayed by a living entity. It accounts for the potentialities it can actualize. The problem of which activities the human soul enables human being to accomplish – and, for that matter, which kind of life this might be – is something that Aristotle tackles not only in *De anima* but also and even more extensively in the *Nicomachean Ethics*. That is because in the latter he does not only describe the constitution of human life and the principle behind it, but also considers the question of its goal and fulfilment, as well as accounting for its tendency towards transcendence.

Happiness and the Goal of Human Life

In the *Nicomachean Ethics*, Aristotle explains human life in terms of the characteristic function (*ergon*) the human soul performs. It is also in relation to this that human being's ultimate end (*telos*) is explained. Human life is fully actualized when human being attains *eudaimonia*, its ultimate end, by realizing its function.

Already in Book One of his *Ethics*, Aristotle offers a formula by which human being's ultimate good might be understood. What he does first is to point out the characteristic *ergon* of human being, identifying it as 'an active life of the element that has a rational principle'.[8] Eventually, he comes up with a very formal

---

6   Ibid., 412a28–b3.

7   Ibid., 412a23–6.

8   Aristotle, *Nicomachean Ethics* 1098a3–4.

definition of *eudaimonia* as an 'activity of soul in conformity with excellence'.[9] This suggests that the goal of every human being is not simply an object external to himself or herself, but an activity which is characteristic of the agent and which is done excellently. What this amounts to in concrete terms, nonetheless, has been a subject of much dispute. Some commentators would aver that what Aristotle means by this is nothing more than purely contemplative activity, whereas there are those who would ascribe many other human activities thereto. Anthony Kenny, for example, adheres to an intellectualist or dominant perspective whereby *eudaimonia* is interpreted as consisting only in the exercise of the intellectual excellence of *sophia* or philosophic wisdom, which is essentially an activity of contemplation. This would then mean that moral virtues and the exercise thereof are nothing but instruments or means towards the achievement of *eudaimonia*. Kenny maintains that the intellectualist or dominant argument 'essentially concerns Aristotle's view of the hierarchy of choice: that is to say, the structure to be given to the pattern, in human life and striving, of one thing's being done for the sake of another, of A's being chosen for the sake of B'.[10] In this regard, he refers to a passage in the *Nicomachean Ethics* (*NE*), wherein Aristotle states:

> We call that which is in itself worthy of pursuit more complete than that which is worthy of pursuit for the sake of something else, and that which is never desirable for the sake of something else more complete than the things that are desirable both in themselves and for the sake of that other thing, and therefore we call complete without qualification that which is always desirable in itself and never for something else.[11]

But one can ask: Does one really carry out virtuous acts for the purpose of attaining happiness? Are not acts of virtue ends for themselves? Are they pursued also for the sake of happiness? Kenny's opinion in this matter would be that while virtues may be regarded as desired for themselves, nothing prevents one from pursuing them to achieve happiness. *Eudaimonia* alone would be the good which is never aimed at for some other end. Or, to use Kenny's term, it alone is a 'supreme' or 'endy' good;[12] one does not desire happiness for the purpose of attaining something else. Accordingly, Kenny asserts: 'The position of *NE* 10 is surely that the contemplative *possess* the moral virtues, but that their exercise will not constitute part of his happiness. That will be constituted by contemplation alone'.[13]

The so-called inclusivist perspective, on the other hand, insists that there is a multiplicity of activities that constitutes *eudaimonia*. Contrary to Kenny's

---

[9]   Ibid., 1098a16–17.
[10]   Anthony John Patrick Kenny, *Aristotle on the Perfect Life* (New York: Clarendon Press, 1992), p. 7.
[11]   Aristotle, *Nicomachean Ethics* 1097a30–4.
[12]   See Kenny, *Aristotle*, p. 16.
[13]   Ibid., p. 91.

interpretation, this perspective understands the completeness of *eudaimonia* as signifying not so much its being the last or the most final in the series of means and ends, as the inclusiveness of its constitution. That is to say, more than being the ultimate point of one's pursuit, *eudaimonia* is the most desirable because it is the most comprehensive and all-embracing. J.L. Ackrill is perhaps the most notable among those who adopt this perspective. He likewise makes use of the same 'for-the-sake' argument as Kenny, but his point is entirely different; namely, to show why *eudaimonia* cannot consist only in a single activity. He writes:

> The idea that some things are done for their own sake and may yet be done for the sake of something else is precisely the idea Aristotle will need and use in talking of good actions and *eudaimonia*. For *eudaimonia* – what all men want – is not, he insists, the result or outcome of a lifetime's effort; it is not something to look forward to (like a contented retirement), it is life, enjoyable and worth while all through. Various bits of it must themselves be enjoyable and worth while, not just means for bringing about subsequent bits. That the primary ingredients of *eudaimonia* are for the sake of *eudaimonia* is not incompatible with their being ends themselves; for *eudaimonia* is constituted by activities that are ends in themselves.[14]

Ackrill thus identifies *eudaimonia* with some sort of a fulfilling life, made up of activities that are themselves fulfilling. In this regard, it cannot simply consist in one single activity like contemplation, but must include all the ingredients that compose a worthwhile existence. Aristotle, according to Ackrill, is thus saying that '*eudaimonia*, being absolutely final and genuinely sufficient, is more desirable than anything else in that it *includes* everything desirable in itself'.[15]

The debate between the dominant and inclusivist interpretations is probably irresolvable. One thing that is often ignored though in these interpretations is the fact that the Stagirite specifically identifies *eudaimonia* as an activity, the Greek equivalent of which (namely, *energeia*) bears a lot of implications. For the very term *energeia* expresses the actualization of the potentiality that the *ergon* represents, a power that is assigned to the human soul. As Aristotle himself points out in *Metaphysics*: '[For] the action [*ergon*] is the end [*telos*], and the actuality [*energeia*] is the action [*ergon*]. Therefore even the *word* "actuality" [*energeia*] is derived from action [*ergon*], and points to the fulfillment'.[16] What we notice here is the distinct manner in which Aristotle plays with words and underlines the significance of these two Greek words, *ergon* and *energeia*, by pointing to their etymological connection. By closely tying up the two words, Aristotle is in effect

---

[14]   J.L. Ackrill, 'Aristotle on *Eudaimonia*', in Amélie Rorty (ed.), *Essays on Aristotle's Ethics* (Los Angeles: University of California Press, 1980), p. 19.

[15]   Ibid., p. 20.

[16]   Aristotle, *Metaphysics* 1050a21–3.

suggesting that *energeia*, translated as 'activity' in English, is in its most basic sense the activation or actualization of *ergon* or 'function'.

That *eudaimonia* is an *energeia* entails that we have to go beyond the distinction often made between means and end. Such a differentiation is certainly clear in what Aristotle refers to as *poiésis* or 'craft', which is a productive activity or an act of making. In this kind of activity, we can easily tell between the act of making and the product generated. But that is not how *eudaimonia* ought to be understood. For happiness is not merely a product or an ensuing effect; it is an *energeia* or actualization. *Eudaimonia* is indeed a *telos* or an end, but it is not simply a consequence. Instead, it consists in an activity that actualizes a capacity or potentiality.

Here Aristotle's distinction between *energeia* and *kinésis* becomes relevant. Translated as 'movement' in English, *kinésis* represents an activity that remains always incomplete in its unfolding. It is never complete because once completed the activity comes to an end. And this is reflected in Aristotle's definition thereof. He writes: 'kinesis is the act of being in potency as such'.[17] This means that movement is an actualization, yes, but not yet fully realized. Thus in *Physics*, Aristotle further states: '*Kinésis* seems to be a kind of *energeia* but imperfect'.[18] Productive activities are basically a *kinésis* type of activity. Building a house, for example, involves a movement whereby a product is gradually being generated. And once the product is finished, the construction ceases. Here, one can see clearly how the activity of building represents the means towards attaining the product, which in this case is the constructed house. *Energeia*, on the other hand, indicates an activity that is complete at every moment. That is because it consists in the sheer actualization of a potentiality. For example, when one sees with one's eyes, one is really actualizing the potentiality of a sense function. And such actualization happens at every moment of one's act of seeing. The actualization of the capacity of seeing is complete at every stage of the act. That is why it cannot be described in terms of speed or slowness. One cannot, for example, say, 'I see the thing quickly [or slowly]', without making a ridiculous statement. But one may rightly say, 'We are constructing the house quickly [or slowly]'.[19]

That *poiésis* resembles the structure of a *kinésis* is probably the reason that Aristotle contrasts it with *praxis* or action. He writes: 'For while making has an end other than itself, action cannot; for good action itself is its end'.[20] Indeed, Aristotle relates the actualization that constitutes *eudaimonia* to the 'actions' (*praxeis* in Greek) that one does. And these include morally virtuous actions. For these actions themselves represent the actualization not only of moral virtues which are states of character, but also of the specifically human *ergon*, which Aristotle identifies with rationality. This is because the exercise of moral virtues cannot take place

---

[17] Aristotle, *Physics* 201a10–11.

[18] Ibid., 201b3.

[19] See Aristotle, *Nicomachean Ethics* 1173a29–b4.

[20] Ibid., 1140b4–7.

without the involvement of reason and the intellectual virtue pertinent to them, namely *phronésis* or practical wisdom. Hence, in defining moral virtues, Aristotle explicitly mentions the role reason plays in exercising these virtues. He writes:

> With regard to the excellences in *general* we have stated their genus in outline, viz. that they are means, and that they are states, and that they tend by their own nature to the doing of the acts by which they are produced, and that they are in our power and voluntary, *and act as right reason prescribes.*[21]

Eudaimonia is thus instantiated even in morally virtuous actions. For they, too, constitute the actualization in which *eudaimonia* consists: namely, the *energeia* giving actuality to the exclusively human *ergon* of reasoning. And if human life finds its fulfilment in *eudaimonia*, then we must understand the dynamics of life as taking place not in a linear or one-dimensional manner, whereby there is a movement from one point to another, but in a multidimensional manner wherein its fulfilment can happen in many ways and in the many activities human being can engage in. Human life thus is not just a *kinésis* or movement. Rather, it is an unfolding of actualization.

This brings us back to what Aristotle discusses in the *De anima*, wherein he maintains that the soul constitutes an initial actuality of a living organism, enabling it to possess a potentiality for a further actualization. 'That is why', Aristotle asserts, 'the soul is an actuality of the first kind of a natural body having life potentially in it'.[22] He further states:

> We must not understand by that which is potentially capable of living what has lost the soul it had, but only what still retains it; but seeds and fruits are bodies which are potentially of that sort. Consequently, while waking is actuality in the sense corresponding to the cutting and seeing, the soul is actuality in the sense corresponding to sight and the power in the tool; the body corresponds to what is in potentiality; as the pupil *plus* the power of sight constitutes the eye, so the soul *plus* the body constitutes the animal.[23]

This has implications for human life. For, in view of the human soul's *ergon* having to do with rationality, the capacity of the human being appears to always go beyond the limits that his or her actual life imposes. And here one can see why, as pointed out earlier, we must not simply understand human capacities in terms of the structure and actualization of potentialities found in subhuman entities, and why the instrument of analogy is to be applied whenever the operation of subhuman capacities is employed as illustration to explain the function of human potentialities.

---

[21]   Ibid., 1114b26–30.
[22]   Aristotle, *De anima* 412a27–8.
[23]   Ibid., 412b25–413 a3.

According to Aristotle, human life is an actualization of a potentiality, which is identified with the rational soul. The life every human being manifests is the realization of a capacity present in it. But this actualization of life among human beings does not happen in the same way as it does in subhuman beings. On account of the nature of the *ergon* characteristic of human beings, human life must also be understood in terms of its openness to what transcends its actuality. For human life tends to go beyond the factuality of the present, in that it seeks its full actualization not simply in the satisfaction of its biological requirements and in the realization of its capacities, but pushes itself towards what the mind can probe into. In other words, aside from consisting merely in a movement from potentiality to actuality, human life involves the act of directing itself towards that which reason discovers and presents as objects for contemplation. And, were it only possible for human beings, they would have to abandon all the other activities in favour of it. But the fact is human life has other and more fundamental requirements, and the pursuit of what lies beyond these requirements necessitates and is built upon their satisfaction. For contemplative activity can only take place when the basic necessities of human life have already been addressed.

Now that gives us some insight as to why Aristotle does not assign great importance to wealth. For we need only so much. And if the bare minimum amount thereof would suffice to fulfil our basic needs, then we need not spend our time and energy accumulating material possessions, because we should focus ourselves instead on the more noble task of contemplation. Aristotle writes:

> we must not think that the man who is to be happy will need many things or
> great things, merely because he cannot be blessed without external goods; for
> self-sufficiency and action do not depend on excess, and we can do noble acts
> without ruling earth and sea; for even with moderate advantages one can act
> excellently … and it is enough that we should have so much as that; for the life
> of the man who is active in accordance with excellence will be happy.[24]

Aristotle thus urges his readers to aim at maximizing as much as possible their engagement in contemplative activity. It is true: human that we are, we also need to satisfy the cravings of our body and the exigencies of living in society. But we must work for the greatest possible opportunity to actualize our highest potentiality and to activate that divine element in us, which is no other than our reason. For our rationality is that one thing that sets us apart from all other living entities. Aristotle writes:

> If intellect is divine, then, in comparison with man, the life according to it is
> divine in comparison with human life. But we must not allow those who advise
> us, being [human], to think of human things, and being mortal, of mortal things,
> but must, so far as we can, make ourselves immortal, and strain every nerve to

---

[24]   Aristotle, *Nicomachean Ethics* 1179a1–9.

live in accordance with the best thing in us; for even if it be small in bulk, much more does it in power and worth surpass everything.[25]

The Transcendence of Human Life

Human life, according to Aristotle, is not simply founded on *ergon*, and it is not exhausted in the mere realization of its potentialities. There is also that aspect in it that pushes it beyond sheer capacities, even to such an extent that, if only it were possible, it would let go of the opportunities to actualize all those capacities and simply allow itself to be consumed by the object that reason presents to it. We can describe the rational function of human being as some kind of an aperture, which allows it to set its gaze beyond the actualities of the present moment. In view of that possibility, the human individual could always embark on a quest higher than their previous challenges. And this only corroborates the fact that human being is meant for something much higher and greater than its mundane concerns.

The implication of this Aristotelian teaching has a far-reaching consequence. For one thing, it provided Aquinas with the material necessary to advance his argument concerning human being's ultimate end as attainable only in the afterlife. Building on Aristotle's suggestion that human beings maximize the exercise of what is divine in them, Aquinas maintains not only that happiness consists in *Beatitudo* or the beatific vision of God, but also that only God can provide human life with the capacity to achieve such a vision. Surely, *Beatitudo*, as the beatific vision of God, quite resembles *eudaimonia*, envisioned by Aristotle as consisting in contemplative activity. But, unlike the Aristotelian notion, *Beatitudo* cannot be attained in the present life, because it requires union with God. Aquinas thus writes:

> But in men, according to their present state of life, the final perfection is in respect of an operation whereby man is united to God: but this operation neither can be continual, nor, consequently, is it one only, because operation is multiplied by being discontinued. And for this reason in the present state of life, perfect happiness cannot be attained by man.[26]

Aquinas's argument is both simple and complex. He certainly acknowledges the fact that, given its rational faculty, human being is able to pursue not only that which is sensible and particular, and is thus valid in the here and now, but also that which is intellectual and thus holds true always and everywhere. That is to say, reason enables the human person to set as their goal something that is absolutely good and most worthy of their pursuit. And that would direct them to some reality that exists beyond the realm of what is finite and temporary. Since human being

---

[25]   Ibid., 1177b30–1178a2.

[26]   Thomas Aquinas, *Summa theologica* I-II q.3, a.2, ad 4, trans. and ed. Fathers of the English Dominican Province (Westminster: Christian Classics, 1948).

has the capacity for something greater than what is earthly, it can and must aim at the best possible good available to it. Eventually Aquinas would identify this with divine reality, which represents the best and most important being. He writes:

> if man's happiness is an operation, it must needs be man's highest operation. Now man's highest operation is that of his highest power in respect of its highest object: and his highest power is the intellect, whose highest object is the Divine Good, which is the object, not of the practical, but of the speculative intellect.[27]

Such openness of human being towards divine reality is quite significant in understanding its ultimate good because, according to Aquinas, the object to which this human aperture is directed is what really defines the beatific activity. In fact, he argues, 'since happiness is an operation ... the true nature of Happiness is taken from the object, which specifies the act, and not from the subject'.[28] This means that the decisive factor in human being's happiness is no longer its *ergon* or characteristic capacity and its actualization but that to which this actualizing pursuit is directed. Indeed, this would be a total departure from the initial way in which human life is understood. For its fulfilment is no longer simply identified with actualization or activity, but with its object and the possession thereof. And this is what made Aquinas differentiate between the subjective and objective aspects of *Beatitudo*. Subjectively, human happiness is beatific vision; objectively, it is the divine being which is the object of such a vision.

Aquinas would further explain that, given its limited power, human being can only go up to a certain extent in its quest for that best possible good. Beyond its natural capacity for knowledge and reason, human being needs to be empowered by God to be able to fully actualize that possibility. Human being's rational and intellectual capability could, of course, direct it to what is absolute and infinite. But to actually pursue and attain such a goal would require a far greater capacity on its part. And in Aquinas's account such possibility and power is provided by God, who is the very goal of human pursuit. He writes: 'the created intellect cannot see the essence of God, unless God by His grace unites Himself to the created intellect, as an object made intelligible to it'.[29] Aquinas further clarifies his point in his reply to the third objection:

> The sense of sight, as being altogether material, cannot be raised up to immateriality. But our intellect, or the angelic intellect, inasmuch as it is elevated above matter in its own nature, can be raised up above its own nature to a higher level by grace ... it can be raised up to know separate subsisting substance, and separate subsisting existence.[30]

---

27   Ibid., I-II q.3, a.5.
28   Ibid., I-II q.5, a.3, ad 2.
29   Ibid., I q.12, a.4.
30   Ibid., I q.12, a.4, ad 3.

Thus, Aristotle's reference to human reason as the divine element in human being acquires a far greater significance and implication when Aquinas states that, unlike the faculty of sight, human intelligence is capable of attaining to the divine when raised above its nature by means of grace. Here Aquinas does not only echo Aristotle's teaching on contemplative activity but also makes a further claim that the object itself provides human intelligence with the means to possess it. Hence, although human being by nature does not have the capacity for beatific vision, God who is the object of such vision makes it possible for human being to attain it. And this happens, in Aquinas's teaching, on account of God's gratuitous offer of grace to human being. This makes grace then into some kind of potentiality or capacity supernaturally implanted in the human individual to enable them to exercise an activity – beatific vision – which they cannot possibly carry out on their own.

What is consistent in these activities constituting life in its various forms is the pattern whereby life unfolds from a capacity possessed by the living being. To use the categories of the Stagirite, life would simply be the subsequent actuality of a being, which is possible only if that being possesses the first actuality, which is the soul and the power for such a life. And in the case of human being, that power goes beyond the realm of what is material and temporal. For that very power that is characteristic of human existence opens it up to something much greater and farther than its bare and unaided power could ever reach.

For this reason, Aquinas argues that human being has to possess a far higher faculty which would enable it to pursue its highest and ultimate good. Such a power is something it can only receive from the very object of its pursuit, which is a being far greater than it. Since the goal that human being's natural capacity directs and opens it to is more perfect than it, the possibility of *attaining* that goal can be realized only when that more perfect goal (God) enables attainment, by giving human being (through grace) the power (human soul and potentiality) to do so. Such is how Aquinas understands God as the object of human being's contemplative activity in which *Beatitudo* consists: it is possible only when God provides human being with the power to take the divine reality as the object of its contemplative vision. Aquinas states: 'Now everlasting life is an end exceeding the proportion of human nature ... Hence man, by his natural endowments, cannot produce meritorious works proportionate to everlasting life; and for this a higher force is needed, viz., the force of grace'.[31]

Aquinas's account of *Beatitudo* readily translates to an assertion that human life ultimately is spiritual in its highest possible mode. And yet even human being's natural capacity, which includes its intellectual and rational powers, is essentially spiritual. The mere fact that human reason can go beyond the materiality and particularity of the sensible data already evidences the human capacity for what is spiritual. This is in fact what prompts Aristotle to describe it as a divine element in us. Similarly, Aquinas points out that the human intellect by its nature is elevated above matter.

---

[31]   Ibid., I-II q.109, a.5.

Spirituality in its most basic sense is contrasted with materiality, in that that which is spiritual is understood as non-material in the same way that that which is material is non-spiritual. But, then again, that is only the most fundamental mode in which human being's spirituality is displayed. For the very reality that serves as the object of human being's highest and ultimate pursuit is spiritual *par excellence*. And this can be understood to be in the form of eternal ideas, as in Plato, or of truth, as in Aristotle, or of the personal divine being of God, as in Aquinas. Aristotle himself associates human happiness with the divine not only because it consists in the activation of that divine element in us, but also because the object of such activity is itself divine and noble. Thus, he writes:

> If happiness is activity in accordance with excellence, it is reasonable that it should be in accordance with the highest excellence; and this will be that of the best thing in us. Whether it be intellect or something else that is this element which is thought to be our natural ruler and guide and to take thought of things noble and divine, whether it be itself also divine or only the most divine element in us, the activity of this in accordance with its proper excellence will be complete happiness.[32]

The Challenge to a Deeper Human Life as Spirituality

To realize thus the best good possible and available to it, human being ought to take the path towards a deeper and more profound spirituality. This requires not only the decision and choice to harness that divine element in us which distinguishes us from other living entities and which allows us to probe into what transcends us, but also the deliberate act of avoiding any reduction of human life to mere biological or perceptual operations. Indeed, both human being's natural characteristic power and the highest good at which it can possibly ever aim are essentially spiritual. And this is because both the highest potentiality it has and the object to which it directs itself have the marks of divinity.

Taken in this sense, human spirituality would no longer simply be descriptive of one's conviction in regard to the existence of a supernatural being. Instead, it consists in a particular mode of human life whereby one exists from the core and interiority of one's being. Nevertheless, very often this leads to the question of the supernatural because the spiritual mode of existence always involves a yearning for the absolute. Reason in itself – the very faculty that makes human life a spiritual existence – is hardly satisfied with the particular and temporal but only with the ultimate and unconditioned. On account of this, human being always finds itself in search of the Absolute.

Of course, human beings are naturally situated in the context of everyday life. As such, it is always possible that they be drawn toward and be preoccupied with

---

[32]   Aristotle, *Nicomachean Ethics* 1177a 12–17.

mundane concerns, which may then lead to a rather superficial existence. But this need not be the case because, in their search for their ultimate goal and in their quest for fulfilment, people discover that no single reality in this world can provide total satisfaction to their yearning. And so, while there are moments in one's life whereby one might think that a project, a goal, an entity or a person could provide the absolute fulfilment one always lacks, it is fairly reasonable to expect that one would eventually outgrow one's need for it and would even become tired of it.

Where is this restlessness coming from? Why are we never satisfied with any state of human affairs? The only way to explain this problem is to point to what we naturally pursue. We cannot settle for anything less than the absolute and the unconditioned. But nothing in this world has ever proven to be such. Accordingly, we are drawn to what lies beyond this life, and we begin to turn to what transcends it. Indeed, by recognizing the absolute and unconditioned character of our ultimate goal, we come to know the nature of human existence. Because our aspiration always surpasses and pushes beyond every object we have so far pursued and attained, we now understand that we are meant for something greater than any reality or state of affairs in this world. This likewise tells us that by nature we are not merely living organisms. There is something in our constitution that propels us to transcend sheer biological existence. And this is what Aristotle describes as the divine element in us, identifying it with our reason and intelligence.

In their life journey, people might at some point be totally consumed by various kinds of undertakings. But this does not necessarily prevent them from discovering the transitory character of such projects. On the contrary, engaging in their daily concerns is an occasion to realize that what they seek goes beyond these endeavours. This similarly gives them an opportunity to activate that which Aristotle regards as the divine element in them. For, even in the most ordinary deeds, one can still exercise one's reason and intelligence, by which one manifests oneself as a spiritual being. We can thus regard human reason and intelligence as spiritual powers because, while they are necessarily employed and involved in all sorts of human activities, they direct us ultimately towards the absolute and the unconditioned, beyond the concerns of everyday life.

Chapter 9
Two Philosophies of Life

Don Cupitt

In late antiquity, and especially during the first two or three centuries of the Christian era, it was common for philosophers to be wandering teachers. In art, and especially in Hellenistic sculpture, the philosopher is simply a Greek man of indeterminate age who carries a cloak, a book and not much else. Arriving in a city, he would seek out a suitable place for his teaching, either by renting a hall or perhaps by simply commandeering a good pitch in the *agora* or market-place. He would then attempt to win followers by criticizing other philosophers and the current state of religion, and putting forward his own teaching about the good life. It was hard work: selling your philosophy to the multitude was quite as difficult then as it is today. But being an itinerant himself, it seemed natural enough to the philosopher that he should picture all of human life as an arduous journey through time in pursuit of the Summum Bonum, the Highest Good, a goal that would be finally attained only beyond death in the eternal world that is our true and last home. At the very beginning of Christian art, Jesus himself was portrayed as having been a wandering philosopher of this type, and so too were those of his followers, from Paul to the Apologists, who had also lived as wandering evangelists.

So then, all of these itinerant teachers taught a 'Way', a version of the good life; but were they *philosophers of life* in the modern sense? Not quite, because at that time many or most thinking people were notably dualistic in outlook. A human being was a rational animal, and rationality was the distinctively human attribute. The best life was therefore the most purely rational life. Reason, reason would lead us to the eternal world. Our reason connected us with an immanent purposiveness and rationality that persuaded the entire cosmos, or with the transcendent intelligible world of timeless values, truths and meanings, or with the supernatural world of religion. And however the Supreme Good was described, it lay altogether beyond the world of our biological life, our senses and our emotions, which was relatively disparaged – so much so that for many or most teachers in that period the good life paradoxically was a life that *denied* life. We should hurry through this world, averting our eyes from its ceaseless temptations and distractions and keeping them fixed on our heavenly Goal, immortality; and so in the course of a few centuries the philosopher turned into the Christian monk.

In retrospect, it is now apparent that the most pernicious legacy of ancient Greek thought was an extraordinary supernaturalism of reason itself. A proper modern philosophy of human life could not develop until the whole Order of Reason had been demythologized and brought down to earth for good. Hume began this work, and Kant and Hegel continued it, but it approaches completion only after Darwin's works on *The Descent of Man* (1871) and on *The Expression of the Emotions* (1873). Then, in the writings of figures such as Nietzsche and William James, we begin to see philosophy working out the implications of a thoroughly immanent and biology-based understanding of human thought and human life. Only then do terms like *Lebensphilosophie* (philosophy of life) and *Lebenswelt* (lifeworld) come into use in Germany. In Britain, we are still cautious about the philosophy of life even today, fearing that it may not be considered a serious subject.

For my contribution to this collection, I offer two specimen modern philosophies of life in summary form. But before we look at the first of them, a few general points need to be made.

First, there is inevitably a close relationship between modern philosophy of life and the older religious naturalism of which Spinoza has usually been considered the greatest exponent. A philosophy of life is usually intended to serve as a replacement for traditional religious belief. It gives us a very general account of what we are, what we can know, how we should live and what we can hope for. Most of all, it seeks to reconcile us to our life, by overcoming various painful splits and oppositions in our experience – for example, between the self and God, between the self and the cosmos, between mind and body, and between language and reality. By closing these oppositions, the philosophy of life hopes to make us feel completely *at home* in the world.

There is a special difficulty about *reflexivity*. During the early nineteenth century, as the focus of philosophical attention switched from the world of logic to the human lifeworld, a world in which everything is transient, contingent and interrelated, it was soon realized that old-style universal philosophical statements about this world always seem to generate paradoxes when applied to themselves. Nietzsche was acutely aware of such paradoxes.

This explains why our first philosophy of life takes the form that it does. It is called Energetic Spinozism, or alternatively The Fountain. It was first published in 1995.[1] It is intended to conjure up a monistic picture of the human situation which, as it all clicks into place, should create a feeling of religious happiness. If it works for you, then you may well believe that it will still work equally well for the last human beings, a century or so hence. It also attempts to ward off the paradoxes of reflexivity as it goes along.

The reader is warned to go slowly, allowing a little time for the picture to build up.

* * *

---

[1]   See Don Cupitt, *The Last Philosophy* (London: SCM Press, 1995), pp. 117–20.

The Fountain: Energetic Spinozism

(to be read aloud) What is there?
1. There is at least *language*. Here we are in it; and in any case, the existence of language cannot coherently be denied, denial being itself a linguistic act. For there to be language, moving as these sentences now are in being produced and received, there must also be temporality and a discharge and scattering of energies.
2. There must be *temporality*, in the sense of unidirectional succession in the production, presentation and scanning of a chain of signs. (There need not necessarily be 'linear time' in any stronger sense, for cyclical time also may be unidirectional.)
3. There must be *scattering energies*, because uttered language needs a material 'body' to ride upon or to modulate. Language is *broadcast*, or *published*.
4. There is at least, then, an outpouring and scattering stream of language-formed events. And we do best to picture the world at large as *a beginningless, endless and outsideless stream of language-formed events* that continually pours forth and passes away. The stream of events becomes real and determinate, or 'formed', in being read as language by us.
5. By being read, in one language or another (natural, mathematical etc.), the elements of the world become experience, and by being described they become public, or 'real'. Thus the real world is the public world, which is the world-in-language, *our* world.
6. Our worst mistake is that of supposing the world of consciousness to be a private subworld within each person. No: the world of consciousness is simply the common world, the world that our language has fixed, objectified, illuminated and made public. Our consciousness is simply our participation in this common world.
7. A chain of signs like this one can claim to be an epitome of everything in so far as (a), it states that the world itself consists of lots and lots more stuff like this; and (b), the signs it contains resonate with and evoke many, many other strands in the flux of world-events.
8. Thus philosophy must (a), represent the world as a many-stranded stream of events-read-as-signs; and (b), must work somewhat as poetry does, by employing highly condensed and evocative metaphors.
9. Human life is radically linguistic, because it is language that gives to the stream of events, not only the flowing continuity, but also the *identifiable aims*, that our life requires. (To live a human life, I must not only have desires, but know what they are. Or at least what some of them are. I must have goals, and I need to be able to make up narrative accounts of how I may achieve my goals.)
10. In practical philosophy, the world is seen under totalizing metaphors that enable us to view it as a fit arena for the successful pursuit of a certain way of life.
11. All readings of the stream of events are highly selective-and-constructive.

12. When the stream of events is read from a first-person-singular standpoint, and in a vocabulary that gives priority to one's own interests and desires, then it is seen as the world of experience or *subjectivity*. (But still, my world is simply my angle upon the common world.)

13. When the stream of events is read from a third-person standpoint, then it is seen as the *objective* world – as, for example, the world of our physical-object language, or the world of some form of scientific theory.

14. In the objective world, we recognize other persons, with angles upon the world other than our own. Thus, the second-person standpoint, and with it the possibility of ethical and political thought and action, arises as a synthesis of the first-person and the third-person readings of the world.

15. This synthesis is *love*.

16. Everything is made of only one sort of stuff, namely the stream of language-formed events, and the very same bits of world-stuff may be taken up into various constructions – for example, into both your subjectivity and mine. Selfhoods overlap, it may be very considerably.

17. The happiness that comes when one realizes that one is completely immersed in and interwoven with the whole endless flux of things is *ecstatic immanence*.

18. As a living being, one is an organism composed of various organs or subsystems which have slightly different aims. (There is, for example, a potential discordance between the need to preserve one's own life and the need, at whatever cost, to pass on one's genes.) Thus there is – it seems, irremediably – some conflict of forces within the self, which shows up in every first-person account of things as the distinction between text and subtext, conscious and subconscious, and so on. This conflict is *ambivalence*. 'Mixed feelings'.

19. Ambivalence within the self is at least partly resolved and relieved by talking, by artistic expression and by theorizing the world.

20. The sign as such is a compromise-formation, and all our symbolic expressions are more unified and beautiful than we who have originated them.

21. As our productive and expressive life-activity is a continual *creation* of the world of experience, so too the happiness that comes when we see our conflicting aims and feelings resolved in the beauty of the world is *our objective redemption*, that is, our redemption achieved in and through our expression. Hence 'expressionism'.

22. When we see in the public world our own objective redemption, we see the world as being *ours* in the strongest sense; that is, we see in it the concrete universal human, reconciled and perfected. (This 'cosmic humanism' is possible because (a), we make the world look the way it does to us; and (b), the world is made of just the same stuff as the self is made of.)

23. Because there is no subjective immortality, we can be happy in recognizing in the continuance of the world our own objective immortality; and because there is no subjective redemption, we can be happy in recognizing in the beauty of the world our own objective redemption.

24. The way to this eternal happiness is by the love (above nos. 12–15) which enables us to escape from a purely first-personal or subjective view of our condition.

* * *

One is tempted to wonder, what percentage of people experienced a *frisson* as they felt all that click together? The answer is, I guess, only a small minority – probably the same minority of people as those who get a similar *frisson* from one of Barnett Newman's great scarlet rectangular paintings. In that case, the painting acts as a swimming pool for the eyes: one dives in and is blissfully drowned in ecstatic immanence.

The parallel helps me to answer the following question: Why is it that a modern democratic philosophy of life, which of course has to be a philosophy of thoroughgoing immanence, can only ever interest a small minority of people? Spinoza himself interests only a very small élite group of people like Jeeves.[2] Why? Presumably because a philosophy of immanence can offer no Grand Narrative, nor any mythology. The best it can do is to show each of us that we are parts of the Whole, that we come to be and pass away along with everything else, and that each of us can make a valuable contribution to the Whole. To this end, it conjures up a poetic image like that of the Fountain, every bit of which pours out and passes away very quickly, but which as a whole is a blissful symbol of healing and repose. Fine, but it can scarcely compete with supernatural religion, for the fact is that for most people absolute monarchy and class society still continue to be much more *interesting* than democratic society. We who are Nature's cooks and footmen, maids and gardeners, love to have that Upstairs world of 'the Quality' to gossip about. *They* set up the entire framework within which we live, *they* are keeping an eye on us, and *they* are very well aware of just how diligently we are performing our duties. *They* give to our life the 'meaning' we need. So will not a supernatural theology always be a more popular and effective philosophy of life than my updated Spinozism?

Maybe. I do have a more 'advanced' version of Energetic Spinozism, called not The Fountain, but The Torus, a second possible modern philosophy of life.[3] Yet I cannot pretend that it will either work any better than the Fountain, or attract any more interest. It was published in 2008,[4] and is here presented with more explicit reference to the religious tradition, which may perhaps make it more intelligible and attractive to those who encounter it for the first time. I call it The Religion of

---

[2]   The butler to the hapless rich gentleman of the P.G. Wodehouse 'Jeeves and Wooster' series of stories.

[3]   A solid ring-doughnut shape. Interestingly, Victorian fountains were often arranged in a circle, to produce just such a shape. It symbolizes a constant cyclical process of outpouring and return. See Don Cupitt, *The Fountain* (London: SCM Press, 2010), p. 65.

[4]   See Don Cupitt, *Above Us Only Sky* (Santa Rosa, CA: Polebridge Press, 2008), pp. 4–10.

Ordinary Life, and make two claims for it. The first is that during the past hundred and fifty years or so, since Darwin, there has been a remarkable shift in the focus of religious language from the word 'God' to the word 'Life'. And the second claim is that the religion of ordinary life really is now *demonstrably* the effective religion of ordinary people. So whereas the first of our specimen philosophies of life was invented by a philosopher, the second was discovered by empirical research. It is here presented in a philosopher's tidied-up transcription, but I do really claim that it fairly represents what, on the evidence of their own language, ordinary people currently think.

* * *

The Torus: The Religion of Ordinary Life

Life

1. *Life is everything.*
   Life is the whole human world, everything as it looks to and is experienced by the only beings who actually have a world, namely human beings with a life to live.
2. *Life is all there is.*
   Our age is now post-metaphysical. The world of life is not dependent upon, nor derived from, any other realm, nor is there any other world after it, or beyond it.
3. *Life has no outside.*
   Everything is immanent, interconnected, secondary. Everything remains within life. When we are born, we do not come *into* this world, and when we die we do not *leave* it. There is no absolute point of view from which someone can see 'the Truth', the final Truth, about life.
4. *Life is God.*
   Life is that in which 'we live and move and have our being' (Acts 17.28), within which we are formed, and of whose past we will remain part. Both our ultimate Origin and our Last End are within life. Life is now as God to us.
5. *To love life is to love God.*
   Every bit of our life is final for us, and we should treat all life as a sacred gift and responsibility. We should see our relation to life as being like an immediate relation to God. We are moved and touched by the way all living things, and not just we ourselves, spontaneously love life, affirm it and cling to it.
6. *Life is a continuous streaming process of symbolic expression and exchange.*
   The motion of language logically precedes the appearing of a formed and 'definite' world. It is in this sense that it was once said that 'In the beginning was the Word'.

Life and My Life

7. *My life is my own personal stake in life.*
   The traditional relation of the soul to God is now experienced in the form of the relation between my life and life in general. As, traditionally, one's first responsibility in religion was for the salvation of one's own soul, so now a human being's first duty is the duty to recognize that I simply am the life I have lived so far, plus the life that still remains to me.

8. *My life is all I have, and all I will ever have.*
   I must *own* my own life, in three senses: I must claim it wholly as mine, acknowledge it and assume full responsibility for the way I conduct it. I must live my own life in a way that is authentically mine. To be authentically oneself in this way – the opposite of 'living a lie' – is the first part of the contribution each of us should seek to make to life as a whole.

9. *Every human person has, in principle, an equal stake in life.*
   This principle is vital to our ideas of justice and of love for the fellow human being. Murder and other offences against the person are almost everywhere regarded as equally serious, whoever the victim is. The love of God is love and fellow-feeling for 'the neighbour' – or the fellow creature – generalized without limit until it becomes the love of all life.

10. *In human relationships, justice is first in order, but love is first in value.*
    We should esteem love most highly of all; but love itself must be based on justice, not least in parental/filial and in sexual relationships. The work of justice is to clear a level space for love.

The Limits of Life

11. *Life is subject to limits. In life, everything is subject to temporality.*
    In life, everything is held within and is subject to the movement of one-way linear time. Life is, as people say, a single ticket: there are no second chances or retakes.

12. *In life, everything is contingent.*
    In life, the one-way linear movement of time makes every moment final and every chance a last chance; but at the same time everything is contingent. This painful combination of finality with contingency is what gives rise to people's talk of luck or fate. More to the point, it also follows that there are no fixed or unchanging absolutes in life. There are no clearly and permanently fixed realities, or identities, or even standards.

13. *Life itself, and everything in the world of life, is mediated by language.*
    Consciousness is an effect of the way language lights up the world of experience, and self-consciousness is an effect of the use of language to talk about itself. Thought is an incompletely-executed motion of language somewhere in our heads.

14. *Life goes on, but my life is finite.*

The only deaths we need to prepare ourselves for are the deaths of others who are dear to us. We will never experience our own deaths. So we should simply love life and say Yes to life until our last day. There is no point at all in making any other preparation for death.

Faith in Life

15. *When I have faith in life, love life, and commit myself to it, I have bought a package deal: life with its limits.*

Whereas in traditional theology 'evil' was seen as a secondary intruder into an originally perfect world, and therefore as being eliminable, the limits of life, which were traditionally called 'metaphysical evil' or 'evils of imperfection', are essential to life. Unlike God, life is finite and imperfect, and has to be accepted as being neither more nor less than what it is. If I want to refuse the package, the alternative for me is 'passive nihilism' or thoroughgoing pessimism. For the religion of life, apologetics takes the form of an attempt to show that pessimism is unreasonable.

16. *The package deal of life cannot be renegotiated.*

There is nobody to renegotiate the deal with. We cannot hope to vary the terms on which life is offered to us.

17. *Life is bittersweet, and bittersweetness is greatly to be preferred to pure sweetness.*

In the classic iconography of Heaven, everyone is 33 years old, everyone looks the same and everything is oddly dead, like a plastic flower on a grave. In real life, we love imperfections, irregularities, beauty spots and signs of frailty or age. The mortal actual is far more loveable than the ideal.

18. *We should never complain, nor even feel any need to complain.*

Life should be loved purely affirmatively and exactly as it is. Everyone gets basically the same deal, and nothing else is on offer. Any sense of victimhood or paranoia or grievance is out of place, and we should get it out of our systems. Never say, nor even *think*, 'Why me?'

Solar Living

19. *Life is a gift (with no giver) that is renewed every day, and true religion is expressive, outpouring 'solar' living by self-giving (as the Sun lives by expending itself).*

By faith, and without any qualification or restriction, I should let life well up in me and pour itself out into symbolic expression through me. Thus, I 'get myself together': we become ourselves by expressing ourselves.

20. *Solarity is creative living-by-dying.*

In solar living, I live by dying because I am passing away all the time. In my symbolic expression I get myself together, but as I do so I must instantly pass on and leave that self behind. I must not be *attached* to my own life, nor to my own products, or expressed selves. My self, and all my loves, must be continuously let go of and continuously renewed. Dying therefore no longer has any terrors for me, because I have made a way of life out of it.

21. *Solar living creates great joy and happiness.*
    My symbolic expression may take various forms, as it pours out in my quest for selfhood, in my loves or my work. In all these areas, continuous letting-go and renewal creates joy, which on occasion rises and spills over into cosmic happiness. This 'cosmic' happiness is the modern equivalent of the traditional Summum Bonum, the 'chief end' of life.

22. *Even the Supreme Good must be left behind at once.*
    I, all my expressions, and even the Summum Bonum, the Supreme Good itself, are all of them transient. Eternal happiness may be great enough to make one feel that one's whole life has been worthwhile, but it is utterly transient. Let it go!

The End of 'The Real World'

What people call 'reality' is merely an effect of either power, or habit.

23. *The Real: a product of lazy, unthinking habits of perception and interpretation.*
    The fixity and unchangeability that people like to ascribe to the real world out there is in fact merely the effect upon them of their own lazy habits. They are in a rut of their own making.

24. *There is no readymade Reality out there.*
    There is no readymade meaningfulness out there, and no objective Truth out there. Meaning is found only in language, and truth belongs only to true statements. Because life is always language-wrapped, everything in the world of life is always shaped by the language in which we describe it, and in a living language everything is always changing. It follows that we ourselves, and our language and our world, are shifting all the time like the sea. Nothing is, nor can it be, objectively and permanently fixed.

25. *We ourselves are the only Creator.*
    As we become critically aware, the objective world melts away. So many supposed features of the world turn out to be merely features of the language in which we describe it. By now, critical thinking has dissolved away objective reality, leaving us with just the human world-wide web, the stream of all our human activity and conversation, and the changing consensus-world-picture that it generates. Our world is our communal, partly-botched work of folk art.

26. *Nihilism and creative freedom.*
    There is no stable real world and no enduring real self. But this situation is not one for despair: it offers us the freedom to remake ourselves and our world. By solar living we can each of us make a personal offering, a small contribution to life, an oblation.

Death

27. *Passing out into life.*
Unattached, but loving life to the last, I am able at the end of my life to pass out into the moving flow of life in general. The only sensible preparation for death is the practice of solar living.

* * *

In a philosophical collection such as this is, I ought to offer some explanation of nos. 23–7. Surely, you will object, I cannot be attributing to ordinary people a version of philosophical Idealism? My reply is that nowadays philosophers do not need, and should not try, to get involved with philosophical cosmology, or 'natural philosophy', as it used to be called. John Locke and others made a mistake there: they thought that philosophers had a clear duty to back up the scientists by explaining how this remarkable new way to knowledge worked. So the philosopher was supposed to justify the objectivity of scientific knowledge, perhaps even to the extent of constructing metaphysical foundations for it. In general, philosophers were considered to have a duty to justify a fairly crude form of scientific realism.

For our present purposes, we do not need to get involved in those debates. Instead, let us ask simply what sort of world-view an animal such as a dog or a chimpanzee can have, and what sort of world-view talking animals such as ourselves can have. From the point of view of life, an animal's world-view must be determined by its needs, its senses, its point of view, its way of life, its *interests*. A social, talking, human-type animal will be able by its daily chatter to develop a shared, public, clarified version of an animal's world-view. In addition, many social animals have been able to develop quite elaborate technologies by trial-and-error methods, so that one can well imagine how a talking animal such as we are might be able to develop socially agreed methods of enquiry, and eventually even experimental sciences of nature. But all this continues to happen within the human life-world, and within the limitations of a talking animal's faculties, interests and the like. We never get outside our own heads, nor indeed outside our own only-human languages, so that in our philosophy of science we should not forget that we are always inside life, and should therefore be consistent pragmatists in our theory of knowledge. We must, of course, acknowledge that orthodox scientific method is by far the most powerful and important way to knowledge that human beings have ever devised, and we should adhere strictly to it. But scientific thinking is a form of critical thinking, and critical thinking is always and on principle non-realistic.[5] It cannot profess, in any field, to tell us how things are *absolutely*. It must limit

---

[5]   The 'critical realism' professed by some theologians (and even some philosophers of religion) is an oxymoron. See Don Cupitt, *Kingdom Come in Everyday Speech* (London: SCM Press, 2000), p. 56.

itself to telling us what theories at present seem to work best, and what is the current state of the debate in that field.

In conclusion, then, I claim that I am not being fanciful in attributing my own non-realistic outlook to ordinary people and ordinary language, and in incorporating it within a 'democratic' philosophy of life.

A further general conclusion. In both of my specimen philosophies of life I go along with what I take to be the common view that a modern post-Hegel and post-Darwin philosophy of life will be non-dualistic. It will aim to give a unified, naturalistic account of what a human being is, and of how a human being should live. So I have deliberately reversed the received rather monastic type of spirituality. No more inner life, no more interior way to a Better World Above, and no more inwardness at all. Instead, we are ourselves only in our expression, our 'coming out'. Hence my slogans, like 'Your mind is in front of your face' and 'We live along the wires, and are ourselves in our interaction with others'. In the culture generally, this is the age of the media, of publicity, of celebrity and of display. The 'outward show' of existence just *is* existence.

Do you like that? For me, it is how things are now. 'All out', is the phrase, is it not?

Chapter 10

Thinking and Life: On Philosophy as a Spiritual Exercise

Philip Goodchild

What does it mean to lead a rich life, as opposed to a long one? A fruitful life, as opposed to a comfortable one? A life filled with meaning, as opposed to bare living? Who are our most truly wealthy souls? Such souls must surely be thoughtful. Is life endowed with meaning by reason, and is the richest life that of the philosopher, the life devoted to pure reason, as many of the great philosophers such as Plato, Aristotle, Spinoza and Hegel seem to have believed? And if our contemporary philosophers bear little resemblance to wealthy souls, is this because true wealth is imperceptible? Or is it rather because our contemporary philosophers are better at mastering concepts than at pursuing philosophy as a way of life? Or even, on the contrary, is it because true wealth is not to be found within, in the life of thought alone?

I admit that such considerations occasionally lead me towards a temptation: to suppose that the richest life is the one that gives life to others. The greatest souls attend closely to life, respond to that which matters and spend their lives by nourishing life. Unlike the philosopher who spends life as a preparation for death, the greatest souls spend life as a preparation for birth. Meaning is given by what lies outside and comes after the self. Human life is conceived in terms of natality rather than mortality, and the good life is essentially maternal: one gives of one's own substance to nourish the lives of others. The greatest souls lead lives of total obscurity, impacting deeply just a few others, perhaps unnoticed and taken for granted even by those whom they serve. On such an account, the philosopher, whose freedom of thought is bought at the expense of a lack of response to the urgent clamour of personal, social and political demands, opts out of any opportunity for living a wealthy and worthwhile life. To think is at variance with being good.

This temptation mirrors its opposite: to suppose that philosophy provides a training in being good. The work of the recent French philosopher Pierre Hadot has re-established that ancient philosophy was a way of life, a set of spiritual exercises.[1] Socrates himself explained the philosophical vocation for which he was condemned: 'I tried to persuade each one of you to concern himself less with what he has than with what he is, so as to render himself as excellent and rational

---

[1] Pierre Hadot, *Philosophy as a Way of Life*, ed. Arnold I. Davidson (Oxford: Blackwell, 1995) and *What is Ancient Philosophy?* trans. Michael Chase (Cambridge, MA: Harvard University Press, 2002).

as possible'.[2] He tried to shame his fellow Athenians, as citizens of the city with the greatest reputation for wisdom and power, for their eagerness to possess wealth, reputation and honours without caring for the state of their souls.[3] In practice, this means that 'the most important thing is not life, but the good life'.[4] And it is the greatest good to discuss virtue every day, for the unexamined life is not worth living.[5] Then Socrates regarded reason as a matter of masculine heroism: 'wherever a man has taken a position that he believes to be best, or has been placed by his commander, there he must I think remain and face danger, without a thought for death or anything else, rather than disgrace'.[6] Heroic and virtuous souls 'despise Being for the sake of the Good, when they voluntarily place themselves in danger'.[7] Hadot describes this as the fundamental philosophical choice: to prefer the Good above being, and thought and conscience above the life of the body. It is in this sense that philosophy is an apprenticeship for death: it subjugates the body's will to live to the higher demands of thought.[8] This moral image of thought requires the splitting of the Good and Being, and the consequent judgement and perpetual disciplining of life in the name of the Idea. Yet there is nowhere to stand outside life where we might judge what is truly good.

Both of these views are mere temptations. Both introduce a division between thought and life, even if they differ over which term is privileged: can a life of pure thought really be rich, if it does not give life to others? Can a life without thinking really be rich, even if it gives life to others? I am reminded of the peasant widower of Saint Marcel mentioned by Simone Weil, an early-twentieth-century French philosopher who was attracted from Marxism to Platonism, Catholicism and Eastern religions. This acquaintance mentioned in passing in her *Notebooks* presumably found his existence pointless now that he no longer had someone to love: 'If one hasn't a being to love, for whom one lives, life isn't worth anything'.[9] The problem, Weil noted, is that if human life is not worth anything in itself, how can another person give one's life a meaning?[10] When the responsibility for fulfilling the purpose of life can no longer be deferred onto others, then the time has come for thought: thought begins in the absence of meaning and fulfilment. For Weil, it is the very experience of futility that makes one wait and look up. Could one even say that a rich, thoughtful life begins when life lacks meaning?

---

2   Plato's *Apology* 36c, translation cited in Hadot, *Philosophy as a Way of Life*, p. 85.

3   Ibid., 29d–e.

4   Plato, *Crito* 48b.

5   Plato, *Apology* 38a.

6   Ibid., 28d.

7   Hadot quotes Sallustius, a fourth-century Neoplatonist, here. *Philosophy as a Way of Life*, p. 94.

8   Ibid.

9   Simone Weil, *The Notebooks of Simone Weil*, trans. Arthur Wills (London: Routledge and Kegan Paul, 1956), vol. 2, p. 498.

10   Ibid.

This is the crucial point: when I appeal to a rich, meaningful life, I seem to refer to a possible state that might already be achieved. If only one could think hard enough to find out what that blessed state might be, one could lead a life of perfection. Philosophy, according to this image, would be the knowledge of perfection. Yet by simply asking the question in ignorance of such a state, I evoke a longing: 'let my life be a rich and meaningful one!' I lead my life in search of meaning. Philosophy, according to this image, is the search for depth and meaning. Instead of being a state of knowledge, a wisdom that can easily be shared, philosophy becomes a way of life, a spiritual practice, a task to be undertaken. Socrates himself claimed not to be wise; the only subject he claimed to understand was erotics.[11] As Weil explains:

> The good represents for us a nothingness, since no one thing is in itself good. But this nothingness is not a non-being, not something unreal. Everything which exists is unreal compared to it. This nothingness is at least as real as we are ourselves. For our very being itself is nothing other than this need for the good.[12]

No content or fulfilment or special bond or even life can satisfy here. Instead, one places one's life beyond what can be touched or experienced, in an experience of waiting or attention to the unknown: 'It is impossible. It is a death. It means no longer being alive. And that is exactly what is wanted'.[13] Meaninglessness and affliction are present at the birth of thought. Moreover, they inhabit thought all the way, leading to 'the revelation that this nothingness is really the fullest possible fullness, the main-spring and principle of all reality'.[14] Or, more succinctly: 'To love truth means to endure the void and to accept death. Truth is on the side of death'.[15] One has to be dead to see things in their nakedness. This absolute blockage to the power of thought and understanding is encountered in suffering when one renounces all imaginary compensations that cover over reality. For Weil, suffering is regarded as a koan, a self-contradictory subject for meditation:

> The thought of suffering is not of a discursive kind. The mind comes slap up against physical suffering, affliction, like a fly against a pane of glass, without being able to make the slightest progress or discover anything new, and yet unable to prevent itself from returning to the attack. ... Suffering has no significance.

---

[11] Plato, *Theages* 128b: 'As regards this subject of learning, I claim to be more clever than any human beings previously or now'. See also *Symposium* 177d, and the extraordinarily rich commentary, James M. Rhodes, *Eros, Wisdom and Silence* (Columbia, MO: University of Missouri Press, 2003).

[12] Weil, *Notebooks*, vol. 2, p. 491.

[13] Ibid., p. 494.

[14] Ibid., p. 492.

[15] Simone Weil, *Gravity and Grace*, trans. Emma Crawford and Mario von der Ruhr (London: Routledge, 2002), p. 11; *Notebooks*, vol. 1, pp. 160–1.

There lies the very essence of its reality. We must love it in its reality, which is absence of significance.[16]

The disutility of suffering is in direct contrast to power:

Power is the pure means. For that very reason it represents the supreme end in the case of all those who have not understood.

The inversion of means and ends, which is the very essence of all the evil in society, is inevitable, for this very good reason, that there isn't any end. Consequently, the means is taken as the end.[17]

Suffering removes the inevitable illusions we entertain to protect ourselves from reality. The imagination, which fills up the void with relative goods conceived as absolute, is essentially a liar because it does away with the material dimension of existence.[18] Suffering focuses attention, and attention is what penetrates reality, so that the 'greater the attention on the part of the mind, the greater the amount of real being in the object'.[19] Suffering enters the body: it is what the body cannot escape from incorporating. For Weil, to 'know yourself' means that you do not identify yourself with your thoughts;[20] the most difficult and fruitful thing is to learn 'not to think *about* …'.[21] There is a dualism here between 'gravity' and 'grace', between the succession of conditions and causes that continually compel imagination and action, and between the moments of shock, suspension, waiting or attention as a result of which thought can be otherwise. If the life of a giver lacks purpose, or if its meaning is perpetually deferred in service of the younger generation who will in turn lead a life of service, then life proceeds as a denial of death. As Weil also noted: 'All sins are an attempt to escape from time. Virtue is to submit to time, to press it to the heart until the heart breaks'.[22]

Life and death, suffering and wealth: are we to imagine these as separate planes of existence between which there is no communication? Is life to be judged by thought? Yet this is to attribute far too much power to our thinking. It is not the imagination that separates soul from body, but time itself in the very movement by which it brings life towards death. Our words will be forgotten, our books no longer read, our bodies are destined for corruption – and this is why they matter. For our very finitude brings our attention back to the present, at the same time that

---

[16]   Weil, *Notebooks*, vol. 2, pp. 483–4.

[17]   Ibid., p. 495.

[18]   Weil, *Notebooks*, vol. 1, pp. 145 and 160.

[19]   Weil, *Notebooks*, vol. 2, p. 527.

[20]   Simone Weil, *Lectures on Philosophy*, trans. Hugh Price (Cambridge: Cambridge University Press, 1978), p. 193.

[21]   Weil, *Notebooks*, vol. 1, p. 134.

[22]   Simone Weil, *First and Last Notebooks*, trans. Richard Rees (Oxford: Oxford University Press, 1970), p. 102.

it makes us long for a truth that endures beyond us. It is the hope for a truth through which we can measure our lives, rather than measuring them by the power of our own thought alone. Perhaps we need to distinguish between levels:[23] on one level it is true that affliction is meaningless and destructive; on another level it is a means of engaging with that which matters. Thinking requires both perspectives. In fact, thinking requires a contrast of perspective, an internal contradiction, a necessary distinction. Purity of heart is to will at least two things, to be double-minded. It is like being consciously atheist but unconsciously theist – to protest and affirm the world at one and the same time. For Weil, this even applies to piety: to make every effort for God, to pray to God, while thinking that he does not exist.[24] The left hand no longer knows what the right hand is doing.[25] Only as such can life be known.

There is, therefore, no question of the philosophical perspective escaping the void to attain some putative content. There is no possibility of condensing some ultimate morsel of wisdom. There is no single point that unites thinking and life. According to Weil, the 'proper method of philosophy consists in clearly conceiving the insoluble problems in all their insolubility and then in simply contemplating them, fixedly and tirelessly, year after year, without any hope, patiently waiting'.[26] This is, no doubt, the recipe for a life of poverty. Perhaps life slips through the fingers in any attempt to consider that its essence should be grasped. Is this the philosophy of life: that any attempt to grasp the concept loses the reality, while losing the concept restores the reality? Is any attempt to bring life into thought, to find the wise word, an intolerable act of hubris? One is reminded of the gospel saying: 'For whoever would save his life would lose it, and whoever loses his life will find it' (Matthew 16.25). As Weil once remarked, 'the Gospel contains a conception of human life, not a theology'.[27] For if one lives without comfort as a driving factor, if one leads a life of attention and waiting, could it not be possible that such a life would not only be impoverished, but also – in its extreme awareness of reality – rather rich? Moreover – and here we move beyond what Weil said, even if not what Weil did – such a life may be the condition for a prodigious creativity of thought.

There is a philosophical formula for such an experience. It can be found in the words of another French philosopher, Gilles Deleuze, a Nietzschean who could not have been more different from Weil: 'Life will no longer be made to appear before the categories of thought; thought will be thrown into the categories of life'.[28] This amounts to a conversion or revolution in thought. The relevant insight is that the question of the meaning of life is a false problem, for it seeks

23   Weil, *Notebooks*, vol. 1, p. 139.

24   Ibid., pp. 136 and 142.

25   Ibid., pp. 173–4.

26   Weil, *First and Last Notebooks*, p. 335.

27   Ibid., p. 147.

28   Gilles Deleuze, *Cinema 2: The Time-Image*, trans. Hugh Tomlinson and Robert Galeta (London: Athlone Press, 1989), p. 189.

to displace a living, breathing, thinking person in favour of a completed thought expressing a meaning or purpose. This would be to mistake the greater for the less, so that one attempts to regulate the greater by the lesser.[29] It is the gesture of taking a perspective produced by life, nature and history as though it stood entirely outside.[30] Rejecting such claims to know transcendent reality, the immanentist revolution consists in encountering life within thought, within the forces that form thought as such. It is no longer what you think about which counts so much as how you think. For immanence means ethos: it is a way of thinking and dwelling, not a proposal about the unreality of transcendent objects. It is not a comment on the existence of God. It does not even express a refusal or abstention from metaphysics. Deleuze's distinction between morality and ethics is, of course, crucial here.[31] Instead of subjecting the body to conscious ideas represented in the mind, as in Stoic or Epicurean philosophical exercises, the life of the body and the mind escapes representation. This overturns the entire tradition of philosophy deriving from Socrates that aims to judge conduct in accordance with what is right. For the forces that shape our lives, our thoughts, and our conduct are much greater than what they produce: a few ideas in our minds. We cannot know what such forces will do in advance.

Ethics becomes a matter of experimentation, rather than representation, in an attempt to discover what the mind and the body can do. Once one has put aside the moral image of thought, such experimentation becomes an art of living, not simply an art of thinking. To think is now to interpret and to evaluate.[32] The question of whether a thought is true or false, right or wrong, is far too infantile and simplistic when we discuss a meaningful life, rather than simply identifying objects or moral rules. To think is to act and to live, and thinking makes a difference to thought.[33] Thinking itself is ethical. The mind is already involved in ethical evaluations – evaluation is the element in which it moves. Deleuze's immanent understanding of evaluations is that they are 'not values but ways of being, modes of existence of those who judge and evaluate. This is why we always have the beliefs, feelings and thoughts that we deserve given our way of being or style of life'.[34] This suggests that philosophy is less the art of judging, or of disciplining the body to conform to the mind, but more the formation of a 'way of being or style of life'. It is not simply about ideas.

---

[29] See Gilles Deleuze, *Bergsonism*, trans. Hugh Tomlinson and Barbara Habberjam (New York: Zone, 1988), p. 147.

[30] See Friedrich Nietzsche, *Twilight of the Idols*, trans. R.J. Hollingdale (London: Penguin, 1990), p. 55.

[31] Gilles Deleuze, *Spinoza: Practical Philosophy*, trans. Robert Hurley (San Francisco: City Lights, 1988), ch. 2.

[32] Gilles Deleuze, *Nietzsche and Philosophy*, trans. Hugh Tomlinson (London: Athlone Press, 1983), p. xiii.

[33] Gilles Deleuze, *Difference and Repetition*, trans. Paul Patton (London: Athlone Press 1994), p. 265.

[34] Deleuze, *Nietzsche and Philosophy*, p. 1.

Yet philosophy remains a cultivation of ideas. It is not simply a matter of habit, lifestyle or character. Indeed, such ideas do exist objectively, whether we embody them or not. There is a second reversal which constitutes in some ways a return of metaphysics. For each way of life belongs to an element, a culture, a time and a place. Each way of life grows in a particular soil. The philosopher, far from finding ideas deep within, has to enter the territory where thoughts are found:

> We only find truths where they are, at their time and in their element. Every truth is a truth of an element, of a time and a place: the minotaur does not leave the labyrinth. ... We are not going to think unless we are forced to go where the forces which give food for thought are, where the forces that make thought something active and affirmative are made use of. Thought does not need a method but a paideia, a formation, a culture. ... It is up to us to go to extreme places, to extreme times, where the highest and deepest truths live and rise up.[35]

We have to set out in search of ideas. We cannot be content with representing received wisdom, with making common sense explicit. So much that passes for philosophy is merely an appeal to the wisdom of crowds, an attempt to reinforce and reproduce a style of life. It is an appeal to the majority. There is, of course, a role for reproducing successful styles of life, but this is hardly the search for wisdom that begins in ignorance. It is not the creative thinking that will free us from our illusions. Philosophy is a way of life, but a dangerous one. Thought itself is decision and evaluation, and it decides and affirms itself: 'There are never any criteria other than the tenor of existence, the intensification of life'.[36] So the world is composed of more than suffering bodies and acts of generosity or attention. It swarms with evaluations. All ideas are evaluations or judgements.

Nevertheless, there does indeed remain a question as to how effective philosophy has been in pursuing the way of life that will give birth to thought. An important insight is given by the contemporary British philosopher Michael McGhee in his *Transformations of Mind: Philosophy as a Spiritual Exercise* – one of the only books of philosophy that, under a Platonic inspiration, does contain personal confessions of erotic experience. It is written amidst pillow-talk, opening thus:

> Listen, wisdom is something dared, and what matters beyond all else in philosophy, which is love of wisdom, is a spirit of inwardness, which you have to cultivate for yourself, a practice of inner silence, even before reflection, which philosophy is thought to start with. ... Philosophy is also a conversation, and what matters beyond all else here is demeanour, how we listen, how we speak or

---

[35] Ibid., p. 110.

[36] Gilles Deleuze and Félix Guattari, *What is Philosophy?* trans. Graham Burchell and Hugh Tomlinson (London: Verso, 1994), p. 174.

write, not seeking dominance, not indifferent to the well-being of the other, but encouraging inwardness, a friendly, even an 'erotic' spirit ...[37]

While McGhee follows in the Socratic tradition of philosophy as a 'cultivation of the soul',[38] he shifts the emphasis of philosophical inquiry from the analysis of concepts, understood through a reason regarded as the highest part of the soul, to the cultivation of a certain quality of attention. For McGhee, a reason is what motivates us: it is a form of feeling;[39] 'a reason is just a thought or perception that moves or engages us'.[40] Yet reason alone is insufficient for truthfulness:

> It is not that the 'objective thinker' does not 'reflect' upon their life or has no self-awareness. *The terms* in which they *reflect* upon their life simply *reduplicate* the established way of thinking; *that* is what they fail to reflect upon, the totality of the established way of thinking itself, of which they thus become the creature.[41]

Reasons do not merely concern objective truths; their habitual repetition may become a form of attention 'as though they arise and their pattern possesses me and I am in their grip and then that is just what I am thinking and imagining and what I am intending and what I am doing'.[42] Philosophy is therefore not merely a matter of ordering life in accordance with reason or justified true belief; a critique of reason requires first of all an *ascesis*, a suspension of mental activity,[43] in order to liberate the forms of attention. Where modern philosophy begins with doubting all objective knowledge, McGhee proposes the more radical step of suspending subjective presuppositions about the form of thought, and what it means to think.[44] For there is a connection between what one attends to and the state of one's desires. Thus:

> All we see of the world is what our attention is focused on and, *a fortiori*, we don't see the underlying reasons for this. We take the focus of our attention to reveal the state of things, but it only reveals what it reveals, and what is outside

---

[37]   Michael McGhee, *Transformations of Mind* (Cambridge: Cambridge University Press, 2000), p. 1.

[38]   Most evident in the Platonic dialogues Alcibiades and Laches, and recovered in the works of Pierre Hadot. See also Alexander Nehamas, *The Art of Living* (Berkeley, CA: University of California Press, 1998) and Robert C. Solomon, *Spirituality for the Skeptic* (Oxford: Oxford University Press, 2002). See also Michael McGhee (ed.), *Philosophy, Religion and the Spiritual Life* (Cambridge: Cambridge University Press, 1992) and John Cornwell and Michael McGhee (eds), *Philosophers and God* (London: Continuum, 2009).

[39]   McGhee, *Transformations of Mind*, p. 28.

[40]   Ibid., p. 29.

[41]   Ibid., p. 21.

[42]   Ibid., p. 69.

[43]   Ibid., p. 74.

[44]   Cf. Deleuze, *Difference and Repetition*, pp. 129–31.

the focus is not apparent to us, so that we don't even know what someone is talking about who points to things outside its scope. And we take our perceived world to be a ground of judgement, whereas it is only the present *scope* of our judgement ...[45]

Our metaphysics is always the measure of our blindness: it names what we are willing to see. How can one attend to life itself if desire is always oriented to matters within life? Hence the widower's sense of futility – he lacks concepts to make visible the meanings in life which swarm around him. Similarly, the prisoners in the cave do not know that they are prisoners: 'Cramped thoughts are projected onto the world and read back as reality'.[46] For McGhee, everything turns on the profundity or otherwise of an 'experience of life': 'It depends on those depths swirling below those "inner reaches of consciousness" mentioned by [William] James. I would say that the investigation of those depths is the real task of the philosophy of religion, and that it has to be a kind of spiritual exercise'.[47]

Why does McGhee invoke religion at this point? It is partly because philosophy here concerns inwardness, and he draws on Kierkegaard's and Tolstoy's discussions of Christian faith to provide a vocabulary for inwardness. It is also because it is impossible to change one's state of soul for oneself through one's own power, for this is precisely what needs to be changed: 'understanding *dawns*, it comes, as it were, from outside, even though that grace depends on a sustained and vigorous effort'.[48] Philosophy depends upon an awakening of a capacity to see, a secret knowledge 'access to which requires the password of a reconstituted self',[49] a new insight welling up within the inner reaches of consciousness. The religious language of 'other-power', 'revelation' or 'awakening' may be the most appropriate. Yet McGhee also finds a further qualification: 'the mind must be set in motion *by* religious ideas, *by* them, and, more radically, *towards* them: if this dynamism is absent, then we are no longer dealing with religion, but the relevant ideas are merely incorporated into mundane thought'.[50]

This dynamism and attraction is almost offered as a defining feature of the religious, although McGhee notes that 'meaning is not to be defined but evoked'.[51] The idea of God, therefore, is meaningful to the extent that it impels the mind towards it – as it clearly did for the likes of Augustine and Anselm. If the idea no longer speaks to us, so that we merely speak of it, then it falls into terminal decline and this marks the end of a spiritual practice. The issue is not one of whether one believes in God, or speaks of God all the time. It is a matter of whether the

---

[45]   McGhee, *Transformations of Mind*, p. 85.
[46]   Ibid., p. 169.
[47]   Ibid., p. 23.
[48]   Ibid., p. 115.
[49]   Ibid., p. 97.
[50]   Ibid., p. 120.
[51]   Ibid., p. 101.

concept of God has its own inwardness, its own dynamic power, that sets thought on its way. It is not sufficient in philosophy of religion to maintain a metaphysical system according to which the mind is oriented towards God in theory, if the mind is not set in motion towards God in practice. Thus the 'death of God' is the death of a disturbance and attraction, the end of a practice, afflicting believer and unbeliever alike. Philosophy of religion is then no longer concerned primarily with the question of the existence of God; it has to be concerned with the conditions under which the mind is set in motion.[52]

So we come at last to the vital question: is the mind set in motion towards a concept of life? McGhee remarks: 'To know what the term "life" refers to requires one to have undergone the transformation it brings about'.[53] Notice that this thinking of life, on this account, would have three dimensions: it would be a liberation and intensification of the concept of life, which now bears the role of the source of the value of values, the immanent criterion of evaluation that generates evaluations, the metaphysical substance that names what matters; it would also be an attention to life, an awareness of vitality, a capacity to feel past the concepts to taste intense life wherever it is to be found and liberated; and the thinking of life would also be the life that thinks, the awakening thought that arises from the swirling depths of consciousness and expresses its vital power in thought itself. So the concept of 'life' fulfils the functions formerly attributed to God: it replaces God, or rather, as a biblical and philosophical name for God, the concept is one of the few acceptable names under which God can be thought outside of the confines of institutional religion, in all God's transcendence, immanence and inspiration. If life does play such a role, then perhaps our sharpest divisions are not between theists or atheists, nor between participants and non-participants in religious practice, but would arise from the thinking that undergirds our ways of life. For the substitution of concepts such as 'God' and 'life' are less significant than our frameworks of thinking insofar as these constrain or enable us to perceive reality, to touch it, participate in it and live it. Moreover, if thinking is at once intensification, attention and awakening, then just as the thinking of God has been shaped by the practice of life within institutional religion, the thinking of 'life' may be shaped by the practice of philosophy as a way of life.

So what actually does shape a philosopher's way of life and framework of thinking? Here I think we must be candid, for the life of a contemporary philosopher is rarely shaped by thought and its structures alone, but more often by the demands, more internalized than ever, of the management of thought within the multicultural university in contemporary global credit capitalism. For our established ways of thinking, which include the formality and impersonality of the conference paper, journal article or research monograph, with its peculiar ranges of reference, attention, affect and demeanour, may shape or limit intensification, attention and awakening much more than metaphysical commitments. Indeed, if Deleuze and Guattari are to

---

52   Ibid., p. 124.
53   Ibid., p. 139.

be believed, our institutional assemblages including their micropolitics of gestures shape desire itself, no, they are desire itself. Who does not derive an erotic pleasure out of the formality of a well-crafted conference paper?

Such pleasures aside, if a philosophical exercise is capable of reforming our desire, what direction should this take? Is philosophy an intimate conversation, an erotic liaison, the most intense expression of life? Here we have come full circle and must return to Plato's *Symposium*, with its hymns to love, its praise of philosophy as the true lover which loves true beauty, and its celebration of those erotic liaisons between older men and the beautiful young boys who wish to learn their wisdom. Is the essence of philosophy expressed in the pedagogical relation, concealed beneath the blanket where the beautiful young Alcibiades' love of wisdom overcame his physical repulsion for his admirer, ugly old Socrates?[54] Did Socrates betray philosophy as well as his love of beauty by rejecting the physical advances of the young man he had sought after for so long? For if physical passion is nothing but incorporation, eating and being eaten, intensification, attention and awakening to life, is it not the consummation of philosophy as well as of life?

There are reasons to doubt that this particular liaison forms the apogee of philosophy, and reasons to doubt that any such liaison is the consummation of philosophy. Since we know that Alcibiades was to become a notorious tyrant and traitor, Socrates appears to have shown little wisdom in his choice of boys, little discernment in his perception of moral beauty and little effectiveness as a midwife for the recollection of justice in Alcibiades' soul. Unless, of course, as an impotent precursor to Christ, he had come to seek and save the lost.[55] Indeed, this might suggest one possible explanation for Socrates' inhuman degree of self-control: the shame of impotence. McGhee, however, has a more moral explanation: appreciation of beauty of soul is the ground of both delight in the presence of another's flourishing and compassion in its absence. What counts, for Socrates, is the preservation of Alcibiades' orientation towards the good, and Alcibiades' turn towards physical demonstrations of affection threatens that orientation in offering to exchange beauty for wisdom, 'bronze for gold'.[56] Indeed, it is the moral ugliness of Alcibiades' bargaining that kills desire in Socrates – Alcibiades offers too cheap a price for thought.[57] But I am not entirely persuaded – it is of course merely Alcibiades' physical beauty that has entranced Socrates. What could be more lovely than a young man who wishes to make love? Socrates' protest of an unfair exchange exemplifies the common but effective banter of an experienced seducer.[58] No, if Socrates does indeed remain a 'cave of every foul lust' as he was supposedly described by the physiognomist Zopyrus,[59] then it is more likely that it

54   Plato, *Symposium* 217–18.

55   Rhodes, *Eros, Wisdom and Silence*, p. 374.

56   McGhee, *Transformations of Mind*, p. 192.

57   See also Rhodes, *Eros, Wisdom and Silence*, p. 400.

58   Plato, *Symposium* 218e.

59   Mentioned by Cicero (*Tusculan Disputations* 4.37).

is his own reaction that Socrates finds repellent, as a double-minded philosopher, a soul whose chariot is drawn in opposing directions by competing horses.[60] If this is the case, philosophy may not resolve the conflicts of desire, nor successfully produce moral beauty – even if religion may serve to do so instead. So one cannot seek philosophy's fulfilment in either physical or moral intimacy.

Yet Plato could have had one way of resolving this dilemma: suppose Alcibiades, with his immense charisma and inordinate desire to rule, had been converted to philosophy. He could have become one of Plato's ideal philosophical rulers, serving the common good. The consummation of philosophy is political. Following the analogy set out in the *Republic*, philosophy produces a politics of the soul rather than an ethics. If our desires are evoked by our institutional contexts, then the ascetic path of philosophy should put aside all that is inessential and merely private, in the sense of putting aside merely individual concerns. For what matters most are social forces, manifest in habitual ways of thinking and living, that shape the focus of attention and thus the ground of judgement. If philosophy seeks the wise word that will forge a special connection between people, it is a word that bridges difference by attending to the shared experience of constraint in life, and by giving back a little intensification, a wider focus of attention, a measure of awakening. For insofar as the forces of constraint pass through the form and practice of thought, then the course of human history is decided within the human soul. Philosophy is the work of human freedom. Its vocation is politics. Socrates was prevented from taking part in politics by his inner voice, knowing that someone who really fights for justice must lead a private, not public life, if he is to survive for even a short time.[61] Now, on the contrary, the philosopher must become exposed to social forces in their most extreme and naked state – only as such can one attend to and diagnose the human condition, and only as such can one speak of what matters. Far from being a therapy of desire, such a philosophy produces a divided, exposed and exhausted individual, a cave of every foul lust, who risks not only being but also virtue for the sake of life. For the exercise of philosophy does not bring life to the soul so much as it brings life to thought and thought to life. Even if philosophy is pursued at the cost of one's own life, soul and virtue, there still remains a life in the absence of the individual: it is the life of thought.

---

60 Plato, *Phaedrus* 253d–254e.

61 Plato, *Apology* 32a.

Afterword

Katharine Sarah Moody and Steven Shakespeare

What remains of life? A reading of the essays in this collection will expose various tensions and fault lines between the authors. Not least of these is whether a true conception of life requires the acknowledgement or refusal of a transcendent dimension. At the same time, however, there are some remarkable lines of convergence. These centre on the ways that thinking life undermines subject-centred philosophies, without abandoning ethical and political agency. Surviving thus requires a philosophy of life, or, rather, philosophy as a way of life. Such a way will resist the fixity that draws lines between self and other, friend and enemy, self and world, passive and active, life and death.

However, we must ask how such an emerging philosophy of life reckons with another important strand in contemporary thought. Speculative realism or speculative materialism rejects the Kantian consensus that the world and its objects can exist only in relation to a subject. Thinkers such as Meillassoux, Brassier and Harman call us in different ways to think the world in our absence. In this perspective, it seems that life in general, and the human perspective in particular, can have no privileged position in truly thinking the 'absolute' – reality as absolved or severed from any point of view upon it. Indeed, our living forms and our awareness of the world are wholly dependent upon unthinking processes formed in an ancestral past and destined to die with the extinguishing of the universe.

Such a prospect makes a philosophy of life appear to be wishful thinking: a light flickering for a few moments in futile defiance of the dark that will consume it. Nevertheless, the way we have characterized speculative thinking is not so far away from where we began this volume. In the Introduction, we already noted the ways in which life and death, the organic and the mechanical, converge and interact. Our authors have contended any escapist flight into a beyond of life, and yet have consistently raised the ethical and political question of what it means to affirm life.

Consider perhaps the most challenging of the new speculative philosophies, Brassier's fiercely unsentimental and austere nihilism. His *Nihil Unbound* ends with the declaration that 'the subject of philosophy must also recognize that he or she is already dead, and that philosophy is neither a medium of affirmation nor a source of justification, but rather an organon of extinction'.[1] The will to know is driven by its subjective trauma, in which it already knows its extinction; philosophy gives that trauma form and voice.

Here, we seem a long way from a philosophy of life. But the question for the subject of philosophy remains: why are you taking a stance towards this at all? Why does the scar of extinction motivate you to think? Without dreaming of escape or reducing meaning to a subject's affirmation, surely this is where a philosophy of life gets its purchase? We are not making the trivial point that speculative philosophy about the inhumanity of the world is written by a human being, but rather that an encounter with the inhuman impels a new thinking of what it is to be born, to live and to affirm.

It is striking that this is exactly where Thacker's seminal *After Life* ends: life is not simply left behind, but pursued to the limits ('we're *after* life, on its trail!') of the unhuman.[2] In common with many of the contributors to this volume, we believe that doing justice to the aporia, wounds and negativity of life is an essential part of doing justice in the world and resisting injustice. None of this need mean romanticizing or absolutizing a concept of life above all else. Instead, we simply take a chance on life: that it is, even in the face of extinction, an opportunity for wonder and solidarity.

* * *

Instructions for living a life:
Pay attention.
Be astonished.
Tell about it.[3]

---

[1]   Ray Brassier, *Nihil Unbound: Enlightenment and Extinction* (Basingstoke and New York: Palgrave Macmillan, 2007), p. 239.

[2]   Eugene Thacker, *After Life* (Chicago: University of Chicago Press, 2010), pp. 257–68.

[3]   From Mary Oliver, 'Sometimes', *Red Bird* (Boston: Beacon Press, 2008).

Index